Points of Departure

By the same author

Gentlemen, Players and Politicians

Dalton Camp

Points of Departure

Deneau & Greenberg

ISBN: 0-88879-020-1

© Deneau and Greenberg Publishers Ltd.   1979

Printed in Canada by John Deyell Company

Canadian Cataloguing in Publication Data
Camp, Dalton, 1920-
   Points of departure
   ISBN 0-88879-020-1
1. Canada. Parliament — Elections, 1979. I. Title.
JL193.C35 324.971'064'4 C79-090101-3

For
Christopher J. K. Bear
and H. L.

Individuals always did and always do take themselves as points of departure.

Karl Marx

PROLOGUE

varlet, n. (Hist.) medieval page pre-
paring to be a squire; (arch., esp. joc.)
menial, low fellow, rascal. (var. of
vaslet, see VALET)
The Concise Oxford Dictionary

To begin near the beginning, and by way of explanation, the varlet is the author's alter ego. More than pseudonym or alias, varlet is the name bestowed upon the author by one discerning enough to realize he had become, after his years in party politics, a Third Person. Consulting a dictionary, he was satisfied that it suited him, even as antithesis, and in the ensuing time, the Varlet Papers came to be produced, marked by an easy flow of candour otherwise impossible for a man of natural restraint and inhibition.

During a career given over to conceptualizing political strategies and reducing them to more or less precise expression — something, at least, a typesetter could get his teeth into — it became a familiar habit to write in the first person singular, or plural, when, in reality, the words were composed for others — some other Him or Them. If schizophrenia could be induced, such a constant exercise, over so long a period, would easily have given him a rash of it.

The transference of so much private thought, blood and nervous sweat to prime ministers, premiers and aspiring opposition leaders yields only tangential gratifications, such as the applause of unseen audiences, distant editorial approbation, or an oblique electoral triumph, all of which is passing solace to an ego consigned to the shadows of anonymity.

1

Furthermore, since ghosts must be invisible, those who valued his advice and penmanship became increasingly anxious that he not be seen in their company. (On their behalf, the Third Person often conveyed his wisdom through other Third Persons.) It was then that he began to enter back doors, ride service elevators, and occupy hotel rooms preregistered under assumed names, the initials of at least one of these still a laundry mark on his shirts and underwear.

Enter now our unlikely hero, the varlet, Third Person incarnate, part pariah, part pimpernel, to celebrate the author's deliverance from the dark nights of a prolonged penance:

The Media Watch

i

I'm a bigger blunder than Big Thunder
What a winless, chinless wonder
Ragged ass ol'
Save the Crow's Nest Pass ol'
Ragged ass ol' Joe.
Parliamentary Press Gallery
Revue, 17 March 1979

A man in search of portents is lucky to be in Ottawa on the night of 17 March 1979, and to have in his pocket a ticket to the Parliamentary Press Gallery Annual Dinner and Revue. The season's accumulation of snow, compacted in a winter's litter, encrusts the nation's capital, presenting a baleful landscape of fading grey and a reminder of the intransigence of Canada's longest season. The Gallery Dinner is a spring's herald: within a week crocuses will appear on the eastern slopes of Parliament Hill, and, soon after, Parliament will be dissolved.

Going to the dinner is something like attending a reunion with a past self, a mingling of *déjà vu* and nostalgia. Sentiment, too, since there is a notion that this will be the last of these events for the varlet, who has been a watchful, reflective spectator at so many before. Adorned in rented tuxedo, struggling with a springless clip-on tie, he recalls a dinner in 1965 during the Pearson era at which he wore a white, formal turtleneck sweater under his monkeysuit.

As the president of the Progressive Conservative National Association, he was then entering the period of his celebrity,

5

soon to be locked in fateful confrontation with his party's leader, John Diefenbaker. That day, he had lunched in Ottawa with the *Globe and Mail*, gently chiding his hosts for their editorial transgressions against his leader and divided party — there were, he argued, more serious divisions elsewhere, turning not on personality but principle — and at the dinner that night he had sat at the *Toronto Star*'s table: a day spent, it could be said, in the camp of Diefenbaker's enemies.

But Diefenbaker had been absent that evening because of a sudden illness, doubtless brought on by thoughts of the dinner. (Tommy Douglas, the NDP leader, spoke in his stead.) Lester Pearson, the prime minister, was present, dutiful and obliging, as his life had equipped him to be, and he had delivered an after-dinner speech which had sent currents of shock through his audience, so heavy was the voltage of his cynicism.

The prime minister, displaying his patented rueful smile, had fished a black leather glove from the pocket of his dinner jacket, which he put on to wear throughout his performance. Thus waving the black hand of the Mafia, he delivered the mordant humour of his ghost-writers to his audience, a discourse which contained all the delights one would find in reading the announcement of a bankruptcy proceeding. Even so, it was done with the familiar detachment of a world statesman who had always felt secure pronouncing the briefs and arguments of others, and whose ambition was always so deeply buried beneath the layers of his congeniality that it was even possible to believe he had become prime minister by accident. Seeing him then, it was no less easy to believe that he held his title lightly and that he would just as soon debase the office or fudge the truth as have anyone not think well of him.

Diefenbaker had been a presence at this dinner, like Banquo's ghost, and the varlet suspected, groping for greater understanding of the prime minister's grotesque performance, that the old man brooding over his nightmare visions at Stornoway had spooked the prime minister, who had guilt enough of his own to bear.

The contrived humour of desperation has not much wit in it, but it allows men to jest at the tragedy of their own lives. To enjoy this sort of entertainment, an audience must be kept afloat on a rising tide of booze, and the varlet, coming off a six-hour cocktail party, went on drinking, even though, like everyone else, he had already drunk enough. Belshazzar's Feast had nothing on the Parliamentary Press Gallery Dinner of 1965.

Even the post-dinner skits had proved too strong for some to stomach. When one of the cast, pretending to be Justice Minister Guy Favreau, sang "I've got a luv-erly bunch of criminals," the CNR's president, Donald Gordon, had jumped on a table to roar "Shame, Shame!" and to shake his fist — the first and only critical review in Gallery history.

Gallery dinners have their fixed, uncomplicated routine: guests and hosts assemble by the Railway Committee Room in the Hall of Honour for an hour's convivial drinking, proceeding then to the Parliamentary restaurant for an hour's eating, followed by an hour's speeches — from, in order of their appearance, the Gallery president, the leader of the Opposition, the prime minister, and the Governor General — followed by an hour's entertainment by the Gallery's writers and performers, after which, the formalities concluded, the drinking resumes until the serving tables are discreetly cleared, and guests and hosts depart to reconvene at the National Press Club across the street, where the bar remains open until dawn when breakfast is served.

The schedule is invariably elastic: an hour need not be sixty minutes, but perhaps ninety or one hundred and twenty. During the night, as the levels of booze lower in the bottles arranged at the bar, and rise in the celebrants, notions of time become ephemeral, and the noise level in the echo chamber on Parliament Hill exceeds in decibels anything one might experience at a hard rock concert. A man of sensible habit or sobriety cannot endure it very long; only the hardy survive until daybreak, a passage the varlet has made but once, which was the bottomless night of Lester Pearson's Black Hand, when the varlet's drinking achieved true gravity flow.

The Gallery dinner is a carnival mirror held up to the national condition, reflecting a distorted reality. Star politicians and star performers create a harmony of mood in the synthesis of past events, present concerns and future anxieties. With the compulsive flexing of elbows around the bar, guards are lowered — the artifice of congeniality dissolving into camaraderie and unnatural candour — and the busy traffic of insult, which is the evening's fun, provides for accidents of revelation. In Pearson's act of self-loathing was the realization that he had earned the contempt of his peers. Throughout the evening's mockery ran a coarse vein of truth: Canadian politics was sick.

The fevers raging through the parties and parliaments during the sixties fed upon the frustrations of politicians never quite in power or out of it. Centre stage, those two egregious aging buskers, end-men in the minstrel show, comported themselves before their audiences with a supporting cast of hoods, spies, whores, union thugs, fixers and pedlars of influence. The Pearson-Diefenbaker Deadlock, to give the show a title, would have fateful consequences for tomorrow's politics. One was P.E. Trudeau. Another was Joe Clark. Still another was the Gallery dinner of 1965.

Out of the night's celebration of that black mass on Parliament Hill came the varlet's strengthened resolve: fortified by the hospitality of his hosts, he would set out to bring down Gomorrah's temple. It had seemed to him, even in the pallid light of the morning after, that a life's apprenticeship in politics had prepared him for the part. Reformation would be his cause, leadership review his strategy and ambition his ally.

To endure his lonely pilgrimage, the varlet practised levitation as an exercise and fatalism as a religion. Believed to be the Tory party's saviour by some, a traitor by others, he gave all alike the benediction of his cool. Only bullets could have deflected him; he knew he was making waves. These would soon engulf the embattled leader at Stornoway and silence the malevolent furies in his court. Then, after the storm, new voices would be heard, new forces summoned, the parties would be led, and the nation governed, by rational men of reasonable purpose, free of the legacy of a decade's acrimony.

For such noble aspirations, he found support almost everywhere, in Toronto, certainly, but even in Regina. Along the way, his course was smoothed by the party's Nestors who gave him the wisdom of their years, while the young filled campus auditoriums to hear him marvel at the excitements of politics, until, nearing the end of his journey, he felt himself vectored on destiny's glide path, become an agent of a new politics, bringing with him the gift of tomorrow's renaissance.

The euphoria induced by so dazzling a vision left him unprepared for the rudeness of a subsequent reality: even were politics made new, politicians would remain the same. Out of the chaotic convulsions that produced the moment of his achievement emerged the discovery of an unexpected consequence: no few of those who had found his cause useful now sought to use him. He sensed their unease.

His recent eminence had made him suspect. With the incident of his success, by which he created a gaping vacancy for the leadership of his party, the varlet became hostage to the aspirations of all those who yearned to fill it.

In a recurrent childhood dream, he would sweat in his sleep from having climbed some rock-faced pinnacle, or steeple's face, only to discover he could not safely climb down again. And so it was with his conquest; throughout the long ascent he had been sustained by a secret, the talisman to his spirits, which was that at the end of it, having reached the summit of his purpose, he would be done with politics.

Imagine, then, when weary from all the small business of his exertions, having left the last table, departed the last hotel, caught the last plane, delivered the last speech — and with the last vote taken — looking down from the climactic heights, he found himself staring into a vast, foreboding abyss, the lofty perch suddenly become precarious, a mere station in a private purgatory.

Signals of his fate reached him even as the delegates at the annual meeting of his party, in a chorus of unanimity, endorsed a resolution calling for a leadership convention. Seized by compassion for his humbled leader, he had turned over the chair to a fellow officer of the executive, Roy Deyell (who would later pay for his subaltern's role in these proceedings), in order to seek advice on healing wounds to pride, and injury to place and position.

On his rounds as peacemaker, he found Davie Fulton and joined him in his suite. The dragon, Fulton told him, his voice shaking with conviction, is only wounded. You must, he told the varlet, take the sword and sever its head.

Transmogrified into a St George, the varlet left the Fulton suite, himself shaking with thoughts of so lugubrious a mission. In the corridor, he met a man from Toronto who asked approval of his plan to raise a subscription for the Diefenbakers — who, he reasoned, would soon be homeless — to provide them with a suitable Ottawa residence. The varlet gave the initiative his distracted blessing; then, taking an elevator to the lobby, he was told by a passenger that someone had spit upon Grattan O'Leary in retaliation for the Senator's offence in nominating the varlet for his second term as national president. It was enough to make any man reach for his sword.

But no. His attitude towards Diefenbaker bore the burden of a considerable respect and, now, an errant sympathy. The metaphor of the dragon was lurid enough to be compelling, and even memorable, but most of all distasteful. Still, the old man had delivered the speech of a mattoid to the delegates, an amphigouri of his own creation, spurning, the varlet knew, the wiser counsel of the venerable Grosart. And he had been heckled, howled at, and humiliated by an audience as contemptuous of him as he had often been of them.

After the varlet had returned to the meeting, searching for an appropriate doxology for uncertain deliverance, Diefenbaker had re-entered the hotel, like a smoking girandole, to proclaim his defiance in an anteroom crowded with wailing witnesses to his martyrdom.

The light of that sullen, threatening day darkened at the windows. Outside, the streets, black with rain, bore the traffic of Diefenbaker's retiring forces — the janissaries recruited in Quebec, who nearly provided him a margin of victory — retreating silently to the precincts of Hull to enjoy the rewards of their mindless exercise. (What delicious irony, the varlet thought, if Diefenbaker had triumphed with these votes from a few score commuters from Hull, impersonating delegates from the graveyards of Tory constituency organizations in Quebec.) Sulphur hung in the air, as though the doors of hell had been left ajar. It was a night for a loser's private remorse, dreams of vengeance, beckoning lusts for blood, lycanthropy stirring in many a bosom, while the victors were left to contemplate their prize, a shambles of a party smouldering in the ruins of their good intentions.

In Ottawa's Chateau Laurier, the chambermaids on their clattering rounds summoned the varlet from his shallow sleep, but the dawn that was to usher in the new age of politics, and liberate him from his long service to his party, brought instead the sentence of a hanging judge. Allowing even for his hangover from the past night's determined celebration, the sour juices within him and the constrictions and leaping palpitations in his breast warned him that politics might yet be the death of him. Having won, he had lost. The battle had been a mere skirmish; now war had been declared.

That it would be war was certain. The old man at Stornoway chose his weapons carefully and turned to the Tory caucus — always his instrument — to be the spearhead of his counterattack. The varlet, in Antigua, inhaling martinis at Howard Hulford's Sugar Mill Bar, heard the news: 71 of the 95 caucus members had signed a round-robin letter voting their renewed confidence in their leader. Now there were two Conservative parties.

ii

Yes, we are a long way from the Gallery dinner of 1979, but a man's thoughts can easily sweep through a decade of history, and more, in the short walk from the Chateau Laurier to the Hill. And even as the cold penetrates his rented garment from Classy Formal Wear, as he overhears the conversation of his companions on this march, words coming between puffs of exertion as they climb the path along the Rideau Locks, the gears of his thought shift from reflection of past events to the business at hand.

His interest in this year's dinner is academic, a political scientist researching a doctoral thesis. He has come to test his postulate, to study images in the carnival glass where he hopes to find portents of future events. Does the Gallery mood — as reflected in its humour — mirror national trends? He is there to study the chief protagonists, Trudeau and Clark, knowing from a long experience how greatly their anxiety of this evening exceeds their enthusiasm for it. Would their conduct on this occasion, on the very eve of a crucial election, reveal some symptom of their interior condition? It is more than a test of a politician's ego to submit himself to these jaded observers; guts and guile are also required. And while the prime minister is known to possess both in quantity, he has become a politician discomfited by the unfamiliar chafe of hostile public opinion and narrowing options.

The winter capital of his shrunken constituency was now Montreal, heart of the Liberal fiefdom, but elsewhere, as a Goldfarb or any fool could tell him, there was a national blight of failed expectation of him that neither policy nor strategy could cure. Still, even among his critics, it was believed that Trudeau was an alchemist and that, somehow, he would convert the dross of his low esteem into a renewed mandate.

The varlet, frequently a victim of his unpredictable sensibilities, feels a nagging compassion for the prime minister. His respect for him has long been cerebral, and lately, sentimental. A man plagued by separatists, retentionists, oil barons, bigots, economic fundamentalists and his own wife deserves sympathy if only for the awesome range of his adversaries.

Compassion, however, must not become a barrier to objectivity. The record offered stern rebuke to the tenure of P.E. Trudeau: the winds of change now blew through the urban plazas where he had once captivated thousands with the novelty of his charisma — more novel by contrast to his predecessors — which hinted at a politics of ecstasy, orgasms in polling booths. Trudeaumania gave blessed release to a nation frustrated by the barren years of a sterile deadlock.

But it had all come to this, eleven years later: that the philosopher prince would be seen — paradigm of irony — up against the wall on Parliament Hill, in the long lobby leading to the Senate doors, now cast in the role of abandoned spouse, grass-widower to a lethal diarist, and, worse, a cuckold in the nation's gossip mills. One glimpsed in him, peering through his retinue, the distracted air of a man whose thoughts are unevenly divided between his perfunctory duty to this social occasion and the busy sorting of tomorrow's contingent possibilities.

The prime minister held briefly in his view, the varlet continues his promenade, greeting some, avoiding others; he cannot find Clark.

But Clark is a hard man to find in a crowd; his magnetic field is small, aura has not yet encompassed him, and in the uniform attire of formal dress, he is easily lost among the looming hulks and protruding bulges of more familiar political properties.

Paul Hellyer, looking down upon the varlet from his height, offers a handshake. They are both lapsed Grits, sometime columnists and — a harder truth — failed politicians. The Don Quixote of Canadian politics, Hellyer has enriched its history with the humours of his romantic, earnest visions. But when he is not running for office, or holding one, Hellyer is easy to like. (Later that evening, Paul will entertain with his rich baritone voice and be awarded an ovation larger than any given him at either Grit or Tory leadership conventions.)

Anyway, the varlet had lampooned Hellyer in a recent column. This encounter allows the varlet to tell him, as compensation, that the column produced an astonishing reaction: a stranger had called long-distance to convey his appreciation, a lady had written from Ottawa to say the column induced hysterical laughter in a dentist's office. The nation is still responsive to the man who homogenized the armed forces.

The crowd moves in swarms, like bees. Back of Hellyer, the head of John Diefenbaker appears, disappears. Diefenbaker?

But then two blue eyelids, resembling lamps on some cruising celestial vehicle, arrest the varlet's eye. The Honourable Iona Campagnolo, diaphanously gowned, passes to his left, exchanges a bat's blink of recognition, turns away, and recedes. Maybe forever, he thinks, always busy with election permutations.

But had he truly seen Diefenbaker? A wraith, perhaps, although the evening is young for apparitions. Richard Jackson, aging *enfant terrible* to the civil servants, comes down range, his smile as tight as the grip on his glass. Has he said hello to the Chief? (Vision confirmed.) Not for ten years, the varlet answers.

Jackson reports a telephone conversation with an editor of the Saint John *Telegraph-Journal.* So what's this I hear, Jackson asks the varlet, about you giving the Tories a hard time? (The varlet had appeared before a group of law students and prophesied a Liberal minority.) Why are you being hard on Joe Clark? After all, Jackson goes on, the Tories have given you lots of nice advertising business.

I say what I think, the varlet answers, over the lip of his glass, a reply that does nothing to narrow the gulf between them. To Jackson, it may even have been a *non sequitur.*

Extract from the Varlet Papers:

November 1965: Conversation between J.G. Diefenbaker, the party's national leader, and D.K. Camp, its national president, in the Opposition leader's office, Ottawa.

It is their first meeting since the election of another Liberal minority government. The national president is fresh from his convalescence, following his defeat in a Toronto riding at the hands of Mitchell Sharp.

The Chief begins by discussing his recent campaign in Prince Albert. I did not do very well this time, he says. Whereas I won in 1963 with a majority of 14,400 votes, I won this time by only 11,400 votes. That's not good, not good at all.

But, he says, brightening, you did well in your campaign, Mr President. Awfully well. How much did you lose by? A thousand?

About two thousand, is the reply.

Oh, the leader says, I thought it was less than that.

It is a warm, bright day in the capital, and a quiet one. The 27th Parliament will not sit until January, and the corridors of power are empty. The national president has steeled himself for this encounter; he has been accused by the Chief of being "equivocal" about his leadership. (Early in the campaign, the press had asked him, "Do you support your leader?" "As much as Mitchell Sharp supports Pearson," he had answered. Could he have said more — or said it better?) The clock chimes in the Peace Tower and strikes the half hour. Round two begins.

Well, now, Mr President (is the repeated salutation meant as flattery or irony?) tell me: what advice do you have for me?

It is an opportunity, an invitation, in the calm hiatus between the campaign and the opening of Parliament, which the national president welcomes. He knows the temper of his party almost perfectly — far better than the man behind the desk, as future events will prove — and is aware of a gathering restlessness that can only produce conspiracies of Catilinian proportions.

Unless, of course, his leader really meant the question and will listen to the response.

His first advice is something of a trial balloon, tossed up to test the currents. Having campaigned in Toronto, and in much of the country, the national president has arrived at the conclusion that many people are sick of a Parliament reduced to a cockpit, and political parties to warring tribes of pygmies. These were the metaphors in his mind, unspoken, but he did say to his leader that the country was weary of blood-letting and longed for a return to a more normal, functional partisanship.

As a step towards achieving this, he suggests that the Opposition leader take the initiative by proposing that Lucien Lamoureux, the member for Stormont, Ontario, deputy Speaker, and certainly the next Speaker of the House, be made permanent Speaker. A peace offering, if you like. But a signal, in more than one direction, of a fresh start.

The leader appears to ponder this, turning Lamoureux's name over on his tongue while he gazes into space. But at least there is a decent interval between the impertinence of the proposal and the leader's disposition of it.

No — he says, slowly, finally — we can't do that. We couldn't do that now, you see, because the French have too much. Now, Mr President, what else do you have?

Someone less foolhardy might have then abandoned the second part of his advice. But no; he would be derelict not to raise this next matter. He plunges ahead, a man seeing daylight from a thicket of danger.

The party, which had been drawn and held together in the recent campaign to allow the leader the fullest measure of his opportunity, would now be concerned as to its future, he says. Plainly, Pearson had led his party for the last time in an election. It would only be reasonable, then, that many Conservatives would expect their leader to begin to consider — at his leisure, but sometime in the next year or so — the appropriate time for the party to choose a successor.

Ah — the leader sighs, after not so long a pause — but you see there *are* no successors. He would illustrate by example. Fulton? Fulton had ditched himself, against all advice, by accepting the provincial leadership in British Columbia. He had no judgement. Fulton could never lead this party.

Hees? Hees had been like a son to him. But he had destroyed himself, running off with Bassett in 1963. Had he stood fast, he would be the next leader of this party. But not now. Not ever.

McCutcheon? A snort for McCutcheon's qualifications.

Who is there? The premiers? He had asked them all — Robarts, Roblin, Stanfield — asked each of them to come and take their place in Parliament. He had even told Roblin, before the last election, there would be possibilities for him if he would come in — that was as far as he could go, you see — but, no, none of them would come forward.

There is no one, the leader says, sorrow in his voice, because, you see, no one can lead this party until he has sat in Parliament. (A message for the president?) Bracken had tried to lead the party from the public galleries. It's easy to be a premier, and they are all good men. But they ought to try being in Parliament. Then you find out. But they don't want to sit in Parliament. They like being premier. Well, there's a difference between being a premier and being in Parliament.

But the leader is glad to have the president's advice. Such advice would always be welcomed, because that's the way he is, always willing to listen to the advice of anyone.

The audience is over. But the national president has one further impertinence, as he moves to the door. It is merely to remark that he had been impressed by the fact that his leader — "you, yourself, sir" — had run for the leadership, against Bracken, only twenty-one months after being elected to Parliament. (He had looked it up in the *Parliamentary Guide*.) So, he had concluded, it does not take long before a member of Parliament feels himself qualified to lead his party. There were, then, possibilities to remedy the leader's despair over the lack of successors — such as a by-election? A passing thought, mind you, from the national president, passing out the door to early oblivion.

Then there was Walpole. The name comes to mind as he descends the marble stairs and walks through the silent corridor to the centre door. Walpole had led his party for twenty-seven years and been prime minister for twenty of them. He, too, lacked successors. But Walpole had been a Whig.

A further extract from the Varlet Papers:

March 1966: a second meeting between the national leader and the national president, in the Opposition leader's office. Also present: Richard Jackson, scribe.

He has not expected Jackson and is prepared to see him leave, but the Chief presses him to stay. Between Jackson's bow tie and his horn-rimmed glasses is the familiar grin — if there was a Prize Day for smilers, Jackson would have no competition — and the national president takes up position on the chesterfield, near the door. Behind him, over his head, is the portrait of Sir John A. Macdonald which, to him, makes the great man look something of a dude.

Winterset in Ottawa, early dark, the office half-lit, the national president is sober but apprehensive. He has no agenda for a meeting with the national leader that would involve the parliamentary corre-spondent for the *Ottawa Journal*; he holds his tongue and awaits devel-opments.

The impression grows that they have business with him.

I know you are interested in politics, Mr President, the leader is saying, and your views and opinions are usually sound. But there may be some things you might not be aware of. Mr Jackson knows these things. Perhaps the president should know them too? (Jackson nods assent.)

It reminds him of a preamble to some secret initiation: the rites of the order were to come, perhaps followed by communion.

After rummaging through a bottom drawer in his desk, the leader retrieves a document, held between cardboard covers. It is placed in the national president's hands, and he is urged to read it.

The document represents the secret testimony of Elizabeth Bentley, given before the U.S. House UnAmerican Activities Committee during the Cold War; somewhere in the shadowy folds of her evidence lies the buried mite: the Red cell meetings in wartime Washington had been visited by a Canadian named Pearson — aha! — Pumpkin Papers in the leader's office! The national president raises his eyes from this Congressional pulp for clues. He looks to Jackson, who is of no help.

No one knows about this, the leader is saying, exaggeration being his emphasis. The most recent to be informed of it waits to be sworn to secrecy, truly an oath he would have gladly taken. But the leader wants it understood, he says, that just so long as this man, Pearson, remains at the head of the government of Canada, then the leader has no choice. It is his duty to remain here. Here, he says, tapping a finger on his desk, the desk of the Leader of Her Majesty's Loyal Opposition.

The national president departs the leader's sanctum to return to the

Chateau Laurier; of late, he observes, each time he makes the walk, it seems longer.

iii

The bars along the Hall of Honour are busy now, stoking the spirits of a swelling crowd; it would soon be time for the running of the bulls. The varlet meets Flora, noting some cool distance in the embrace which has been the lifetime habit of their greeting. Does she suspect his irreverence of politicians is the fermented product of his envy? Probably so. That, and his publishing, at the time of her race for the Tory leadership, a column that expressed his dour presentiment that many of those who would betray her candidacy in the balloting would be — women! Sexist outrage! Yes, a man who sets out to write the mere truth as he sees it breaches a hundred friendships and seeds a thousand misunderstandings.

There is a touch of hubris in Flora MacDonald now, as there would likely be in anyone who has triumphed over national trends, captured a Liberal stronghold, made Queen's University her thralldom (the hardest trick of all) and become the only politician whose first name would suffice for an introduction to any crowd, in any city or tank town in the land. She is, really, a romantic heroine out of the pages of a Harlequin paperback; the red-headed slip of a girl from Cape Breton who caught on at Tory headquarters because she could type, do shorthand, and, soon after, even parse the sentences of John Diefenbaker. She could also remember names, dates, places, conversations, and where everything was filed, and could do without sleep longer than camels can go without water. Furthermore (can you believe a furthermore?), she owned a ravishing smile and bore herself with the proud, sure grace of a high-wire artist. Flora power!

Even so — comes the desideratum. Our heroine, who gave herself so resolutely to the ambitions of others, a striking figure in any politician's private commando, wearing the ribbons and medals from a hundred long marches, stands isolated now by her hard-won eminence, the grand marshal of her own parade, mistress of a private coterie whose serious flattery and singular loyalty serve as mother's milk to an insatiable ambition.

And here the varlet chides the reader, a pre-emptive plea: there is surely nothing wrong with such ambition, which, to be worth its sweat, needs to be insatiable. He had observed it in others: in Stanfield, who wore it casually, like a garden hat; in Roblin, who could be made to blush with it; or in Clark, who seemed nearly the last to know he had it, until, one night at the Ottawa Coliseum, he discovered it in some corner of his mind, like a winning lottery ticket.

But such potent drives and appetites, commonplace in men of infinite variety and even of unlikely possibility, are simply disconcerting in women. For some months now, observing rude ambition daily in Margaret Thatcher, he imagined Britons writhing in their discomfiture. The varlet was not alone in his vague unease with Flora's chimera.

The difficulty with Flora's candidacy for the leadership was that the varlet, like others, did not see her as a future leader of the Tories, but as a friend, which is not a put down, but a tribute to her capacity for friendship — a capacity which, celebrated in the stresses of politics, was all the more remarkable.

Men are raised to politics, their competitive skills nurtured in the games they play; sly cajolery and chicanery become as familiar to them as the act of shaking hands. They accustom themselves in life to being used, as blocking backs, pitchmen and pallbearers, and to using others. Utility is the current that drives them, builds their estates, provides purchase for the ladder's ascent. They spend their productive years as shameless buyers and sellers in a free market of human flesh, muscle and mind.

But Flora? The varlet would need to leave his skin behind (and some of his parts) to reverse the roles of nature and serve as some impersonal conduit of her restless pursuit of a job only a man is mean enough to hold.

Still, and here the varlet stumbles upon another of his contradictions, he regrets not voting for her at the last Tory convention (he voted mostly for Clark). That he did not has been a shadow on his conscience; it would not have mattered in the result, but it might have redeemed some small portion of his debit account with her: IOUs of politics and friendship substantial enough to correct the imbalance of Canada's foreign trade.

They agree to meet tomorrow, somewhere between Flora's duties in the Commons and office rounds. (Which they did, and the varlet noted, from his low-slung seat on the chesterfield, that she sat behind her desk and above him, as though she were on a dais.)

This dinner is nearly a ladies' night. Older hands could remember when these things were stag, when boys would be boys, and the girls, if any, came later. But for some time now the Gallery has been into unisex. When the women came, dressed right out of Mary Quant and Calvin Klein, striding to the Press Club bar in their Courrèges boots with pointed toes, it was a quiet revolution. Almost everyone let their hair grow, and a lot of the guys went out and bought themselves hair-dryers; on a night like that of a Gallery dinner — especially such a night — many of the male coiffures were wonders to behold, enough Final Net around to manage the hair of a hundred Medusas.

McLuhan would love it: this dinner, a mere leap in technology from a-wayzgoose, at which the pols come to stand close to the media stars; a chance to see them close up, in all their glitter and dazzle, just about the way they look from the neck up on television and without the oracle's squint. A man from out of town, finding himself alongside Geoffrey Stevens or Don McNeill, might wish he'd brought his daughter's autograph book with him.

Allan Fotheringham approaches to introduce Mrs Edward Richard Schreyer, of Beausejour, Manitoba, and Rideau Hall, who is on his arm. The varlet uneasily recalls yet another of his columns in which he confessed his surprise and scarcely concealed displeasure on the appointment of the lady's husband to the office of Governor General. (Is there anyone here he has not savaged?)

The encounter is brief, but enough to remind him of Canada's good luck with the consorts to its recent Governors General. The daughter of Jake Schulz will likely be no exception. On this night, the Press Gallery's biggest guns convoy Lily Schreyer as though she were a troopship. With Fotheringham at her side, resplendent in his wine-coloured dinner jacket, the varlet recognizes that he is now in the presence of the new forces in the nation's life, weighty enough to give a westward tilt to Ottawa's old vertical establishment: the lady, who represents the introduction of prairie ethnology to applied political science, and her escort, who proclaims belated recognition of a western sophistication previously detected in reprinted Vancouver cartoons.

It had once been the fashion of those western journalists who came down to the national capital not only to join the establishment, but to sign on with the government as well; after all, a journalist without sources might end up an iconoclast, in which case he could also end up without a publisher. But no longer.

Fotheringham is a media star, the brightest yet seen in the western firmament, whose lay-about-him, irreverent, last-page columns so dominate the editorial pages of *Maclean's*, that subscribers now read their national magazine from back to front.

It took more than a little doing to interest Canadians in the standings in the western political league, even when the money got big out there. It was like Japanese baseball; you knew it was somehow different and, anyway, you probably wouldn't like it. Few of the western transplants really blossomed in the Big Time. But Fotheringham opened up the politics of the west to a long-dormant eastern curiosity.

And Marjorie Nichols, who had been the Foth's perfect twin, was not your ordinary media starlet but an avenging angel. Between them, Nichols and Fotheringham revolutionized Ottawa journalism. For the first time in Gallery history, the clean-up hitters were up from the western leagues. (Nichols was soon waived to Washington to allow the brazen takeover to appear more like a mutative, decent process.) The new far-western journalism, if it had a school, would have been founded by David Halberstam, who, the varlet remembers, once instructed him in the rubric of his craft: all politicians are liars, and their chief currency is gratitude. Hence, any journalist who allows himself to become grateful to a politician will find himself obliged to lie for him.

Such musings suit the varlet's mood as the lights are switched on and off to signal the closing of the bar, and to permit the assembled guests their opportunity to bring a drink with them to the dining room. The Gallery has changed since the varlet first knew it, but the thirst of politicians remains the same; last-minute business at the bar is brisk.

Thus far, there has been little in this evening to weigh on the scales of his hypothesis. Heavy with foreboding that perhaps this maieutic device of the dinner might fail him, the varlet seeks distraction in the *aloyau de boeuf rôti* placed before him, which proves to be tough. Across from him, at his table, sits Donald Doyle, Clark's media flack, a man much belittled in the Gallery, and a francophone. The gods make mischief with the painstaking efforts of Tory leaders to proclaim the presence of French-speaking Quebecers in their councils, sending them men with Irish patronymics — O'Hurley, Flynn and Doyle, to name three — who sound more like a Dublin firm of lawyers than Tory obeisance to the French fact.

The varlet spends most of the meal in Pieria, having found himself wedged between two pillars of sobriety, one of them NDP, and, when not visiting the muses, he reads the evening's lyrics printed on the back of the menu and the four-page mock newspaper, "Not the Globe and Mail."

If there is a needle for Trudeau in all this, there are cudgels for Clark:

> . . . everyone is having shit fits
> Wondering why my office staff
> Is full of ninnies, nuts and misfits . . . .

And:

> A High River boy not long on the scene
> Shockingly handled by Neville and Green
> Bit neurotic, too much exotic, full of vim
> You can tell by his smile, you can judge by his style
> Alberta's the place for him.

The butt of the fun, however, was to be neither Trudeau, Clark nor Broadbent. It was to be Ed Schreyer, become His Excellency by the Grace of God, the Queen, and Her Majesty's Principal Canadian Adviser. It was something for the varlet to ponder, this first demonstration of *lèse-majesté* in the history of Press Gallery annual dinners. But not for long.

iv

John Warren is the president of the Parliamentary Press Gallery, whose duty it is to introduce the after-dinner speakers in starkest terms and make a few opening remarks himself, generally in the disguise of announcements. Gallery presidents rise unfailingly to this occasion and Warren is at least as engaging with his wit as any of his predecessors had been; winning the varlet's heart, he also pays graceful tribute to two parliamentarians who will pass from this scene after the next election, Tommy Douglas and Robert Stanfield.

The diners proffer ungrudging applause to Warren's valedictory salute. Douglas, the pocket evangelist of prairie socialism and a man who, during his forty-five years in politics, has addressed himself to all the torts known to God, is a life member in good standing in the varlet's esteem. Had they not marched, shoulder to shoulder, against the war in Vietnam? But more: had they not, following a fit of managerial unction, both been tossed out of the lobby of the Chateau Laurier that same November afternoon, out into the bitter chill and into a storm of Maoist invective? Yes, the varlet had learned from much experience that there are worse companions for life's adventures than socialists; as, indeed, there are no better hostelries from which to be ejected than the Chateau Laurier.

The first speaker to follow the Gallery president's opening gambit is Clark, introduced as the leader of Her Majesty's Loyal Opposition. The room seems suffused in shadow and uneasy expectation, the audience seized by some dull premonition. The varlet stands now at the entrance to the parliamentary dining room, alongside Richard O'Hagan, a third or fourth cousin of his, once Trudeau's press officer, now the eighty-fourth vice-president of the Canadian Imperial Bank of Commerce. They have a clear view of the proceedings.

To explain the coming of Joe Clark to the post he now holds would be no easier than explaining the cosmos. Of greater import to his audience is that Clark may be within some sixty days — a cat's whisker as history is measured — of running the country and rearranging the lives of everyone in the room. It is a heavy thought, but there are furies and fevers, so many of them to stretch possibility to — well — to Clark, a Clark government. The burden of such conjecture weighs on the crowd, which receives the Tory leader with a

Tossed out of the lobby of the Chateau Laurier that
same November afternoon, out into the bitter chill
and into a storm of Maoist invective... there are
worse companions for life's adventures than
socialists.

sitting ovation, adequate for a man who, at the very least, threatens the comforts of many of those present.

Future considerations alone do not account for Clark's restrained reception. No, the varlet clearly recalls the first time Diefenbaker had appeared at this function as leader of the Opposition, to be given two standing ovations, supported throughout his performance with whoops of sheer delight, awarded both ears and tail for the sharpness and thrust of his wit, all of which, in the varlet's hypothesis of media osmosis (among other things), signalled the coming of a Diefenbaker government.

In those days (it was the winter of '57) Diefenbaker was neither more nor less than a known quantity, a product of Gallery ink and establishment indulgence, which had created the image of a safe man. Indeed, one veteran journalist had wept openly, so great had been his relief, upon Diefenbaker's election as leader. (Some Tories had wept with him, but for different reasons.) Not everyone in Ottawa wanted him as prime minister, but no one thought he deserved to do badly either, and their favourable bias would ensure that he didn't.

Clark, however, is perceived very differently by those assembled in this same room, twenty years later. Unlike Diefenbaker, he was not the choice of the Tory caucus. His candidacy did not have the weight of a political base; indeed, he had no political base. His native Alberta support was negligible. The establishment, including the ambassadors and high commissioners, had no briefing book on Clark. Head waiters, from the Chateau Laurier Grill Room to Louis IX would have been inclined to seat him by the kitchen door. The media had been stunned by his convention victory; the post-convention cry of "Joe Who?" perfectly expressed their consternation, and the lack of hard information.

No national capital enjoys surprise. It is uncomfortable with mystery, and the baffling mystery of Clark soon became an irritant, something under the skin, further inflamed by the swoops of his fortunes in the public opinion polls. Any national leader of the alternative party is a natural force to be reckoned with; Ottawa deals in futures too. But Clark had appeared on the scene like some foundling left on the steps of Parliament, without a full name or established lineage. There was not, alas, even any gossip about him: no one knew his habits, foibles, predilections, tastes, or appetites, or even if he had any.

It is a truth about Clark that his political elixir has been mixed in another batch; his chemistry is unfamiliar. It is also true that he has been around Ottawa for a long time, a careerist in aidesmanship, only since 1972 a backbencher, but thought no more likely to become the Tory leader (or prime minister!) than a Swiss Guard to become Pope. And now that he is at least identifiable, he is no less easily explained, but is perhaps the consequence of some chain reaction in an unknown galaxy.

Worse than the mystery of Clark, for which Ottawa was unprepared, and remains so, is the threat of discontinuity. Clark is the first politician to succeed to the leadership of a national party without the blessing of his elders. There are few lines or connectors to him. He comes from nowhere, without sponsors. It is one of the neural discomforts in his audience: the awareness that if Clark becomes prime minister, everyone in Ottawa will need an introduction.

As Clark begins to speak, the evening promises reward for the varlet's research.

"Mr President, Your Excellency, distinguished guests..." But will he not acknowledge the prime minister? If not, whether oversight or insult, neither could be helpful to the speaker's interests: Clark would have to be a man of leaden sensitivity if he does not understand that he is not among friends, but in the company of appraisers.

Had there been a text released in advance of Clark's delivery, the substance could not have been recovered in the reading of it. What remains in memory of Clark's performance was its effect, a numbing sense of alienation. Part of the trouble was in his delivery. When on his feet, at the podium, he gave to every spoken word the same weight: adjectives and adverbs marched through the mind like so many sized platoons in a ceremonial parade; diphthongs and gerunds thumped like boots on a drill square, and the words tended to overwhelm his meaning. Hearing Clark was like listening to a man ordering his breakfast in the presence of his elocutionist: the cup was emphasized as much as the coffee, the cereal given no more inflection than the bowl it comes in.

Yes — the varlet recalls a line in it, which was a mock complaint of Ian Green, who, Clark said, failed to warn him of the fact that the president of India drank a cup of piss for his breakfast. Clark's listeners groaned at this, hearing the cupboards rattle as far off as Rockcliffe. When he finished, to muted applause, only a handful stood, expressing a defiance suitable to the tenor of the speaker's remarks.

When the prime minister is introduced, the varlet detects a shift in mood; tension dissolves in the room in the presence of a man whose mystery is at least familiar. As with theology, the mystery in him need not be understood to be believed. If they do not know what he is up to, they know what he is about, and if his motives are often unfathomable, they are presumed to have purpose.

Insouciance is a fitting mask for a consummate actor of ineffable diffidence: nothing Trudeau has heard or seen from Clark, on this evening, would have improved his opinion of him or given any urgency to his ritual task, and it becomes plain to all that his tactic for the occasion is to act the role of a player in a puppet show, wherein all his words come from offstage.

He does not pretend to give a speech, but deliberately sets out to read one, making sure his audience see his notes, impressing upon them, with his halting delivery, his lack of familiarity with their contents. Where the humour of his ghost-writers fails him, he shrugs — a critic's objective observation — but he then proceeds. It is as though he were opening up a platter of fortune cookies, removing himself from responsibility for the banalities inside. If you don't like that joke, he is saying, wait until I crack another.

The varlet, whose feelings for the prime minister are well shy of idolatry, is nonetheless impressed by the perfor-mance. There is even a sally aimed in his direction: that he had leaked a portion of the Tory platform, which is to build a fence around the two-hundred mile offshore limit to pre-vent Clark from leaving the country again. (The varlet would have preferred a less feeble jape; still, it contained the seed of prophecy.)

The enthusiasm of others for the prime minister's act is restrained, but he rates higher on the applause meter than Clark, explained in part by the fact that a good percentage of his audience is in his immediate employ. Still, for the curious seeking clues, if Clark's belligerence has been the hint of Tory election strategy, the prime minister gives nothing away as to his own. To the varlet's trained eye, the prime minister looks like a man intent upon survival; strategy would come later, possibly in the gift of Joe Clark, but he would waste nothing here.

So now to His Excellency, the Governor General, the somewhat tentative toast of Ottawa, and the roast of the evening's sport. Standing ovations are in order for Ed Schreyer. The newest tenant at Rideau Hall bears no resemblance to Alexander of Tunis, whose chest of medals could be read like world history, nor does Schreyer have the patrician air of Massey, who was the first Governor General to lack a peerage or royal connections, and the last to look as though he had them. Nothing of Vanier's gentle dignity, nor anything like Léger, for whom the job had al-ways seemed, even before his stroke, like something to be dutifully endured, without complaint or prospect of relief from its pretensions. (The varlet marvelled at a mother who could rear such sons!) As for Michener, there was only some general geography in common with Schreyer — he had been born at Lacombe, Alberta — but there was always more of

Oxford, the Middle Temple and Upper Rosedale than of Lacombe in Michener.

As a Governor General of Canada, Edward Richard Schreyer has minimal military credentials: he had served as a second-lieutenant in the C.O.T.C. His intellect had been honed at United College, St John's College and the University of Manitoba, all of Winnipeg, and his good works all earned in the generalist's field of politics. He is, therefore, in this latest of his callings, an original.

His curriculum vitae, alongside those of his predecessors, seems woefully short, but perhaps one could measure the long march of Canada's history, from its days as a British Dominion, by comparing the biographical embellishments of an Imperial predecessor, such as Field Marshal H.R.H. the Duke of Connaught and of Strathearn, K.G., P.C., K.T., K.P., G.M.B., G.C.S.I., G.C.M.G., G.C.I.E., G.C.V.O., G.B.E., with those of the Honourable Ed Schreyer, M.A., a successor some sixty years later.

To say Schreyer is an original suggests that Canada's most recent Governor General owns qualifications enough, but of a different kind. Upon the man "who's neither French nor Limey," as the Gallery songsheet has it, neither from Ontario nor Quebec, and neither Liberal nor Conservative, nor even a lawyer, devolves the unique task of representing, yes, proclaiming, to the country not only what he is but all that he isn't.

As the Governor General approaches the lectern to acknowledge the greetings from Ottawa's élite — could more of them be represented in any one room? — the varlet imagines the flourish of egalitarian trumpets. If Ed Schreyer were coming to the microphone to accept the trophy for the winning rink in the annual East St Paul Curling Club's closing bonspiel, it would seem about right.

But as His Excellency twins his tongue to the exertions of his scriptwriters — remember, it is all in fun — the varlet, now shifting from one foot to the other, as the words of the first citizen of the land plod through his mind, consoles himself with the notion that there has been some slight distillation from the evening's ferment. He is nearer to finding expression for his thesis.

There is some elaborate convolution, meanwhile, during this first public display of His Excellency's wit: he is saying, by way of comparing western and central Canadian terms of opprobrium, that back home in Winnipeg they have an expression (pause for effect): Bugger you!

The effect of this vice-regal sally upon the audience is to draw from it an involuntary groan — oooooh! — followed by suppressed titterings like those which occasionally interrupt scripture readings in boarding school chapels.

It was, as they say, an inside joke. Enough to say that buggery had recently become moot to the courts in Winnipeg (and in journalistic circles in Ottawa), the salient, and poignant, feature of it being that charges relating to acts of sodomy had been brought against, among others, a publisher of an esteemed Manitoba newspaper. It did not seem a likely topic for vice-regal humour, but it was a further gift to the varlet's thesis.

His Excellency is good for several minutes more and when he sits down his audience stands again, conspicuous in its politeness, but as well to move nearer the door. This has been a lot to endure.

The crowd which reassembles in the Hall of Honour downstairs is subdued; drained of the evening's expectation, they have little to look forward to, or back upon. Like reviewers of a bad play, their talk is as to which of the actors has been the least worse. But most seem aggrieved.

The varlet is canvassing opinions among the Grits until a nudging voice behind him asks: Are we still speaking? He turns to find Clark. Routine greetings and assurance follow. Then: he had not, he tells the Tory leader, thought highly of Shreyer's performance.

A cherubic smile puckers Clark's face. Perhaps, he says, it's because he's too young for the job.

In any game of verbal shinny, Clark is quick around the net. But in a long night, growing longer, it has been his only score.

V

Now there is a strange encounter with Robert Muir, the Tory member for Cape Breton — The Sydneys, who has burst from a scrum around the bar to greet him with unexpected warmth and cordiality, revealing the hustling *bonhomie* of a man who knows something you don't and will need all the friends he can get. The varlet does not linger with Muir, but he marks the moment, putting it aside as a small puzzle with a good piece missing.

His book on Muir was dismal reading, but even so, a part of his education in politics. When Diefenbaker fired Flora MacDonald, the party's dutiful servant at the national office, thus signalling that a state of war existed between the leader and the national president, consternation over the firing had been expressed in the Tory caucus, by way of a resolution.

There were those who came to her defence, believing, in their incredulity, the official line that the deed had not been done by Diefenbaker, but represented merely the clumsy attempt of a newly-appointed national director to establish his authority down at Bracken House. Muir, however, knew otherwise. He intervened to give the caucus his opinion — as one Cape Bretoner sealing the fate of another — that any move by the caucus to restore Flora to her job would be to strike against the leader. This closed the debate on the subject.

Had Flora never left home, she would have been a constituent of Muir's, doubtless his most effective supporter, but, in Ottawa, she was a one-person marching band and cheering section for him, and it was believed she would go down a coal mine without a lamp in his cause. But when she was abruptly removed from her job at national headquarters, Muir was neither the first to come to her defence, nor even the last.

Thus did Flora MacDonald pack her bags, to arrive ultimately at Queen's University, and become, in Diefenbaker's widely quoted oxymoron, "the finest woman ever to walk the streets of Kingston." As for Muir, his credentials as a leader's man continued to be improved, along with the majorities awarded him by the voters back home. People rated him as a solid, safe man of uncomplicated loyalty and modest ambition. In 1974, however, a majority that had been counted in thousands slipped to a few hundred. But he was a survivor, an example of the virtues of fealty, to which testimonial dinners are the inevitable reward.

In June 1977, Joe Clark came to Isle Royal Hotel in Sydney, Nova Scotia, to heap tribute upon the honoured guest who was celebrating twenty years of perfect stewardship: "I am pleased to be here to honour Bob Muir tonight," Clark intoned, as preamble to the evening's essential hyperbole. "No member of Parliament has been more forceful or effective — whether it has been his attack on the present government for its failure to solve, or even take seriously, the economic problems of this island, or his recent demand for a transportation policy for Atlantic Canada, Bob Muir has been the best advocate and spokesman this island could have."

"Had the Diefenbaker government remained in office," Clark went on, unfolding a dazzling hypothesis, "this would have been a better Canada today — more prosperous, more dedicated, and, above all, more united."

Those who attend testimonial dinners come to be impressed by the worthiness of the occasion and leave their normal scepticism at the door. The varlet, however, has retrieved the text of the function's principal speaker, preserving it as an example of how pure moonshine can be employed by an orator to rewrite history, rearrange reality, and recant his own role in it.

Four months later, in October, Clark announced the names of fifty-six caucus appointments, ranging from Caucus Chairman to Youth: "The best advocate and spokesman" Cape Breton could have was not one of them.

No mystery, then, that the encounter with Muir in the Hall of Honour, on the eve of the 1979 federal election, struck him as somehow different than others had been — the varlet has a long experience in detecting nuance in social intercourse — and it was not until sometime later, when the writ had been issued, that the dawn broke.

It broke after a light shower of dispensation which fell from the prime minister's office: Doris Anderson, a sacrificial lamb in the October by-elections, appointed to the Royal Commission on the Status of Women; one of Jack Horner's brothers to the Energy Board; sundry Grit MPs to the Energy Board, Parole Board, or the Senate; and — and! — Tory MP Robert Muir to the Senate. On the eve of an election in which every Tory seat would count as dear, the loyal member of Cape Breton—The Sydneys became a willing accomplice to the burglary of his own political estate.

But politics, alas, becomes, out of all that initial caucus collegiality, finally introspective. The longer one lasts, in the rhythm of government seasons, the shorter the odds against survival. A simple thing, at the outset, before actuarial possibilities infect the mind, to stand four-square, upright and counted; but another thing, when ritual wears, as the blood cools, as life's options narrow down to yet another writ, until, finally, the hunter senses he has become the prey.

So Muir had gone to the Senate, knowing he was being incorporated into Liberal strategy, that they did not want him there, but wanted his seat. Still, what an offer: fifteen years would lie ahead of him now in the Red Chamber, years without care or constituency, and with all the polls reported. A man whose life is suddenly made up of such pleasant

certainty, enjoying an inheritance larger than prior calculation or ambition, is bound to recast his mould, finding himself suddenly devoid of familiar friends or enemies, in a
world without anxiety.

The varlet is feeling like Scrooge, confronted by ghosts of
his past. Had he been hurled into some fatal dark abyss,
rather than merely levitating amid this hugger-mugger in the
Hall of Honour, would not the same images appear to him?
Yes, a part of his life is passing before his eyes, that part of
it ending; the smoke in his nostrils is of bridges burning
behind him.

It is during this reverie he encounters Jim Gillies, who appears to him, through the haze of reflection, as a conduit in
the busy circuitry of politics' eternal continuity. His attitude
towards Gillies is ambivalent, but they had been friends, in
the urban sense of social acquaintances, and were also
friends of friends; indeed, he had celebrated many a New
Year's Eve with Gillies and mutual friends — the Jack
Leitches, the Westcott Cherrys, the Murray Rosses — but,
true to Toronto's buttoned-down urbanity, he did not know
him at all.

In the federal election of 1968, in the first hot rush of
Trudeaumania, the varlet had run and lost to Robert
Kaplan in Don Valley. After that, finding himself strangely
comforted by the result, he had put his future political plans
in limbo, sensing all the while his growing awareness that he
would have none.

Gillies, meanwhile, had made an unsuccessful run for the
presidency of York University, following the retirement of
Murray Ross. He emerged from the ordeal visibly shaken by
the ferocity of the opposition from a few of his peers but
consoled by the more realistic among his friends, who
thought him fortunate to be spared such a fate.

There began, then, a series of genteel canvasses of the
varlet as to his intentions in Don Valley. Would he stand
again? If not, Gillies surely would. Over many martinis, and

a calendar year, the varlet detected in himself an unnatural resistance: not to the notion of giving up his lock on the Tory nomination in Don Valley, but of giving it up to Gillies. Somewhere, in the layers of reluctance, lurked the notion that the defeated candidate for the presidency of York had fallen in love with Don Valley on the rebound. A strange way, you might say, to decide whether to contest the riding again or abandon it.

Finally, he had arrived at a terminal decision, when the president and the treasurer of the Don Valley P.C. Association called upon him at his home. (The president was Ann Austin, later to become Mrs Robert Stanfield.) The nomination was his, they assured him, if he wanted it. They produced their surveys, confirming that his recognition was high among the voters and his prospects as good as any.

It was then that he relinquished his prize, the Don Valley candidacy. He had liked the Don Valley Tories and would miss their company. They had worked hard for him and some even wept for him when he had lost. Political wars forge fast friendships; only a few outlast the political involvement. Still, they were all good people to be with, their politics, much like his own, a blur of shifting concerns and concepts overlaid with an unapologetic and enduring idealism. None of them seemed to ask much of the process to which they gave so much of their time, other than it seem worthy of the effort.

Having renounced the nomination in Don Valley, like a distant relative forsaking any claim upon the family estate, he saw Ann Austin and her colleague to the door; they took leave of him in a properly sombre, reluctant way, as though he were going to the moon and might never be seen again. A few days later, he had invited the Gillies to his home and they had sat, stiff with unease, while he once again renounced his interest in Don Valley. Afterwards, remembering the awkward, even mawkish nature of the occasion, the ritual had reminded him of an amputee giving away his favourite pair of boots.

Gillies was a hot prospect for Don Valley; with his academic *bona fides*, a published tract on urban housing to his name, connections with the downtown financial community, an aura of expertise in business — after all, it was his academic field — and a string of directorships for credentials, he was the natural candidate for a constituency that was very nearly the locus for the opinion that government ought to be run like Brascan. There was room for such an entertaining notion now that the romance between Trudeau and Toronto was cooling.

In 1968, Robert Kaplan had campaigned extensively on his good fortune to have been once a close companion of P.E. Trudeau during a journey into darkest Africa; there were hints of ineluctable benefits to both Kaplan and his Don Valley constituents should the prime minister's safari companion be elected. Further, Kaplan had married into a family of developers, the new élite of the mercantile class, and he spoke of interest rates, debentures and fiscal responsibility with impressive credibility over wine and cheese in the rumpus rooms of a score of high rises, some of which were in the family.

Four years later, the African junket with the leader dropped out of the campaign literature, and, in the flashy esoterica of high-rise high finance, Kaplan was no match for Gillies, who had a well-honed knack for speaking to lay audiences on the politics of fiscal-monetary policy in a genial, periphrastic way which always seemed commandingly authoritative and lucidly clear, even though the gist of it was hard to remember. Still, it is among the gifts of lecturing academics, especially when popularizing so slippery a subject as economics, to be able to persuade listeners to blame themselves for their failure to grasp the import of oracles who are plainly telling less than they know.

Then, too, Gillies had earned the friendship of many who were able and willing to finance his launch into politics. Kaplan, who had declared $86,000 spent in his previous campaign in Don Valley, enough for an entry in the Canadian equivalent of the *Guinness Book of Records*, found himself in a contest against an opponent whose underwriters would not have blinked at a six-figure budget. Gillies not only defeated Kaplan but chased him out of Don Valley to the more secure environs of York Centre, where Trudeau's onetime travelling companion could enjoy the compatability of an ethnocentric electorate with Liberal allegiances impervious to trends or the waning of his leader's charisma.

vi

A puzzle, this seeming parachronism, these leaps in memory; a reader will do well to keep his footing. All the while, however, the drinking at the Gallery dinner goes on, the higher levels of his brain now certainly awash, even though the varlet's true condition of euphoric levitation has become stabilized. So that when Gillies says to him, in his distinctively compressed voice, as though his bronchi were packed with Kleenex, that he hopes his columns during the campaign will have some kind words for Joe Clark and the cause, the varlet's reply is perhaps a better one than he would have given had he been clear sober.

Don't worry, Jim, he says, if I can think of anything good to say about you fellows, I'll say it.

Having dined poorly and fared worse with the speeches, he must now endure the entertainment traditionally provided for the occasion. The night is gaining on him, and, after the guests have taken their seats for the performance in the Railway Committee Room, he stands in the doorway, as Californians do during earthquakes, so that he might easily escape.

The entertainment proves to be arresting; not the best, but far from the worst of these annual follies. As a sort of secular apostasy, the chemistry of its cleverness is not found in the players but in the audience, which gleans from the fierceness of the satire a reaffirmation of its collective importance. You cannot make serious sport of trivial matters or of nonentities; satire needs highly visible targets, and ridicule would be wasted on abstractions.

Thus the audience gleefully submits to the lampooning, knowing the risible wit of the Gallery players would be lost on a lesser audience. Indeed, the Gallery traditionally holds a Sunday-after "reprise" for unranked staff, members' secretaries, ministerial juniors, lower echelon aides and relatives. The varlet, attending one of these, found the performance flat, as compared to that of the previous evening, not only because the performers were in the depths of their hangovers, but also because the assembled guests, who were cold sober, seemed as much puzzled by it as amused. When deliberate insult is entertained as flattery, the basic characteristic of the audience must be its impregnable conceit; only occasionally are there individuals in the crowd with peculiar vulnerabilities for whom the performance might be an ordeal, and who sit through it with the strained composure of a man in a medical clinic awaiting the results of his tests. Such as Trudeau, engulfed in a sea of troubles, private and public, or Clark, surrounded by the palpable scorn of his hosts, each of them isolated from all others by the remoteness of their ambition.

There is a mood, an almost visible consensus of apprehension and despair, that runs like a weft through the evening's confusion of ceremony, civility and egregious humour. It is as though we are all at history's bedside: not so mundane as an old order passing, although that too, but the terminal condition of a hopeful spirit, an imminent sense of loss, an interior silence heard above the din. This party is not as much fun as we all pretend.

The Gallery players take their bows now; it has been a long night of applause, some of it deserved. Among those so deserving, the varlet notes (as though a critic for the *Times*) are William Grogan, once Stanfield's number one in the upstairs office, who has genuine talent for these affairs, which, apart from his wit, includes an ability to sing on key; then, too, Charles Lynch, acknowledged as the Gallery's virtuoso and become its Falstaff, who has, over his many years on this stage, perfected a polished, artless style best described, admiringly, as *agitato bravura*; but also, Ms Martine Savard of *La Presse*, whose cigarette-puffing René Levesque has stopped the show two years in a row; finally, Bruce Phillips, CTV's first man in Ottawa, resembling a Gregory Peck, amiably awkward in the art of foolery but who succeeds only by playing himself, rising above his material, which must be a trick first learned in television.

As soon over, as soon forgotten. There is much too much serious business in this affair to be overcome by song or drowned in drink. At one o'clock in the morning, the revelers begin to dissolve into the outer dark, some to the Press Club bar, others to their beds, making grateful, swift departures. Hardly any of them, certainly not the varlet, would not feel an ebb within him, on this night, a marasmus of the soul.

More than that, he feels weighted with unwelcome auguries, as though all the liquid in him has jelled into sour presentiments. He had committed himself to writing a book — about Clark? Trudeau? the campaign, perhaps? — but the book would be a poor thing if only about the campaign. What he had sensed from this evening and its preambles was a campaign that would be dull and full of dread. It would be dull because, even now, before the writs, the result seemed as good as predetermined — that Clark would win, and in that likelihood lay the dread.

It would be a contest between Clark the Unthinkable and Trudeau the Unready. Pity the prime minister, for no man could prepare himself to run such a gauntlet of manitous: the bad indices; the fury-driven wife, bartering her notoriety; the metastatic escalation in tension between French and English Canada; more, more, and yet more. It would need a miracle to overcome all that, and Trudeau did not look as though there were any miracles left in him.

So why not Clark?

Indeed, it might be thought the coming of Clark would offer the varlet a vista of unrelieved delight: he had known Clark as an ally, had employed him in his office for a summer, had tutored him, sponsored and cajoled for him, voted for him, and even hailed his ascendancy to the leadership. More than that, a Clark victory would vindicate the decent stewardship of Stanfield and offer the final, telling rebuke to the Diefenbakerites, who had celebrated each defeat of the Tory party as vindication of their fuscous opinion that the party had been destroyed in 1966, when it voted to rid itself of Diefenbaker's leadership.

Few among the celebrants of a Clark victory would have so many reasons to celebrate. But fewer still the number who, even before the victory, would feel a strange disturbance in the mere contemplation of it. The varlet had as much trouble with it as did the Gallery players, their audience and the prime minister himself.

Returning to his quarters, piloting his rented car with suspicious caution through empty streets, the varlet could only construct the despairing hypothesis that if Clark lost this election, the party might be lost for another decade. But if he won, might not the country be lost for longer?

vii

A society which eulogizes the average
citizen is one which breeds mediocrity.
Pierre Elliott Trudeau
October 1971
Winnipeg

Over his breakfast of Gravol and coffee later that morning, the varlet brooded upon the events of the night before. He could not account for this gathering scepsis, this rage of feeling. It might be that time had passed him by, a sorrowful conclusion any man might balk at, that he was now in a capsule of his own making, isolated from events around him, and that the signal running through the elaborate plexus of his concerns was that he was not meant for today's politics or tomorrow's Canada.

A generation of poll-takers had usurped his role. No man could afford improvisation in the face of so much confirmed opinion and when politicians abandoned private judgement and experience for samplings compiled from the rudimentary examination of strangers. Public opinion — a noxious phrase — had become the karma of men who dream of power in the concubinage of computers.

But what sort of system is it in which the leaders follow and the followers lead? What is the role of the political parties, other than as claques? Who will test the firmness and fervour of unfavourable public opinion if politicians only flinch before it? Finally, who would bother with such a business?

It would become a good exercise for automatons, he thought, in which every man would march and manoeuvre to the dictates of the numbers — so many for, against and undecided — while politics became an industry for actuaries. Worse still, in an age of anti-heroes, courage and idealism would be secreted in many a mental jockstrap, protected from the incidental blows of the occasional over-achiever.

Even in the throes of his hangover, he could detect self-pity in the murk of his introspection. After all, had not Hatfield won again in New Brunswick, defiantly ignorant of the dire prophecy of the pollsters? But even a luckless sawyer might have enough fingers to count the exceptions to his rule. Elections are henceforth to be preordained, issues determined and strategy decided, out of the tabulations of the Teeters and the Goldfarbs. This would be the new cleared ground upon which the wars of politics would be contested. Nothing need any more be left to chance or to wait for inspiration.

The varlet felt his age and obsolescence.

At least, however, he would know from his sources the numbers by which the next game of politics would be played, knowing too that Clark would be as much married to his data as Trudeau would be the prisoner of his.

The Gallery dinner had been a feast of mediocrity but it provided a tentative thesis: the prime minister had no sorcerer's alkahest for this coming age. Elitism was passing from fashion and with it the spirit of innovation and the ethic of excellence which had lingered in the country since 1967. Nothing so truly marked its decline as Trudeau's appointment of Horner to his cabinet and Schreyer to Rideau Hall. Goldfarb's numbers had finally conquered the man. Normalcy must already be rampant in the land, a message not read in the stars but in the polls.

Rallying from his torpor, the varlet began an earnest search for the ingredients of a Bloody Mary, something to cauterize his internal injury. The thought occurred to him, his brightest of the day, that he would be able, for the first time in his life, to attend an election campaign as an impartial witness, with enough wariness of both Trudeau and Clark, and enough sympathy for them, to allow him the luxury of an unfamiliar objectivity.

The Death Watch

i

In the opening weeks of the campaign, the varlet watched from his television chair, and with muted enthusiasm, the rites of the candidates and the unfolding layers of their strategies. It seemed to him like the early rounds of a boxing match, much feinting and weaving, clinching along the ropes, each man waiting for an opening for a clean shot against a defence of predictable behaviour. The cut-men in the corners stood idle.

In those early rounds, it was clear to him, Clark was piling up points. He was the aggressor, in constant, cautious pursuit, nimble-footed, with a good, stinging jab — unemployment, inflation, debt, credibility — a mixture of crisp blows to the body and head. And the crowds were with him.

As for Trudeau, the varlet marvelled at a champion's conceit which had left him and his handlers so surprisingly unprepared. (The Liberal commercials were showing five-year old film clips.) And yet there was a certain fascination, since it seemed at first, despite the occasional futile round-house swing (showing how bad his timing had become), that he was the only man in the ring with the power to end it all with one punch. After all, his advertisements billed him as "tough," a quality undetected in the sparse frame of his challenger, and the writers had hinted, long before the match, that Clark might easily beat himself, running out of gas at the end, or impaling himself on a ring-post. It is the sort of pre-fight speculation that helps at the gate.

Scholars know the building suspense in any contest between a man who can hit and one who can box, in which the boxer's skill appreciates as the puncher's legs weaken, de-

47

priving him of leverage for a lethal blow. There comes a time, if the boxer can survive, when he has the advantage of his quickness and near parity in power. And so it appeared to the varlet, viewing the contest: while Clark began to step up the pace, Trudeau was running out of legs.

It seemed a good time to join Don Dunphy at ringside.

ii

Arrangements have been made for the varlet to join the media team accompanying the prime minister at Halifax. Now, early on a blindingly bright May morning, he squints painfully behind his shades as he seeks out the local Liberal organizers who are preparing for the arrival of their leader. He finds his quarry gathered at the south end of Halifax International Airport: a huddle of young men in dark suits standing by their black limousines as polished as their earnest, sober faces. Behind them loom the empty press buses awaiting their cargo, and among the machines and the men there is a traffic of officiously busy young ladies, badges and buttons pinned to their blazers, seeking reconfirmation of exhaustive details. It is a beguiling feature of politics that so much importance can be allowed for mundane functions. Yet there is so sombre and serious a mien to all this that a passerby might think the prime minister would be arriving in a coffin.

He was late coming out of Ottawa, someone says, but another reports that he will arrive nearly on time. Minutes later, further intelligence advises that the prime minister will deplane at the north end of the airport. The drivers start their engines and the line of cars and buses is convoyed by the RCMP across the tarmac to take up new positions. The varlet travels in one of the buses in the company of Arnie Patterson, the prime minister's novitiate press secretary, himself from Halifax, and a familiar figure in many a past political skirmish.

Richard O'Hagan's successor as media buffer to the prime minister is without the nervous intensity O'Hagan brought to a thankless job. Unlike O'Hagan, who concealed his partisanship beneath the mantle of his professionalism, Arnie's credits have been earned in the chicanery and hustle of basic Maritime politics. While rising from radio announcer to station manager, to the owner of a Dartmouth FM station, he has been more than once a Grit candidate.

With O'Hagan, who is built close to the ground like a scrum half, eye-level talk came easy. Patterson is long enough for basketball, so that, in conversation, most people are obliged to look up to him. Among Trudeau's entourage on this day, Patterson is highly visible, standing taller than Jim Coutts would were he perched on Trudeau's shoulders. The Press Gallery nurses a collective suspicion of Patterson if only because, apart from the prominence his present position gives him, he would as soon be in Halifax counting his money; one needs to be wary of those who hold important jobs they do not need.

Still, as a sometime peripheral adversary, the varlet likes Patterson for his natural congeniality. Besides, as one Maritimer studying another, he has already detected in him clues to confirm his own suspicions. The campaign has been a dog. While the day augurs well for the prime minister's visit, a bright sunlit morning tossed in a brisk, clearing westerly, the press secretary stands apart from the welcoming party, the dull cast of his distant gaze reflecting thoughts of a man bemused by unaccustomed uncertainties.

"Tell me, Arnie," asks a functionary, coming alongside, "how do you think things are going?"

Patterson kicks at the tarmac with the toe of his shoe as though to make a hole in it. "Pretty well," he says softly, frowning upon his foot. "Pretty well, I guess." He moves away, leaving behind further equivocation. "Yeah, I'd say things are pretty good."

Bob Anderson

Arnie Patterson's credits have been earned in the
chicanery and hustle of basic Maritime politics.
While rising from radio announcer to station
manager, to the owner of a Dartmouth FM station,
he has been more than once a Grit candidate.

The mood of the awaiting hosts brightens only a little as the prime minister's jet taxis to its station and shuts down. Senator Al Graham, president of the National Liberal Federation, a Nova Scotian, and the ranking personage present, stands by as the media file from the plane. Then Coutts emerges, cherubic, alert, smiling, to be followed by Trudeau, sportingly attired in yellow corduroy, a raincoat folded over his arm, a rose in his lapel. The prime minister seems smaller, reduced somehow by the brightness of the day, and the teeth displayed in his mannered smile appear too large for his face. The wind tosses his hair, disassembling the Caesar's wreath of his remaining locks, artfully combed back and interwoven, which conceals the essential baldness.

He is poor at small talk, and this talk, within earshot of microphones and pencils, is minuscule; there is only a slight lingering until he is in his car, the buses loaded, and the caravan, with its freight of doubt, moves off.

The scene along the Bicentennial Drive is unremarkable to the varlet, offering outcroppings of glacial rock amid stands of stunted conifers and sugar maples, a good location for a simulated moon-landing. In another day, the varlet would have noted it as yet another modern highway built by Nova Scotia's Stanfield government. He could not number the times he had driven this road, but had he still the fares he could buy his Chivas by the case. It struck him then, a true pilgrim in the back of a bus, that he had never come to Halifax on so strange an odyssey.

He would have been more at home riding ahead with Coutts, hatching strategies. Were he up there, right now, he would only ask of Coutts what in the name of national unity any of us were doing here.

The varlet has the latest Ontario polls in his pocket. According to Teeter, they read 39-31-17: voluptuous figures for Clark, in the only province that would count on election night. But the prime minister has brought his campaign to Halifax, lending his presence to the candidacy of Brian Flemming who, according to the Liberal Party's briefing notes, "is portraying himself as a dynamic, multi-talented individual who, because of his background and his standing with the prime minister, would forcefully represent Halifax's concerns within the government."

Not even pap needs to be that bad, but the varlet is not yet aware of the afflictions of incompetence and — not too strong a word — stupidity visited upon a party that once occupied the only corner in town dispensing expertise. The awareness grows, however, with each paragraph and page of the hand-out. Brian Flemming, it reads, has focused his campaign on five issues, the fifth of which is — Brian Flemming! "He is playing up his role as adviser to the prime minister . . . his attachment to Halifax [he reportedly lives in the oldest house in the city] and his knowledge of local concerns and issues." Honest to God.

If that were not enough of Brian Flemming, by far the brightest star in the Nova Scotia firmament of candidates (save only Allan MacEachen), there is more. This, on "National Unity," which is merely Issue No. Four:

> Flemming is suggesting that an independent Quebec would hurt the Atlantic provinces more than the rest of Canada and has been using the image of East Pakistan to strengthen his argument.

Benumbed, the varlet pauses over this material, meditating upon Brian Flemming's long stewardship in the prime minister's office, those years seated at the Maritime desk; only heaven would know how many policy pies had felt this adviser's finger! Would logic have been his suit?

Yes, it said something of the Liberal party, perhaps of Trudeau himself, that a day in a desperate campaign would be given to Flemming. If the varlet's travelling companions had read of the Halifax candidate's "issue-focus," nothing was said. Anyway, they were used to it.

The motorcade halts at the Bedford Institute where the prime minister is greeted by the candidate and some two-hundred supporters, spectators and onlookers. Trudeau climbs out of his car, always the hardest exercise of any in a campaign, to move among the crowd, Flemming at his side, looking bookish and bearing the weight of his years in Ottawa. The sun hangs at the day's meridian, but Trudeau bears his raincoat with him, as Linus would his blanket. ("For God's sake," the varlet says to Coutts, ever the stage manager at such events, "strike the raincoat. It looks like a statement." Shortly after, the garment disappears.)

But there is something about the people in this crowd, even though friendly, and most of them young, that a man would notice who had once been mobbed by crowds, adored by them — it was as though now they had not come to greet him but to see him off. That was it, the varlet concludes: it was something a friend had said a few days before, speaking of Trudeau's big crowds. "They are coming to say goodbye," the friend said, and a Grit he was, too, a French-Canadian Trudeau Liberal. "People aren't coming to hear him. They just want to see him one more time, before he's gone."

They see him off from Bedford, literally, as he boards the *MV Haligonian III* to cross the harbour to Halifax, the boat slowly edging away from shore, the silent crowd standing along the pier. No one cheers, a few wave, a brief, shy fluttering of hands. Below deck, the media fall upon the sandwiches and beer as if tomorrow would be for fasting.

As the good ship *Haligonian III* churns through the chop, heading for the Historic Properties wharf, her passengers are invited to gaze upon the naval dockyards, the new, abuilding container pier, the deep-sea oil rigs, and a half-dozen destroyer escorts and lesser craft of the Canadian Navy docked along the waterfront. It is less impressive a sight than the fleet at Scapa Flow, but is a vivid reminder of the politics of Halifax, whose basic ingredient is the salt of the sea. ("Industry, Trade and Commerce departmental officials," reads the briefing paper, as though speaking in a whisper, "have suggested . . . that the federal government is not sympathetic to a request for a shipbuilding subsidy. Brian Flemming is hoping that this information will not become an issue, or if it does that Mr Honer [sic] can be prevailed upon to re-examine the circumstances.")

Nearing our destination, a native Haligonian points out the pen where the abandoned, federally funded hydrofoil is now stored and, nearby, the *Bluenose*, a replica of Nova Scotia's most illustrious vessel, the felicitous contribution of a local brewer whose best-selling product is Schooner Ale. And for backdrop, inescapable to the eye, is the profile of the new city, with its rising towers of commerce. Would there be a skyline anywhere in Canada without the banks?

We are now close enough to the Historic Properties wharf (a site admirably redeveloped with federal funds) to measure the crowd, which is dense, and to hear boos drifting across the water. The weather has rewarded Liberal plans for this outdoor event but there will be a tariff imposed by hostile elements, now visible, in shirtsleeves and placards, who occupy prime positions along the wharf. The media, quick to exploit the possibilities in this evident confrontation, hasten to film and record the scene; as they do, the baying and hooting reach a crescendo. When *Haligonian III* berths and lowers its gangplank, it becomes audibly plain that the organizers of this event have been outflanked by the organizers of the Canadian Union of Public Employees and the Canadian Union of Postal Workers, "Kewpie" and "Cup-W" in the vernacular.

"We want jobs," goes the chant.

"Tru-deau, Tru-deau, Tru-deau," comes the alternative cry from the faithful.

"Boo! Boo! Boo!" shouts a woman among the demonstrators, holding a child in her arms. Following these primitive imprecations, she smiles.

"We want jobs!"

A woman, suitably attired for the day and the occasion, shouts above the dissonance surrounding her: "Get off your ass and look for one." She too smiles, as part of the crowd

Bob Anderson

The prime minister emerges from the crowd and, like a cork tossed up by the tides, reaches the platform.

Bob Anderson

Hostile elements occupy prime positions along the wharf... the organizers of this event have been outflanked.

rewards her with a cheer. It has been very likely her first intervention in active politics.

By this time, the prime minister emerges from the crowd and, like a cork tossed up by the tides, reaches the platform. Most of his audience is gathered in front of him, pressed between two oblong buildings, but there is another crowd on his right, backed by the harbour and the *Bluenose* and between a restaurant and the front of a tourist information office. The demonstrators, themselves now outflanked, are left standing behind him. Temporarily, there is a chagrined silence, and most of the crowd, at least, can hear Brian Flemming introduce the prime minister as a man of great modesty and humility, something he had noticed while serving as his friend and adviser. Such is the strain upon the varlet's credulity that he feels himself wince.

The varlet has taken himself to the rear of the crowd, and, while he cannot see the platform, he can hear Flemming twice, the words of the candidate's introduction bouncing off the walls in the narrow mall. Scanning the audience, he is surprised by the number of children who have been brought by their mothers, each of whom seems stunned by the turmoil of sound. There is also a good deal of flux in this midday crowd: early departures, late arrivals, shifting of vantages, so much mobility that it might not ever become an audience, at least not one to listen.

The cadres of CUPE and CUPW are now revived by the sound of the prime minister's voice magnified by a loud-hailer. What follows is a contest of decibels between sheer lungpower and the strident amplification of Trudeau's voice. The varlet has not attended a Liberal rally for de-cades and has never heard Trudeau speak from the stump; it could be that he has not missed much.

If the organizers of this yell-in expected the prime minister to make a speech, they were fools. But if the prime minister expected to give one, he was a greater fool. Still, he tries, inflicting damage on himself and frustration upon those who would have liked to have heard him.

A man cannot make a speech through a loud-hailer; he can give simple commands, or call for help, but he can't deliver a speech. The most the varlet hears, and he does not always listen, being frequently engaged in conversation by strangers, is something shouted about fish, a subject of remote concern to an audience obliged to eat it while historically unwilling to worry about it.

No, the politics of Halifax does not deal in fish, but Brian Flemming's first line of defence of the Liberal government's record is the achievement of the two-hundred-mile limit, which (and where would any of us be without the briefing paper?) "ties in with his experience in drafting Canada's position on the law of the sea."

So the prime minister, extolling the merits of Brian Flemming, declares that not only had his man drafted Canada's position on the law of the sea (in such a way as to suggest Flemming may have invented it), but that it was this upstream flow of events which pushed the international fishing waters out to the two-hundred-mile barrier, which was why you need a strong federal government, and why you couldn't turn over the Fisheries to the provinces, as Joe Clark would do, and as Premier Buchanan and Premier Moores wanted Clark to do.

"Because," bellows the prime minister, concluding his argument, "fish don't stay in the same place. They move around."

The varlet, struck by this refinement of the case for federalism, his mind's wheels spinning, begins to conjure a hasty essay upon the place of fish in Canadian politics. Is not Harold Innis's *Cod Fisheries* the seminal work in Canadian economic history? And was not the nation's first solo venture into international waters — the original proud moment of the creation of its identity — when it became a signatory in its own right to the Halibut Treaty signed with the United States? It would do for a Master's thesis: "The Influence of Fish Upon National Sovereignty and Liberal Hegemony, 1921-79."

A man standing beside the varlet says, confidentially, "That's bullshit, you know. The fact is fish don't move around."

He could be a Tory usurper, come to infect the crowd with sly counterintelligence, but he sounds too serious for mischief.

"Some fish move around," the varlet counters. "Tuna sure do."

"What about shellfish?" asks the man, his voice rising. "Why do you suppose they call 'em scallop beds? How come every fleet in the world comes to fish on the Grand Banks?"

And are there not always eels in the Sargasso Sea?

It was unlikely that any further defence of the prime minister's piscatory case for a strong federal government would be productive. The varlet, anxious to regain his neutrality in this as in all other matters of public dispute, produces his notebook and, adopting his manner as a journalist, writes upon a page: "Fish — do they move around?" He would ask Jim Coutts about that.

Still, this day finds him unprepared for such absurdities: the prime minister battling his hecklers in this sunlit trapezium of reverberation, struggling to hold any part of his audience, flooding the air with a strident voice no one has heard before, coming from a source few could see — were there a spine stiffened anywhere, or a vote changed between the Historic Properties wharf and Water Street, wherein the crowd was contained, it could only be to give a jolt of confidence to a Tory poll captain, or switch a vote to Clark.

There are now three, maybe four, crowds: surrounded Grits, imprisoned bystanders, CUPE and CUPW, and the curious. The choir from the union chapels, still baying, expresses the nub of their complaint, which is that the CUPW boss is on his way to jail for contempt. Jean-Claude Parrot was going to jail for defying Parliament, a sentence well-received by the general public and possibly the only substantive matter a heckler could raise that the prime minister would welcome. Indeed, in all the lengthy litany of complaints against the government, among all that had misfired, aborted, wouldn't work, or couldn't be fixed, the Post Office, which was surely one of them, was also the only one for which Trudeau could escape blame.

Parrot was a man who lost his case each time he appeared on television. It was not only his accent, which was French and, being so, brought the blood to instant boil in English Canada, so often has it become the accent of trouble, but Parrot also had a seemingly malevolent face — just right perhaps for eyeball-to-eyeball confrontation with Postmasters General but not the sort a mother would like even if viewed on Sesame Street. True, no man can help how he looks, but union leaders, from John L. Lewis to Dennis McDermott, look too much like men who would shut down the incubators of a hospital nursery to get another teabreak for a union of clerks. As a breed, they ought never to go on television without counsel.

When the hecklers begin their braying about Parrot, the prime minister knows that finally they have thrown him a pitch he can hit:

"Listen," he says, "in this country we don't have one law for the unions and another for everyone else. We don't have one law for the people of Canada and another for Mr Parrot."

At last the crowd has something to cheer, and it is the only moment in which the speaker is able to fuse his fragmented audience into one. But it is the only moment of the day thus far; the rest of the rhetoric now plunges into anticlimax, bathos and the inevitable closing banalities of the pitchman about to pick up his samples, shut his valise and move on.

Be sure and get out and vote for Brian Flemming, he says. Send him to Ottawa for a strong, united Canada. Something like that.

Kids scurry among the crowd, voicing their sentiments in piercing adolescent shouts.

"What a fucking jerk," one of them says, speaking of a man in whose acne scars mothers like his, a mere decade ago, perceived stigmata.

"Vote NDP!" shouts another, wise to ways of giving offence to such a gathering.

It is one of the problems of outdoor political meetings, and by far not the least of them, that the environment prevents the possibility of agreeable consensus. In a closed hall, the crowd is captive and, even if the speeches are dull, or the hecklers disturbing, as the crowd moves out, milling around the doors, greeting friends, shaking hands, whether commiserating or celebrating, its members can be persuaded, in the communion of like-mindedness, that things went rather well after all. A meeting worth attending must be deemed to have been worth the effort. While captive audiences need little persuasion, barring the catastrophic, this one, emerging from the shadows of Historic Properties, was fatefully fragmented, already intermingled with irreverent youths, self-satisfied hecklers and bemused spectators. The partisans, sensing their isolation and driven by doubts, are left to weigh the value of their dutiful attendance.

A young man clad in a toga appears before the varlet, addressing him familiarly by his first name. They shake hands.

"How are you?" the varlet asks.

"You don't know who the hell I am, do you," the man in the toga replies cheerfully. It is a statement of irrefutable fact.

"I'm sorry, I don't."

"Here," he says, producing a card from within his garment, "take my card."

The varlet does so: it is plastic, solid blue, and has nothing on it.

iii

The buses, lumbering in the van of the Trudeau-Flemming cavalcade, head into the old northern precincts of Halifax, into the Irish Catholic wards, along narrow streets whose rows of weather-worn, wood-frame houses shelter traditional Liberal majorities. The politics of Halifax were once more of an arrangement, and less a struggle, between Catholic Liberals and Protestant Conservatives, each imbued with a prior religiosity which decreed every other mayor should be Catholic, a careful balance of Catholic and Protestant members among the provincial constituencies in the city, and, in a dual federal riding, one Catholic on each party ticket. The north end produced the men and the majorities to guarantee a Catholic presence in ruling circles.

The decline of neighbourhoods and of patronage, the ranks of bungalows in the sprawling subdivisions on the outskirts of the city, and the restless ambitions of the downtown developers are all harbingers of a new ecumenicism. All that remains in the north end, amid what was once believed a Liberal mortmain, are the memories of Angus L. Macdonald, of Harold Connolly, and Gee A'Hearn, of days when you saw your politicians in the flesh, and when every faith, belief and trust was held in common.

The buses grunt and huff, labouring to round corners, until they arrive at the Northwood Centre Senior Citizens Complex, "regarded," according to a release from David Harrigan, (902) 423-6129, "as one of the finest in North America." And so it seems to be: a substantial high-rise looking out over the harbour, with a spacious lobby now crowded with the hostages to Brian Flemming's ambition — the media, the organization men, the prime minister's personal bodyguards, and, along the walls, the residents turned out in the fashion and finery of their years, a palpable excitement upon every face.

The media take up station in an auditorium which, at first glance, provides a vista of blue rinse; most of these senior citizens are women, mute confirmation of hard actuarial realities. Nearest the platform, the lame and halt have gathered in their wheelchairs. There is an almost inaudible buzz in the room, as though the occasion were too fragile to sustain more than whispers; but this is, after all, a political event, and in Nova Scotia, so that when the prime minister and party enter the hall, they are preceded by the wail of bagpipes. The varlet, discomfited by this room full of reminders of his own mortality, is relieved.

The prime minister's face is masked by the slightest smile. After the jostling and jousting on the waterfront, he has at least repaired to a place where the compliance of his audience is guaranteed; he could be no safer hidden in the sacristy. Even so, he is never entirely safe from the embrace of Brian Flemming's endorsement.

For Flemming will introduce his leader to this audience as one whose children played with his children, laud him as parent, father and family man. There is a suspenseful silence gathered in the room, as though Margaret's ghost were suddenly present. The varlet, who cringes at this conjurer's ramblings, recalls how many times he has vetted, edited or ghosted introductions to leaders of his own party and, when he did not, how often he regretted it.

But this is a house of mothers, grandmothers and maiden aunts, histories of uncounted hurts and wounds, and with dreads and certainties close enough to make the tribulations of a prime minister seem trifling by their very transience. And, besides all that, this is an exquisitely Liberal function; these are not only Senior Citizens — how bleak and felicitous a phrase! — but as well the true benefactors of the ultimate triumph of the welfare state, the conscience of society nicely institutionalized, expiation of guilt achieved in tidy bedsitters with a harbour view.

Liberalism, of which the Canadian model must be exemplary, has meted out its rewards and punishments with an even hand. That what is designed to be the provision of security might appear to the recipient more like a sentence, seems heretical to the donors. But how many of these here present, the varlet wonders, were nudged and cajoled by sons and daughters to apply for entrance as relief for their own responsibility? And how many of those sons and daughters could so cheerfully chuck their obligation, brimful of heart's ease and satisfaction, were not the state so eagerly compliant?

This is a business for bureaucrats, for case-workers, for the politics of brick and mortar, plotting the flow chart for the building of a national geriatric ward.

The prime minister's address, then, does not belie his sense of his audience. It is a poor place for a political speech and the varlet is mildly curious as to how Trudeau will satisfy the attending media without offending his listeners. But he has always been at his best when certain he will not be interrupted, and his performance in this group is flawless.

It may be that his faults sustain him; a man less intellectually arrogant or certain of himself might falter, just as another less sensitive and introspective might tend to be patronizing. Or it may be that a prime minister so familiar with modalities, norms, trade-offs, options and structures must feel at home in this synthesis of Liberal beneficence. But he is able to use his own voice, which he reduces to the level of a conversation, and he deals so gently and circumspectly with his theme of national unity that the reporters are hard pressed to find a sentence in it which they can elevate into a lead.

He praises his listeners for their contribution to building a strong, united Canada and is quick to say that he knows they are still making a contribution — it must have occurred to more than one in the room that he was, after all, not much younger than many of them — and he expresses his hope, which does not emerge as a piety, that the country would make use of their considerable wisdom. There is nothing of Clark, or Petro-Can, or of fish in these remarks;

Bob Anderson

A vista of blue rinse; most of these senior citizens are women, mute confirmation of hard actuarial realities.

Bob Anderson

A virtuoso performance, and few politicians could have matched it for its quality of natural sweetness.

indeed, a less knowing audience could not have guessed his politics, if he had any.

It was, the varlet concludes, a virtuoso performance, and few politicians he knew of could have matched it for its quality of natural sweetness. The applause for him is earned and it might have been one of the rare ovations he has heard, since the campaign began, that is genuine.

Afterwards, the residents and the campaign retinue take tea in an adjoining function room which is flooded by the afternoon sun. It is as though this were not an election campaign after all, but a strangely uneven day to be neither counted nor quantified.

iv

After the teabreak, this *voyage du premier ministre* resumes. The city of Halifax behind as the plane flies over Pictou County and out across the Northumberland Strait to Prince Edward Island, the varlet, for the first time travelling in the back of the plane with the media, reflects upon what he has seen and heard.

Plainly, the prime minister cannot find the handle on the campaign, a fact revealed by much that has transpired before and that has been reconfirmed at the last stop. The possibility that Clark would stumble, blow his lead by blunder, which seemed so alluring a prospect at the outset as to be thought a certainty, has become remote. No, the Organization Man out there, setting the pace, is running well within himself; the Tory campaign, finely tuned to its data, has taken on the momentum of a space age juggernaut, manoeuvred by men, including Clark — especially Clark — with sure hands, knowing where the levers and handles are.

The trick for Trudeau is not the art of patience, waiting for Clark to fall back, or down, but to overtake him. The truth about Trudeau is that his life has made him a front-runner. While there has been nothing in his political career other than unrelieved success, since he has always been sure to win, there is no evidence of his ever coming from behind, out of the pack, to do it. The novelty of his present experience suggests that he is little prepared for such an effort. Habitual winners, as well as chronic losers, nurse the same notion of fatalism. There is that to explain the seeming reluctance of the man, sitting alone up front, to make a run of it. But there are other explanations to ponder, some more soulful than obvious.

The aircraft shudders with the changes in pitch and the lowering of flaps. Prince Edward Island — "Disneyland East," someone says, not unkindly — rises beneath, green as Ireland, basking in the sunlit afternoon. The varlet puts aside the snarled threads of his thoughts on the Liberal campaign; perhaps the prime minister has saved something of this day for his evening speech in Charlottetown.

The Garden of the Gulf is also the Cradle of Confederation, both appealing to tourists who prefer contemplation to action on their vacations. No sooner have we been transported to the Charlottetown Hotel than a holiday mood settles upon the entourage.

Arnie Patterson, familiar with media lusts and appetites, has laid on beer and lobster for his charges in an upstairs room of the hotel, but he is dealing with a group whose impulse is to flee his hospitality and seek their sustenance elsewhere, at their own, or company's, expense. Within an hour, as if by a miracle of telepathy, the media have filled a downtown restaurant, gathered about tables piled with plates of lobster and clams, glasses of beer and wine, boisterously regaling one another with Lucianic irreverence. Cleaned up, the scene might have made a good commercial for the Island's tourist bureau.

The varlet, nagged by visions of Patterson now contemplating a sea of empty tables — a restaurateur without a clientele — is impressed by this spontaneous demonstration of the media's contemptuous disregard for a well-intentioned gesture. It is as though these younger practitioners of political journalism, none of whom were around when the media first embraced the prime minister as if he were their own creation, have nonetheless taken a lesson from the experience and would not themselves ride a campaign plane imagining it a bandwagon. The country was changing, even as they flew over it, but they would leave either rumination or remorse to the editorialists. While some of them would privately confess that they did not yet know how they would vote — as between "that prick and that jerk" — nothing of such doubts infected their coverage. But it was not perhaps a stern enough test of their objectivity; had they liked or admired Clark, it might have shown.

The varlet found their lack of bias sterile. Their passion was in the ferocity of their neutrality; he did not know what to make of it, other than to mark its likely influence upon the electorate. But he had been too long in politics to pretend that his own bias, no longer so partisan, was not a good part of his confused perspective in this election as between the prick and the jerk, and their parties.

The country had changed more in the past two years than in the previous ten, and the differences were largely in all that had been lost, including confidence, a long familiar expectant optimism, and, finally, patience. True, there were new power and wealth, along with old impoverishments, shifts in the balance of things, which put further strains upon the ingenuities of federalism to balance the needs of supplicants against the demands of the country's luckily advantaged.

What was fully shared were the grievances, too disparate and tedious to catalogue, and what was lost was the presumption of some common purpose, neither a syllabus for the nation's learning experience nor an agenda for its business. Above all, there was no communal sense of sharing in an uncommon adventure which, even in the hardest of times, had sustained the faith of a people in the pursuit of a national destiny.

The country had lost a sense of the commonality of its experience; all the races, tribes, provinces, regions — everyone — had come to prize only their *own* history, too much of it either of conquest or grievance, but each providing a unique exclusivity. An oddity, the varlet mused, that the man who had come to unite the country, in 1968, had not so much divided it as he had partitioned it. (A hard question for the strategists of the national parties: how to campaign in a land of fragmented electorates, not of parts but in pieces.)

It was not the magnitude of Trudeau's failure that produced this rage against him in English-speaking Canada — indeed, their animus was the nearest thing we had to shared opinion — but rather it was what they remembered of their expectations of him, which were not less than the children of Israel had expected of Moses. So that when the seas did not part for Trudeau, but instead became more threatening, a pall of disenchantment fell upon the people. The fact that the country was still afloat was of small consolation; a population expecting miracles was in no mood to admire mere seamanship.

Had history the wit to laugh, a propensity not even given historians, it would surely have been convulsed in noting the apogee of Trudeau's popularity, the summit of his power and promise. It was in the period of the "apprehended insurrection," when he threw hundreds of his Quebec compatriots into the slammer. With the British trade commissioner, James Cross, a captive, and Canada's most unlikely martyr, Pierre Laporte, found strangled by assassins, the prime minister of Canada reaped the easy harvest of approval in English Canada: from Westmount to Victoria, this was his finest hour.

A smog of deception hung over the land, the phenomenon of so many inversions of truth, reality turned upside down.

English Canadians sat spellbound by their televisions, fixated by the virile strength of this hot-eyed, fiercely calm prime minister, hearing his muscled rhetoric and imagining, at last, that all the troublesome forces in that troublesome province were now at bay. It was a catharsis for those who had long nursed the opinion that things there could only be resolved by force. And with the troops visible on the streets of Montreal, resembling nothing so much as an army of occupation, and with hundreds of citizens behind bars, few could doubt the moment had come: One Canada had joined its manifest destiny. It is possible that many of those in jail could not believe their luck; for them, it was a catharsis flavoured by sweet hints of martyrdom.

The author-sponsor of the Canadian Bill of Rights, the man who properly refused to reinforce the RCMP in Newfoundland after the murder of a provincial constable, and who had always found his voice to oppose whatever the prime minister proposed, became a silent onlooker upon this spectacle of folly, silence being the most eloquent expression of his approval. But while Diefenbaker fell mute, Stanfield was compelled to speak and, even though pitiably uninformed, one could hear in the awkward, laboured words he found to support the government some echo of his despairing doubts. It was, he said much later, the source of his greatest regret in his political career. But Stanfield was the abject prisoner of his caucus, which was in turn the willing captive of popular passion. When the critical moment came for Parliament to sanction the government's actions by passage of the Public Order Temporary Measures Act, one member, David MacDonald, a United Church minister from Prince Edward Island, stood opposed, the only elected member of any constituency in any chamber beyond Quebec to do so.

There were, though, a few "bleeding hearts", as Trudeau had called them, in Toronto, such as Alan Borovoy, Cy Midanik, Terry Meagher, June Callwood, Barbara Frum, and the varlet (their token Tory), who met to worry the small bone of their protest.

The Canadian Civil Liberties Association is something of a misnomer, never more so than on the night of the emergency meeting of its executive, held in a boardroom of a trade union office, when, after the day's canvass, it had become clear that no one of their membership or kith outside of Toronto, not from Ottawa or Montreal or Vancouver, not even F. R. Scott, would be with them in either body or spirit.

Walter Gordon was present, an elder in political circles, a man of amiable goodwill to whom crises of conscience were familiar enough. He had just returned from Ottawa, a capital seemingly under siege (a national state of mind) and, when he had listened to the words of protest intended for immediate dispatch to the prime minister, with copies to the media, coming from this lonely civil libertarian cell in Toronto, he had advised against it.

He had been in Ottawa and had discussed this apprehended insurrection with his Liberal friends and former colleagues, as one privy councillor to another, and had learned from them that the prime minister had done only what was essential. And if we knew what he knew, we would agree.

There was compressed silence in the room, as much because of Walter Gordon's earnestness as his listeners' embarrassment. Tell us, someone finally asked, what you know so that we can know if we agree. Because, while no one doubted that he had been told something, how could we know it was something that would staunch the bleeding hearts gathered around that table?

Beneath Gordon's geniality there is steel. No, he could not tell us anything of his private conversations. These were secret and could not be divulged. We would have to take his word for it; let his word be the cachet of his personal reassurance.

Anyway, Gordon went on, he had not come to persuade

anybody to anything. If we wished to proclaim our dissent, he had no intention of standing in the way, ill-advised as we were to do so. And, of course, he could not support it, which meant he would have to resign from the Association.

One would have to squint to see, in this microcosmic and decent confrontation of so much good intention and so little menace, the small genetic fluke which makes a few doubt what everyone else is certain of: that the earth is flat, popes are infallible, kings have divine right, or the truth has been told to Walter Gordon.

The system, including the politics of it, is very much a numbers game. The sanction of a majority vindicates all, even stupidity, duplicity and betrayal. The wonder is in this recurring phenomenon of perversity, a mere fraction in the larger equation, which encourages a few to busy themselves with the irrelevance of their concern.

Even the varlet, in this October crisis of conscience, had advised Barbara Frum not to lend her reputation to futile public protest. When she had called him to ask what she should do, he had advised her to keep silent until, at least, the hysteria had subsided. After all, he reasoned, even the CBC had been warned off practising journalism at the expense of national security. Why risk the credibility of a Barbara Frum when an entire national institution had coughed up its own? It would be like, he thought — metaphors of autumn upon his mind — using a damaged quarterback with the game already lost.

Civil libertarians lack numbers, endowment, subsidy, leverage and clout. What little they possess is the small change of moral suasion, which would not be enough credit for a loan at HFC, unless they had a co-signer. No, as well to advertise yourself as a public nuisance in the Yellow Pages as have your name on the letterhead of the CCLA. (Even so, nine years later, the letterhead still bears the varlet's name — and that of a newcomer to the list, Robert L. Stanfield.)

Those around the table, a coterie shrunken by one with Walter Gordon's departure, the compelling need to express their collective dismay lessened not a whit by it, concluded the business of their singularly intransigent telegram to Trudeau with due solemnity. So far as they knew, or know yet, they must have represented the only body in English Canada to feel so obligated. One thing to be said for being in this lifeboat, mused the varlet, was that it was far from being overcrowded.

After the October crisis, Cross retrieved and his captors given safe passage to Cuba, through November and December 1970 the popularity of the Liberal party soared to 60 per cent in the Gallup polls; the prime minister and his government would never again stand so high in public favour. He would win the country — narrowly, in 1972, and with ease two years later — but he had all along been losing hugely from the second thoughts of the several élites and estates of power and influence. There had been a steady attrition in his following among the professors, who at first were enchanted by the panache of a politician who wrote like a scholar and spoke like a philosopher. A decade later, it could be said that he had become, like Keynesian economics, simply unfashionable. In the faculty clubs the prime minister was now cheerfully disliked.

Another constituency whose affection visibly withered after 1970 was that of the performing arts. Trudeau had come to power supported by the impressive testimonials of Canadian theatrical celebrities in New York and from as far off as Hollywood. Everyone, from Kate Reid and Lorne Green to Johnny Wayne, seemed eager to be billed among the Canadian Performers for Trudeau, the first such fan club for a Canadian politician, a familiar phenomenon in reverse. If Lux be the beauty soap of stars, Trudeau was their preference as prime minister. The varlet was nonetheless impressed by these endorsements, which, he knew from the experience of Lever Brothers, sold soap.

There were no testimonials for the Tory product; an adjunct of idolatry is loathing and, for Stanfield, the campaign of 1968 was the hardest, since it was his first experience of being despised for being himself. Yes, it needs saying, the constellations of luminaries surrounding the prime minister lent an awesome substance to his image as the ultimate leader of the nation and consigned to Stanfield an ill-deserved obloquy from which he would never recover.

As for Trudeau, he swept into office in the campaign of '68, not on a bandwagon, but in a coronation procession. Even the media marched in his parade: never before was there an election in which an office-seeker was the only event — a photogenic, televisible, quotable, unpredictable, modern, mobile man whose economy of rhetoric and elegance of phrase bestowed upon whatever he said the wit of aphorism or weight of parable.

All these various élites — there were others, such as the haberdashers, decorators, architects and the children of inherited wealth, all of whom saw something in him related to their own fantasies — all these and other adjutants to influence and power had sorrowfully, reluctantly, abandoned their dreams of him and the promise of his leadership, a gradual falling away of support, never so potent in numbers as to deprive him of his mandate but so telling in its subtle pervasiveness as to be deadly to any of his ambitions for it.

The press were the first to recover from their exposure to the blinding light of his novelty. Within a year of his overwhelming triumph, they had tracked him to a doxy's assignation, had begun to parse his parables to find their contradictions, and thus begun their personal disengagement from a public man who was more than a little the creation of their own indulgence. It was, as many would admit, something of a wrench.

v

The prime minister, who has come to Charlottetown for the day's final events, is plainly a man in reduced circumstances;

even his retinue seems shrunken. And yet, moving through crowds, he is somehow further removed. In this tormented age of politics, men in power are accompanied by the presumption of unnatural danger and they travel amid phalanxes of plainclothed security police. In the short passage of the prime minister from his car, drawn up at the entrance to a Charlottetown high school, to the front door, leading to the auditorium, there is a brief tableau to illustrate the point.

Trudeau is three strides from the entrance when a child — she could be no more than ten — holds out for him a piece of cloth which, at an instant's glance, plainly is a potato sack somehow embroidered. A hand reaches out, snatches the cloth from the child, and flings it behind the prime minister (to be caught in mid-air by a curious journalist). Trudeau is suddenly, immediately, engulfed by his guard, and literally disappears among them, as they propel their property through the door to safety. The episode consumed no more than three seconds of time; so quickly did it transpire that the mind was slower than the eye comprehending it.

A gentler time, which most of us could remember, would have seen a prime minister accept such offerings with grace, and even with the awareness that the opportunity might provide a photo-event; surely there would have been some felicitous exchange, a paternal pat upon the head, a smile for a proud mother, even a kiss.

"Well, you know," a man said to the varlet afterwards, "the kid could have had a gun under that sack."

If such hypotheses place no strain upon credulity, think of the mortal perils immediately in front of us! This school auditorium is packed to the walls with Island Liberals; so dense a crowd, there is scarcely room enough for all the media down in the front rows. Perched on a press table, the varlet looks out over the ranks and rows of faces to imagine the threat their radiant presence would pose to the vigilant guardians of national properties. And what a wholesome, handsome crowd this is: possessed of all the sturdy, substantial virtues of the Scots, sustained by the good land beneath their feet, purified by the sea surrounding them. There are more pickles, relish, jams and jellies stored in the cellars of this audience than anywhere else in Canada. Goodness, like the smell of farm kitchens, permeates the hall.

Three-quarters of the full complement of the Island's Liberal candidates are on the platform — "Don, Gord and Bill," the prime minister will call them, when he speaks — and the fourth candidate, in hospital in Ottawa, is the Honourable Daniel MacDonald, the minister of veterans affairs. Of those present, some are stewards of the United Church, active in Rotary and boards of trade, dutiful to such causes as the United Fund, the Canadian Arthritis and Rheumatism Society, and the Canadian National Institute for the Blind. The four candidates have a total of eighteen children.

Don Wood, once a CBC farm commentator, more recently a member of Parliament after a by-election in 1977, is given the task of introducing the prime minister. Wood, it is noted in a campaign biographical sketch of him, "won the 'Gold Award' for leadership in extra-curricular activities" while attending Macdonald College during the 1950s, an achievement more noteworthy for the recollection of it than for its relevance. Still, the varlet thinks his introduction of Trudeau also something of a prize.

"The prime minister of Canada," he tells the crowd, "has brought us where we are today!"

A statement of that kind, in the dismal context of recent political events, is desperate for some predicate, or at least disclaimer. Joe Clark has often said the same. Only an audience such as this could wait upon the remark in perfect silence, without so much as a nervous titter. Days earlier, the Island Tories had taken over from the last Liberal government extant in the provinces. These are Liberals whose recent grief and pain has made the need to express their homage and fealty to the prime minister more compelling. Nuance is lost upon them.

But Wood would tax them further: he had come to know Trudeau as "a personal man with humility." If there was any trace of a federal strategy in these introductions, it had to be that, the varlet thinks. In three introductions of the prime minister on this day, all had stressed his modesty and humility. But in the Liberal television commercials the operative word was "tough."

The introduction lurches to climax:

"The Just Society," says Wood, who plainly will stop at nothing, "we're living in it today!"

There is something touching about the introduction: in its total absence of cleverness or guile, in the earnest sincerity of the candidate for Malpeque who has, you can bet, laboured over the preparation of his material, and in the awesome innocence of his listeners, who, with obvious exceptions, like it just fine. An ovation follows, rising out of the darkened auditorium, as Trudeau walks to his single, upright microphone, emerging into the glow of the television lamps, which, beaming upon his yellow corduroy suit, give him the aura of a Golden Boy; he could as well break into song as make a speech.

But no, he is happy to be here — "with Don, Gord and Bill." He pays a tribute to MacDonald, the absent one, who he says "will soon be back on his feet" — then, remembering that MacDonald had left an arm and a leg on the battlefields of Europe, he corrects himself to say, "on his own good foot and the other one" — and then, encouraged by the crowd's reaction, adds, "Anyway, Dan MacDonald is a better man flat on his back than a dozen Tories running around on their good legs."

The prime minister is soon launched upon his theme — the need for strong central government — and, throughout, his audience remains respectful, attentive and nearly motionless. It could not have been a better audience had it been rehearsed. Indeed, it seems more like a congregation: already persuaded, and whatever it does not comprehend, it will accept on faith.

Bob Anderson

"The prime minister of Canada," Don Wood tells
the crowd, "has brought us where we are today!"

Bob Anderson

He could as well break into song as make a speech.

"Now that's the way you have to think in this election," the prime minister tells them, in his quiet, arresting voice, reminding them of the importance of this election — "the most important in our lifetime" — and that they must give their support to a government of all Canadians, for all the country, and that the federal government has to have a role in all the country, which is why we shouldn't give Loto Canada to the provinces, or sell Petro-Can, or . . . .

The varlet, meanwhile, has moved to the side of the platform, near the exit doors, where Jim Coutts is standing, in a bevy of plainclothes men. Head down, Coutts listens to Trudeau. In many a hall like this, the varlet has done the same and knows the private torments of a man who lives in another man's skin.

It is a good house and would be in any port of call in the Maritimes. And it is a good speech — coherent, sensible, persuasive — but there is the feeling that between the audience and the speaker there is no chemistry; that, as much as they need some fusion of his purpose and their commitment, there is not the spark for it. He cannot stir them, as he has done before, and they are too placidly compliant to lift him from his fatigue and growing apprehensions. But even Islanders, forever governed by one dour Scot or another, Campbells, Stewarts, Mathesons, Shaws, MacLeans, can be stirred and aroused; yes, could have been brought to their feet by this man who, God knows, has a case to be made.

A politician could use a crowd like this one to fire up his cause, let the media feel the fervour of it. Instead, watching Coutts pacing in the small exit hall, the varlet surmises that another opportunity has been lost. (When Trudeau had mentioned Clark's name, they had jerked forward in their seats, a current of anticipation passing like a shock through the house. The speaker had plunged ahead, forsaking the opportunity. But, the varlet noted, how they had wanted to hear more about Clark!) When Coutts resumes his station at the door, gazing wistfully now at the stage where his man is winding down a thoughtful dissertation on confederation, the varlet detects tears in his eyes.

The meeting concludes with the prime minister's speech. Somewhere along the campaign trails, they had learned how to end political meetings: abruptly. It may have been Diefenbaker's example. He always insisted that his be the last voice in such proceedings, since, as he said, he could always clean up any heresies made by those introducing him, whereas the remarks of those who thanked him, remarks sometimes extending into full-scale speeches, were beyond his opportunity to redress.

While some of the media go off to file their stories, others mill in the crowd or walk slowly in the cool evening air to the waiting buses. On his way out, working his way past the curious gaze of Island Grits plainly puzzled by his presence in Trudeau's entourage, the varlet encounters a young man who announces himself as a Tory defector.

"You're a Liberal now?" the varlet asks.

"I'm a campaign manager," he says.

"Good luck to you."

"I quit the party after Clark was nominated."

"You were at the convention?"

"I was working for Claude Wagner."

"My God," the varlet says, editorially.

"You don't think Wagner would have been better than Clark?"

"I think almost anyone would have been better than Wagner."

"You mean his health?"

"I mean his head."

vi

The varlet had forgotten, in his long absence from the political wars, how little of it he truly missed. He had also forgotten what a bullshit business it was. Here he was, flying to Toronto with the most potent political force in the country but a man who had not struck a blow for his cause or hit a good, strong, resonant note all day.

"What did you think of the speech?" Coutts had asked him, meaning the Charlottetown meeting.

"I thought it was a good speech." Half a truth is the most one can tell in this business. There is never enough time for a whole truth, unless you can afford to be insulting. It was a good enough speech for a man who is losing and knows it. And for all that, it was nearly a brazen speech, even to an audience of ardent Liberals, telling them more than they wanted to know about the need for "a strong federal government," all of it professorial and passionless, as though he were saying they could take it or leave it.

The varlet would have told Coutts, in the fullness of an honest answer, that while Trudeau was waiting for Clark to make a mistake, the country was waiting for Trudeau to get off his rump and start running. What we were getting from him now were elliptical hints, fragmented thoughts, perhaps left unfinished out of weariness or funk, like his saying, in Charlottetown: "They [Quebec] will vote according to how the people of Canada tell them to vote."

The man almost always speaks in complete sentences; only rarely are there lapses in tense, or a participle left dangling. What little he means to say, he says. But there are these occasional cerebral balks, as though he could not express the rounded thought, as though he dared not risk epexegesis lest he reveal too much of himself.

So the thought is abandoned to conjecture, swept away by the relentless flow of logical argument: that you can't give away Petro-Can, or Loto Canada (has there ever been another nation in the world in which a lottery was a burning issue?), or control of the Fishery, or some of the jurisdiction of Industry, Trade and Commerce, without giving away the store. This is dull food for thought, mere sustenance without much satisfaction.

In truth, Quebec is his only issue, but a poor one for a man who will not risk his pride on it. There is even a little hand-wringing in his dealing with bilingualism — "We aren't cramming French down anyone's throat; no one has to learn French" — as though apologies were in order, when he might better say it was a policy essential to any rational commitment to One Canada, which every party and party leader in Parliament had endorsed.

As for the country telling Quebec "how to vote" — a reference likely to the referendum — were he to expand on his unaccustomed ambivalence, he would tell them that only he and his party will have any influence upon that pregnant consideration. Further, it will not be enough for the federalists to win the referendum, but imperative that they win it convincingly. Meantime, he could say, with Clark out in British Columbia dilating upon how much French needs to be on how many cereal boxes, that the voters could judge for themselves how effective the Tories would be in lending leadership and moral force to the federalist cause.

Never mind that Clark had the Tory premiers, and vice versa, could anyone doubt that the Liberal party was the only viable federal presence in Quebec? Would Trudeau not have at least fifty seats or more? Would Clark dare say his party might win even ten?

The varlet had figured that Trudeau would parade his strength in Quebec during the campaign, pack the halls and preach the gospel of federalism, and use the leverage of his unassailable base to force the Tories to join his issue in Ontario. He had been so sure of the sense of it — a no-lose strategy, since the separatists had gone underground for the campaign, although should they come out, all the better — that he had confessed his concern to Clark, Stanfield, and to Lowell Murray. (He was not now sure how to account for his chagrin: whether because Trudeau had proved him wrong, or because of his clinical dismay at seeing a campaign in a peculiarly studied disarray.)

How to account for this strange campaign that better resembled a lecture tour? (Worse was still to come.) His travelling companions in the back of the plane were as puzzled, but less troubled by it. They too found the prime minister's performance lacklustre and distracted, which many of them put down to Margaret, a spectral presence of uncertain dimension, and her book, evoking a more vivid imagery, which bore heavily on the passenger up front. Yes, the varlet reckoned, we are doubtless travelling with a neutered man.

What else could it be? The varlet recalled the stuttering starts and misfires in the early going, remembering how they would bring the prime minister on to the theme music from *Rocky*, until someone got on the blower to say, "Listen, for Chrissakes, didn't you see the movie? Rocky lost!"

Some other wizard tactician must have volunteered the prime minister to the Petroleum Club in Calgary — a haemophiliac among piranha — but, instead of telling them what they wanted to hear, which Clark would do, or telling them the opposite, as he once would have done (and even as Stanfield had done), Trudeau had fudged the energy issue, and so they had eaten him. Which didn't stop him from climbing all over some jerk of a college student at UBC, or a half-lit heckler who needled him about jobs, or all the farmers in the country who, he opined, were always complaining.

But something — someone? — had put him off his stride. He had lost his concentration. It was noticeable even in his small talk: coming down the ramp to meet the welcoming party in Halifax, he had said, "Hello, how are you?" as though hoping that would be enough to fill a void of uneasy silence, in which you could hear the maple leaf pennant on the nose of his plane flapping in the winds, since he had nothing more in mind to say to anyone and, if his greeters had anything more to say to him, he would rather not hear it. He was somewhere else, off in his own space.

If he had no strategy of his own, the media developed one for him. They concluded that the campaign had been programmed to take off from the Toronto rally at the Gardens Thursday night and peak in the confrontation provided by the television debate with Clark and Broadbent the following Sunday. Everything up to now had been lateral motion; the next four days, 10-13 May, would see a breakthrough. That, at least, was the master plan. The four days would be, indeed, a significant conjunction of events: the old politics of the mass rallies and the new politics of electronics. And the loaded question to be asked concerned the man up front, now shrunk in his seat and alone in his thoughts: was there any smoke left in him at all?

The varlet's seat companion is an American journalist, a foreign affairs specialist from a Florida daily, who has just joined the prime minister's tour after a week with Clark. He had been flying with the Tory leader when one of the plane's engines had aborted over Oshawa and they had made an emergency landing. The journalist was understandably shaken by the experience.

"But I gotta hand it to this guy Clark," he says. "He got out of his seat and walked down the aisle to see how we were. One of your television guys was crying. But Clark was cool." He pauses for reflection. "Of course, that's the politician in him, I suppose. What did he have to lose?"

Still, points for Clark; after all, the engines on this aircraft are humming admirably but there are signs of a failure of nerve up front.

"Do you know Clark?" asks the Floridan.

Recognizing the novelty of this conversation, the varlet decides he too will fish: "A little."

"What do you make of the guy?"

"I'm not sure I know. What did *you* think of him?"

"Well, you know, I can't get over how much he reminds me of Nixon."

"A fellow has to be careful when he says that. He has to make it clear that he's not saying something about Clark's character —"

"No, no, no, no."

"— that would be very unfair. Clark is a very decent guy."
The varlet has done his good deed for the day.

"That's not what I meant, of course. No, no. But, my God, he does remind me of Nixon. I mean, he walks like him — he's not a graceful man at all — and he sounds a lot like him. He even has Nixon's wave; you know, the 'V' sign with the four fingers?"

"You'd wonder why someone hasn't told him about that."

"But he sure doesn't impress me as a prime minister. Compared to this guy," he adds, nodding to the front seat, "he's not in the same league."

"You admire Trudeau?"

"Yeah, I do. He's got a lot of class, you know. But I just can't see Clark as your prime minister. I mean, you've got a great, rich country up here." There is wonderment in his voice. "I just can't believe a great country like this with a guy like that as prime minister."

Hearing this Eric Severeid of the Everglades reminds the varlet of the eternal faith in goodness and greatness and their natural propinquity in American politics.

"Good constituents produce good leaders," John Gardner, the earnest champion of American liberal causes, had said in 1975. "When citizens begin to feel that they can have an impact on politics and government, they're going to send better people into politics and government. They're not going to show the distressing taste for mediocrity which has so often characterized the American political system."

There is a syrupy concentrate of natural goodness in Gardner's philosophy, the sort of wholesome liberalism you'd expect from the man who had sired Common Cause — the varlet suspected some of it was also stored in the cells of the Florida journalist — and the kind of radiant moonshine that warms the faith of true democrats even in the face of awesome contradictions. But good constituents don't produce good politicians, any more than good mirrors produce good looks. (The varlet had never seen so many

Ted Grant

"He even has Nixon's wave; you know, the 'V' sign
with the four fingers?"

good people under one roof than at the Miami conventions that nominated and renominated Nixon.) But it was the rest of Gardner's thought that had puzzled him: was political mediocrity the consequence of a lack of a public sense of involvement? He doubted it; in fact, he suspected the opposite might be true, since the outbreak of political activism in America during the sixties had produced an epidemic of mediocrity.

No, after that orgy of involvement, protest, and citizen's coalitions for women's liberation, peace, abortion, sodomy and full disclosure, there had been a sea change in American politics. Despairing winds moaned over miasmic swamps, thick with the debris of abandoned dreams and ruined hopes, even as the last echo of the final eulogies to John F. Kennedy was lost to memory; he was the last president to be admired by his countrymen.

Among those who followed, Gerald Ford was tolerated, Lyndon Johnson had been resented and feared, while Nixon always had been disliked, until he came to be despised. All of them were awkward, disjointed, cumbersome men — Johnson had once said of Ford that he could not chew gum and fart at the same time — but, while Ford had stumbled on stairs, struck his head on doors, sometimes wobbled walking away from Airforce One, and spoken much the same way, Johnson was crude and vulgar, the fine-ground grime and dust of the Pedernales still under his nails and in the deep crevices of his face, a man who would hold up dogs by their ears, and display his post-surgical scars for the cameras. And if Johnson was a usurper to the presidency, and Ford merely an interregnum, Nixon was to be America's vengeance for the lost war in Vietnam. Steeped in self-pity, as Johnson had been, vain yet not proud about his origins, Nixon became the only American president in history to insist that he was not a crook and tell a lie at the same time.

As for Carter — Jimmy Carter, mind — the varlet had stood in his crowds during his run for the presidency and had sensed the lurking doubts and vague discomforts the candidate engendered in his listeners, as though he evoked the sour memories of something irretrievably lost. In the long troughs of restless silence between perfunctory applause, the varlet could read the sorrowful minds of many: Carter was all there was left to America, and he would have to do.

The moral authority with which leaders govern, and cannot do so without, is affirmed by the affections of their citizenry. It was said of George Washington, the first president, whose tenure laid the foundation for much of America's necessary political mythology, that he was "first in the hearts of his countrymen." But for close to sixteen years now, since Dallas, no president has been near to claiming that essential bond of fealty, and this bleak deprivation has drained American politics of its passion and has emasculated the presidency of inspirational purpose.

What would a John Gardner say to such ruminations? Where have the good constituents gone, that the American presidency could become a showplace of mediocrity? Two presidents driven from office, another dismissed, and a fourth who cannot raise his voice above the disputatious factions around him; was there not another Roosevelt, a Truman, or even an Eisenhower, among 220 million people?

The varlet would not burden the Floridan with his keening concern for America's democracy. To do so would risk exposure of his anxiety about his own country, which would lead back to Clark. No, serious consideration of Clark was still a few days away. Still, he wondered if the television tube were not a carrier of this plague of stunted leaders and the pox of cool opprobrium that lay upon the presidents chosen by so many good constituents of America: a cosmic paradox he would leave aside while he attended the last rites for the dying campaign of Pierre Elliott Trudeau. He could now see the phosphorescent glow of Toronto under the wings of the prime minister's jet: the Age of the Klutz was at hand.

A worried man, such as he, would have felt some dull premonition as they deplaned in the warm, close dark of midnight in a corner of Malton reserved for unloading such cargo as the prime minister and his entourage. It could just as well have been a reception for a man being transferred from Springhill to Millhaven. If there were a welcoming party, it was outnumbered by the police and their ring of cars with revolving, blinking lights, and there was only the sound of muted serious bustle, of door-latches clicking shut, the pulsing of V-8 engines, and the moving of baggage. There had been times when Trudeau could not have set foot on Toronto turf without being engulfed by humanity. But this was a midnight arrival, and the entourage and its prominence would not so much enter the city as infiltrate it. The Liberals of York must early to bed these days.

vii

If you haven't come to terms with Toronto, you haven't come to terms with your own life.

Children of the regions learn the catechism of envy of Toronto, an instruction that comes from adults, to be confirmed in literature, finding echo in the streets, and whining like an eternal wind through the legislatures of the provinces.

Most of us learn what the child could not know: Toronto is more than a city or city-state. It is the mother lode, awaiting only the insolence of ambition; it is everyman's nexus, the great Canadian cornucopia, where the simple dreams of immigrants and apprentices are distilled into visible assets.

In Toronto, upward mobility is elevated to ethos, one so powerful as to overcome a newcomer's natural apprehension. A man soon finds himself rising in his work, borne

Bob Anderson

The prime minister arrives in Toronto. It could just as well have been a reception for a man being transferred from Springhill to Millhaven.

aloft on the invisible thermals of capitalism. Making it in Toronto is not a difficult passage, even for modest talents, and a man's value to his commerce, like his real estate, appreciates with his years. The miracle is in the inevitability of his ascent; the only uncertainty is the rate of it.

Like the Florentines, Torontonians believe their city-state to have been posited by a higher power, and, like the Venetians, that the Deity's gift of terrain offers refuge from the hordes of Barbarossa. The stench of mine and mill are found in a Sudbury or a Hamilton; Toronto wears the subtle scent of increment.

In the confluence of river and ravine, a citizenry inspired by an abiding renaissance spirit of individualism built a city worthy of their civic virtue and heaven's indulgence. The city-state's reputation for greed has been earned by the fact that it has everything: museums, galleries, theatres, public parks ¬private clubs, cathedrals and basilicas, a towering stand of banks, a row of investment houses, a stock exchange, a planetarium, a zoo, the tallest buildings, the deepest vaults, two racetracks, four tiers of government, twenty-four seats in the federal parliament, more lawyers, doctors and tenured professors than most of the provinces of Canada. Three daily newspapers.

The *Toronto Star* is Canada's biggest newspaper, by circulation and weight; the *Globe and Mail* is Canada's national (English) newspaper; the Toronto *Sun*, the born-again tabloid of former *Telegram* staffers, is brightly illustrated with cheesecake and pop conservatism. Toronto is the nation's word factory, headquarters of the English-language communications mandarinate, of CTV, Global Television, the CBC, of the national magazines, the trade publications, house organs, the syndicates, most book publishing companies. Nearly everything Canadians read or hear is written, published or spoken within the city-state.

From the media's minarets, various oracles, prophets and harbingers summon English Canadians to the urgency of thought, much as muezzins call their flocks to prayer:

Canada AM, The World at Eight, The National, CBC Evening News, The Fifth Estate, W-5, Man Alive, Sunday Morning, What Was Said, Insight, a parade of talking heads and disembodied voices flooding the attention span of an unseen audience with news and views beyond the parameters of provincial comprehension.

Accustomed to affluence, confident in their hegemony, Torontonians are the most self-assured of all Canadians, as suits a society whose prosperity is built upon the silent accretion of interest and dividends. The city-state resembles an imperialist power with dominion over a colony of provinces, and an arbiter's role in their politics.

The arbiter's role is discharged through a pervasive influence. Money is the imperative of party politics, and the ways and means come largely from Canada's corporate donors, most of whom are found within a bagman's walk through the canyons reaching out from Bay and King. But more than that: almost all the provincial parties are wards of the same principal officers whose contributions, judiciously meted out, represent the proxy tithe of their shareholders to a political system to be saved from socialism.

Yet it would be merely gauche to assume that Toronto money subjects the parties to corporate dominance. Such may be a suitable mythology for the gullible (and harmless, even if believed) but the reality is more subtle. Toronto money merely maintains access to the parties, keeping open essential lines of communication, corporate hotlines, so to speak, to the right ears at appropriate times. For the wise donor, the financing of the political system may very well be a duty and an obligation to the system, but it is, as well, insurance against the unlikely — such as the ascendancy of socialism — or against occasional political aberration, a Walter Gordon budget, say, or a Carter report on tax reform. When such contingencies arise, the price for access is modest indeed.

The influence of big business (a term fallen into disuse just as it has now become appropriate) upon the politicians and parties is most often nugatory. Mature politicians secretly believe board chairmen and company presidents to be political cretins and would as soon take their advice as harken to a herd of mandrills. The politician knows the boardrooms are full of men with a common purpose, as he knows their special interests are often contradictory and conflicting.

But there is such a thing as corporate-think: men in higher executive echelons move in the same elevated circles, club together, and relax at common watering holes along southern shores. Just as with the members of the Parliamentary Press Gallery, propinquity homogenizes opinion and outlook. And just as the biases of journalists are known to their audiences, those of tycoons similarly influence their juniors downstairs, a process of osmosis that is hastened by an alert attentiveness. When the members of the Toronto Club shut the door on John Diefenbaker in 1962, the click of the latch was heard wherever else businessmen gathered to seek solace for their exertions.

Even so, it is important to note, closing the door did not mean closing cheque books, a first principle of insurance being continuity; and with the risk of socialism a constant, one must always be indifferent to the degree of probability. But they did withdraw even their money in 1963, forsaking the normal posture of neutrality, so that the whole world — certainly in London and Washington — knew the ultimate opprobrium of Toronto's corporate-think, which was its terminal disapproval of Diefenbaker.

It is God's own ordinance that, at this hour in Canadian history, Toronto will decide the destiny of the nation. Even the novice strategist, working his calculations from the root of certainty to tendrils of speculation, will discover that Toronto's bulge of seats, its megamedia complex and corporate influence represent the unknown factors in the election equation. The itineraries of the leaders confirm the battle plans of the parties: the city-state must be won for Grit and Tory alike. The problem in the exercise is to find the seats to win a plurality. Simple arithmetic confirms that Toronto holds the key to the election of 1979.

It is, when you think of it, only just. Toronto, the principal beneficiary of Confederation, stands to be the largest loser should the country dissolve. No imperial power may survive the loss of its colonies; should the tariff walls, which have long protected the city from the full rigours of international competition, be permitted to fall, the city-state would perish in the rubble. Assuredly, the burghers of Toronto will come to this grand assize of 1979 with the compelling interest of Confederation's majority share-holders. How they will order their concerns, and vote their shares, is to be part of the suspense in the unfolding drama.

If the dimensions of the present national crisis are unfamiliar, Toronto's role as arbiter is not. When a Liberal government last fell, in 1957, the city-state gave all but one of its seats to the ascendant Diefenbaker Tories, and corrected the single oversight in 1958. Though the corporate community was wary of prairie populism, it was also circumspect. But by 1962, Toronto had cooled on the Tories, and, as Diefenbaker's huge historic majority plummeted to a bare minority, Tory representation in the city was reduced to a corporal's guard. By 1963, one year later, not a Tory seat remained in Toronto, a drought that lasted until 1972.

To Torontonians, politics is theatre. While political patronage in the provinces is crude, basic and even comprehensible, it is dispensed in Toronto in the invisible disguise of national policy. This illusion of personal detachment from self-interest shields Torontonians from the struggle; upwardly mobile citizens act out their political roles under the cover of wine and cheese or coffee parties, rarely lending themselves to the undignified mummery of election campaigns. If Winnipeg is the New Haven of Canadian political theatre, Toronto is the Big Apple. Party leaders who bring their acts to the big city find crowds which behave more like audiences than supporters: already enlightened, they expect to be entertained. Besides, in Toronto everyone gives at the office — to both sides.

In truth, politics is an abstraction to self-made men, most of whom suspect party politics of being frivolous and who, deep down, remain unimpressed by the efficacy of universal suffrage. The presence of two different but indistinguishable parties involved in a constant struggle for office seems to many to be both inefficient and extravagant.

viii

The solemnity that marked Trudeau's arrival in Toronto left its residue of melancholy even as the varlet wakes in the morning somewhere in the tower of the downtown Holiday Inn. But it is a bright spring day outside, the sort of day Toronto often affords for high political occasions (he could never remember a mass rally here nagged by weather), and looking down on University Avenue he can see flowerbeds in bloom along the boulevard and pedestrians in the light attire of summer. He conjures the picture of five thousand suburban matrons sitting under dryers in hundreds of plaza beauty parlours on this day, preparing to turn out for Trudeau, and imagines the adrenalin pumping in the committee rooms of the Metro ridings, enough epinephrine flowing in the bodies of Liberal yeomanry to fuel the buses mobilizing to bear their cargo of defiant hopes to this last stand at Maple Leaf Gardens.

The varlet has missed the press bus which took the media to the Gardens for a briefing on the evening's event. This was fortuitous for him since he takes a cab and gathers insight from his driver.

"Who's going to win the election?"

The driver, a youthful black, has noted the varlet's press badge, which serves to elevate the conversation to an interview.

"You ask me who's gonna win? I tell ya, man. Trudeau's gonna win."

"I thought Toronto was voting for Clark."

"Ain't nobody around here votin' for Clark. Nobody."

"What do you think of Clark?"

"Nuthin', man. Zero. He can't make his mind up about anythin', you know? All 'a time he's changin' his mind."

"What about Broadbent?"

"I don' know Broadbent. I know Trudeau. He's a guy I like, an' I don't like this guy Clark at all."

"So you're voting Liberal?"

"No. I ain' got no vote, man. I ain' been here long enough to vote. I never say I'm votin' for Trudeau, I only say I like the guy. You know?"

The varlet had always factored into his election permutations the fallible opinions of cabdrivers. This one, plainly, was one worth weighting. "Have a good day," the cabbie says, driving off, pleased with his illusions of celebrity. (Still, the varlet would never meet anyone in downtown Toronto who said they were voting for Clark.)

Inside the Gardens, where the ice surface usually is, the media are huddled around a Liberal spokesman who bears the high shine and neat threads of a public relations impresario. Considering the hour, and the casual dishevelment of his audience, he seems almost indecently elegant. The shoes alone, the varlet guesses, cost more than the clothes on the backs of a random sample of any ten of the assembled journalists, camera crew, photographers and sound men. The contrast neatly separates him from his listeners, a distance that grows to a gulf as he fields their questions, like Joe DiMaggio gobbling up fungoes.

"How many seats? We'll fill seventeen thousand seats tonight, including those on the floor. There are four hundred seats we won't be using; they're the seats at the north end, behind me here, where the platform is. When the seventeen thousand seats are filled, we will be closing the doors. No one will be allowed to stand in here tonight."

"How much will this thing cost?"

"How much will it cost?" A flicker of disdain, like a tic, a signal indication of his remote concern for so vulgar a consideration. "I can't give you a precise answer to your question. I can only say that a figure was suggested in this morning's *Globe and Mail* and I have no quarrel with that figure."

"Does that include the cost of entertainment?"

"Yes, it includes the cost of the professional entertainment. For tonight's entertainment, before the prime minister's appearance, we'll have Sylvia Tyson, Lisa Dal Bello, the Good Brothers, Downchild and — I forgot to tell you — not all the floor will be occupied by seats. Some seats have not been set out at the south end because we will be having performances at that end presented by various ethnic groups.

"In addition," says the flack, "we hope to have one surprise appearance during the evening."

The vision of John Turner, in a tuxedo, careens through the varlet's mind; he is singing "My Way" to an ecstatic crowd. Blue Eyes is back!

"Who's Lisa Dal Bello?"

The vision of Turner dissolves in the answer.

"She's from Toronto. A singer. At six o'clock, one half-hour before the prime minister is due to arrive, the doors will be closed. No one will be allowed into the building after six o'clock."

"Except the press."

"That's right, except the press."

The general public, the man had said, would be seated in the greys, high up along the rim of the Gardens. Members of the press peer into those reaches as though gauging the speed with which invective might travel from the greys to the platform. You could boo a referee (or a national anthem) from there, but could you needle a politician? The varlet suspects that the greys will be well packed with the faithful.

(Toronto remained the last bastion of Grit organization, where nothing was left to chance.)

The question period is over; the possibility of any of these churls breaking through the starched barricade of big city suavity had sunk from unlikely to never. Besides, the prime minister would soon be making an appearance at Forest Hill Collegiate in relief of his candidate, the Honourable John Roberts, who was engaged in a media-billed "battle of giants" (Tory Ron Atkey being the other) in the bellwether seat of St Paul's.

The media are looking forward to this event with unusual anticipation. The students of Forest Hill Collegiate, they know, will be a tough audience, too bright and attuned to endure political smarm. Indeed, they might be an audience to flush the bilges of the prime minister's mind.

At the entrance to the high school, the varlet notes there is no gathering of the neighbourhood (although the school is surrounded by apartments and backed by rows of middle-class homes). The prime minister's coming could not have been any secret; there are, after all, the parents of all those children inside — and, as confirmation, here are three middle-aged ladies, sporting the deep tans of the Florida Gold Coast and holding placards.

OPEN YOUR HEARTS, their signs read, VOTE LIBERAL.

But they, and their sentiment, even allowing for its poignancy, seem as out of place as Arabs in the Primrose Club. Nor is it clear for whom their message is meant; certainly the distinguished visitor who would soon see it might read it not so much as a plea as a warning. For, if the hearts of Toronto are shut against his party, this forlorn reception offers some evidence of it. To the varlet, who has found himself involuntarily flinching from so much he has seen of the Trudeau campaign — as though he were in a swarm of bats — the placard bearers need only a cauldron to become the witches in *Macbeth*.

Inside, the students are gathered in the school gymnasium, appearing to have been seated by seniority —

the older students in the bleachers, the younger ones on the floor. A better-than-average high school band is playing "Moon River" over a high-pitched adolescent hum of conversation. From wall to wall, the gymnasium is a sea of denim.

The music is briefly interrupted by the principal, a man of imposing cool, who reminds his students that "we have only a very limited time with the prime minister" — the varlet could, on this day, glean prophecy from a laundry list — and instructs them to "ask questions, but don't make speeches," a caveat probably no principal of any other high school in Toronto would have needed to make. Something else, too: there seems to be a discernible rapport between them, the teacher and the taught, an understated sense of place and pride, held in common. There is, the varlet notes, the look of young eagles in so many of these kids. Forever uneasy with ethnocentric musing, he puts aside the question of how or why these children of Abraham came by their supple quickness and precocity; besides, the band has broken into "Jericho." Struggling to remember the words, he can recall only "and the walls came tumbling down." Still more portents!

The prime minister receives an ovation on his arrival, striding briskly into the gymnasium alongside John Roberts, but there is an undercurrent of boos in the wave of shrill cheers, as though the home team and visiting team would each have their rooters in this game.

Roberts is the pluperfect establishmentarian Grit: a handsome face which, one reckons, will be forever boyish, enough flesh around the jowls to suggest sources of affluence, a face that has hovered over many a good table, and a countenance of ineffable blandness, one which, even in repose, bears the hint of a smile. He is dressed in a discreet dark blue synthetic, a nice contrast to his leader's harvest-gold corduroy, which is the only striking colour visible in the gymnasium's denim motif.

A novelist seeking to create authenticity for the characterization of a Toronto Liberal Wasp politician (of the sort who would represent the hero of a romantic novel in an urban milieu) could do no better than borrow extensively from the life of John Roberts. The writer's hero would have graduated from the University of Toronto (with the Breuls Gold Medal for studies in political science), attended Ecole Nationale d'Administration in Paris (he is, of course, bilingual), and earned a doctorate at Oxford. He would have then served as a foreign service officer with the Department of External Affairs in its Paris embassy, been an executive assistant to a federal minister, as indoctrination into practical politics. He would have proceeded from there to election to the House of Commons, and, after serving as chairman of a few exotic committees (on peacekeeping, the United Nations, and the Official Languages Act), he would have become a parliamentary secretary to a minister before entering the cabinet as, say, secretary of state. And he would be happily married: her name would be Beverley Rockett, and she would be a photographer. John Roberts would not be a bad name for him either.

As sub-plot, this gathering at Forest Hill Collegiate could well mark the denouement of the hero's political career. If one could find John Gardner's syndrome — that good constituents elect good members — applied anywhere in the land, it would be here in St Paul's. For a quarter of a century, since 1953, the good constituents of St Paul's have elected Oxford men, beginning with Roland Michener, a lawyer who had been a Rhodes Scholar and would be Speaker of the House of Commons, then high commissioner to India, then Governor General of Canada. He was succeeded by Ian Wahn, another lawyer and Rhodes Scholar and a good clubman (National Club, Royal Canadian Military Institute, Toronto Cricket, Skating and Curling, Empire Club, Liberal Union). Wahn was dislodged by a Tory — another lawyer, Atkey, who had missed out going to Oxford, and who had served the riding for only two years until Roberts, retreating from a previous defeat in York-Simcoe, wrested St Paul's from him in 1974.

Although he was not Oxford, Atkey did not lack credentials worthy of consideration by his electors. He was Osgoode Hall, as was Wahn, and had taught at Western, as Roberts had at Toronto. The Conservatives had customarily found high profile candidates for the riding, such as Fletcher Markle, a prominence among the Catholic laity, Barry Lowes, a former chairman of the Toronto School Board, and Joel Aldred, whose commercial voice for Rothmans and Household Finance had made him a media star.

After his loss to Roberts in '74, Atkey had kept on running, busy in party organization, policy development, and with appearances on cable television. A youthful, smallish man with a round face behind horn-rimmed glasses, under a Roman-style hairdo, Atkey appeared to most observers as obviously bright, stylishly academic, and a Tory of promise in his party if he could get elected again.

Getting elected as a Tory in St Paul's, for any candidate capable of rudimentary logic, meant winning a fair share of the nominally Liberal Jewish vote. After his defeat, Atkey wooed the Jewish vote, going as far as Israel in pursuit of it, leaping to his feet whenever a Jewish nerve was touched, and, as of the time of this narrative, persuading Clark, through a mutual friend, Jeff Lyons (who had tutored Maureen McTeer for her law exams), to promise that a Conservative government would relocate the Canadian Embassy in Israel, moving it from Tel Aviv to Jerusalem.

This was among the reasons why the media had looked forward to Trudeau's "Question & Answer Session," as it was billed, with the youthful students at Forest Hill Collegiate. The prime minister had initially responded to Clark's statement on the proposed embassy move with — the varlet could not tell which — incredulity, disdain or a knowledgeable cynicism, but left no doubts of his disagreement. It was, therefore, with this in mind that the media were at the least mildly curious, which is as wrought up as any of them could be this early in the day. For the varlet, Trudeau's appearance in the gymnasium at Forest Hill was like watching an old lion entering a den of young Daniels.

Roberts's introduction of his leader is a safe one, and brief. He has not been plodding the streets of St Paul's these weeks without discovering the shoals and currents in the consciousness of his listeners. The nearest he comes to effusion is to call the prime minister "a great guy." It seems, for the moment, a plausible enough endorsement.

"In this place," the prime minister begins, referring to a previous visit, "even the hecklers are intelligent."

If there were mischief afoot among the young cadres of Atkey supporters, it is suppressed by the leaden, earnest, early questions. They are mirror-images of conventional issues, as though each of his interrogators had studied the editorial droppings of the Toronto press: the budget deficit, the swollen ranks of the civil service, the RCMP, and a question on defence policy in which both the questioner and the prime minister become mired, to the audible despair of the audience. Still, the varlet notes, there is a pejorative nettle in each question, an accusatory tone in the cracking uncertain voices of these adolescent offspring of Roberts's majority, that signals doubts and division at home.

What will he do, someone asks him, if he loses?

Obviously, that prospect has occurred to him lately. As he brings it to the surface again, one can sense the stiffness in rarely used gears: "if there were a better man, or a better woman [an inserted clause that wipes out the possibility of this being a spontaneous answer], I would turn it over." He makes no effort, however, to discount the possibility of his losing.

Someone, detecting new-found humility in him, recalls that he had been arrogant in some of his answers when he had visited the school seven months ago. Well, he hadn't meant to be arrogant, "but some of your questions were also, you know, kind of arrogant." Arrogance was not in his nature, then, but a weapon in his arsenal; he would use it on your grandmother if she asked for it. The varlet ponders the tactic of tit-for-tat in a grown-man. But had it not been the very essence of his style?

Finally, the question comes: since Jerusalem is the national capital of Israel, when will Canada move its embassy there "in the name of social justice?" The emotional flourish at the end is followed instantly by an explosive burst of cheering and applause. Acetylene could not have dissolved the small, tight smile on the face of John Roberts.

The prime minister's answer is lengthy, ornate in its detail, and, strangely for him, intriguingly anecdotal. President Carter had asked him not to change Canada's position: "You don't have to ask me [he had told Carter]... I understand that it would be counterproductive in terms of peace." And when the Israeli prime minister, Menachem Begin, had asked that Canada's embassy be moved, "I told him... I admire you, but you're playing a very clever game of moving your policy and your chesspieces. I respect your decision, but that's *your* decision. Don't ask me to take your side, if that will mean the Arabs will break off talks and we'll be involved in another thirty years of war."

He is very much now paterfamilias; whether or not he does speak that way with his global peers matters less than commonsense in the answer he is trying to give (although, saying to Begin, "don't ask me to take your side" would have a familiar ring to western wheat growers). Remarkable, to the varlet, are the lack of hooks, the absence of guile. There is no mention of Clark, and, while he says that of the thirteen nations who have agreed to settle embassies in Jerusalem "only the Netherlands is of any great significance," he could have, were he pressing his point, named some of the others: Chile, the Dominican Republic, Panama and Haiti. At the end of it, the students reward him with a warm burst of applause, not as vociferous as that given his questioner but genuine enough to indicate approval of his candour, if not his answer. The media, busy with ballpoints and pencil nubs, at last have something to file.

Anticlimax attends the closing ceremony: the prime minister is presented with a beanie and obligingly dons it for the photographers. On his way to the media bus, the varlet notices a number of youthful partisans hovering at the exit, stickers fixed to their T-shirts. "The Just Society Just Failed," they read.

The day is now half over, although, for the purposes of high Liberal strategy, not yet half begun: the campaign is scheduled for take-off before the day is out, down in the nether end of St Paul's in Harold Ballard's jockery. The varlet feels the need of strong drink.

In the company of fellow-travellers, he repairs to Yorkville to assuage his thirst and expose his neuroses to the sun. He could not recall a campaign in which the hiatuses allowed for so many leisurely lunches, afternoon naps, even long weekends — enough down time to make a wire service reporter an indolent for the rest of his life.

Having spent two morning hours at the high school, the campaigning prime minister would take the next six hours and twenty minutes at his leisure, or, in the slyly arch language of his printed itinerary, would be attending to "government business."

But if the prime minister was unavailable for combat, what could a wavering Tory, such as the varlet, do to save the country, other than put down his double martinis, matching his companions glass for glass, and watch the conspicuous wealth and pulchritude of Toronto parade among the boutiques of Yorkville?

In support of the theory that vodka escalates depression — melancholia being a Russian norm — the martinis filling the void of his despair, he contemplates the final days of the campaign, which he would spend with Clark. While he would be moving, next week, to Clark's tour, his two companions were remaining with Trudeau, who was, all agreed, "the story" of the campaign, as well as its only mystery.

"So you're going on the Wimp Watch," one of them says.

"And you're staying on the Death Watch," he replies.

"If you get a chance," the other advises, "watch how Clark eats."

ix

The Liberal party had become an ironhorse party, reverting to the age of steam; the rally as a public spectacular is out of the railroad age of politics, when you counted your crowds, compared them to other crowds, and argued about the numbers with the journalists whose professional code it was to underestimate them. There was a time when nothing mattered more to a campaign than filling halls. A full house in the old Winnipeg Auditorium, or the Forum in Vancouver, meant something. A sequence of full houses in Halifax, Hamilton, Regina, Edmonton and Victoria gave a campaign momentum; it used to be the only sure way of telling if it had any.

The Carnegie Hall for Canadian political rallies was Maple Leaf Gardens. Not everyone was good enough, or confident enough, to try it. (So you might book Varsity Arena.) In fact, even in the steam age, it was risky: filling it meant a crowd of seventeen thousand, which was a lot of bodies, but a crowd of ten thousand in the Gardens would be a bust. Whenever anyone considered holding a rally there, the first question asked was, "Can we fill it?" And the next was, "Do we need it?" There was an old maxim about hallsmanship: better to fill a high school auditorium with a thousand than have five thousand in a half-empty hall, and all those vacant seats yawning at the press.

Putting big crowds in the biggest halls remains an irresistible allure to the Grits. The varlet puts it down to the authoritarian streak in them, their Nuremberg syndrome; Liberals were true believers in the mass psychology of the big rally — lots of noise, crowd chants, colour, music, bright lights and that dramatic entrance of The Leader! With Trudeau, in 1968, they didn't need to organize crowds. They simply had to produce their man and the crowds jammed the plazas and overflowed into the streets. They could have charged admission and filled any hall in the country. But when that magic was over, they still put him in the Gardens, as they were doing now, wheeling the crowds in by the busload, pumping them up with Lisa Dal Bello and the Good Brothers, and when the varlet enters the rink around six-thirty the place is packed and the amps are flooding it with rock. He has to keep his mouth open to prevent the sound from blowing his mind.

Outside, on College Street, someone says, shouting in his ear, there are maybe five thousand more Liberals and music lovers who couldn't get in. He confirms this himself, moving through the security checkpoints and out into the alley with its rows of hot-dog and pop stands, and — yes — there they are, pressing around the doors, peering through the glass, some of them waving their Liberal party membership cards. He guesses there might also be a good number of undecided voters out there who would now be switching to Clark.

He returns to the media area, which is just below the stage, cordoned off from the floor seating. The rink is in darkness, save for random spotlights flickering over the heads of the crowd, and spots shining down on Downchild doing their set in a wild cacophony of noise, their's and the babble of seventeen thousand others. The noise, the body heat of the crowd, and the hot lamps around the stage area begin to unravel his nerves, the multiple martinis, distilled in his cells, escaping through the pores of his face. He feels himself marooned on an island on the river Styx.

The media luminaries, like ringside celebrities at a heavy-weight championship fight, mill about in their exclusive en-closure, greeting one another with mock formality and

Bob Anderson

Putting big crowds in the biggest halls remains an
irresistible allure to the Grits...their Nuremberg
syndrome.

exchanging shouted observations. Since this is Toronto, their numbers are swollen by the city's vast armadas of print, radio and television journalists. Not only is this an event to be seen, he suspects, but an event at which to be seen. Like the final, final fight of a Muhammad Ali.

Adrienne Clarkson is there; and Stephen Clarkson, with Christina Newman; John Harbron, who had been among the first of Trudeau's hagiographers; and Peter Newman, clenching his pipe, forever looking like a man burdened by private sorrows: he had found every prime minister of his time — Diefenbaker, Pearson, now Trudeau — full of promise. All had failed him; none more than Diefenbaker, who had been the subject of his polemical genius. *Renegade in Power* had been a masterpiece of demolition, written with cool fury and elegant disdain. Still, it did more to elevate Newman in the world of letters than to put down Diefenbaker, whose relentless rages were visceral, and eternal.

Newman had written to a friend late in 1963, after the success of *Renegade* and the defeat of Diefenbaker's government, explaining why he had not been harsher on the man from Prince Albert. A hysterical tone would have wrecked his mission. The book was understated with a purpose — to convince the reader that this man must never again hold office of any kind.

And what were the rewards for a polemicist of such powers? Even Newman, in the flush of his publishing triumph, seemed uncertain, for, as he wrote his friend, he was getting a great deal of abuse from some powerful quarters and no help from other powerful quarters, and he lamented that Canada was no easy country in which to be "a patriot."

Could any cuts be more unkind than this abuse and ingratitude for a man who had broken the spell of a thousand castrated journalists upon the writing of contemporary politics? Newman was the author of the first bestseller ever written about Canadian politics. But, apart from the royalties, the deep-down satisfactions had been few. Indeed, Canada is not an easy country for patriots; the word itself is all but lost in the language. Patriotism is an Americanism, a solid, substantial American virtue, with its legacy in the revolution that changed the sweep of history. It is a nothing word in Canada; in this country, the only word like it, in our vernacular, is loyalty. America has her patriots. Canada has the loyalists.

Patriotism is a word with a great utility in the United States, a rallying word to summon the ultimate civic virtue in the American society. "Some things don't change," an embattled President Carter would say to the Future Farmers of America, addressing them in the Rose Garden. And the things that don't change are "the fundamentals" — a string of them, but climaxed by "the beauty of nature and genuine patriotism." Genuine patriotism! The patriotic heart, in the breast of every American, beats with love of country, a transcendental passion stronger than the rights of kings, the divinities of priests, and the laws of men, a genuine power of love sanctified by every man's right to bear arms in the eternal frontier wars against arbitrary authority.

Poor Newman; it is not merely difficult to be a patriot in Canada, but impossible. The mere notion of it is repelled by history. In the genes of the forefathers and founding fathers, and in all the mutations since, the dominant strain has been loyalty. (The confusion in Newman may be the explanation of his romantic nationalism, the idea of a Canada like America — a nation.) No, Newman did not reckon with the petrous loyalty in Canada's psyche, forgetting (or never knowing) that allegiance is the requisite of every oath of public office, and loyalty the shim in the hand of every politician, grand vizier, battalion commander, sales manager, headmaster and prefect in the land. It is our native ethic, the ultimate virtue to which we subscribed even as we fled the rabble of the first American patriots, or expelled the Acadians, or sent our sons to war.

Newman's *Renegade* stirred the interests of a considerable public, and when his readers closed the last page, they had come to know more about the quirks, foibles and eccentricities of the authority that governed their lives, more than they ever wanted to know. But not enough — never enough — to do more than offend their habit of obeisance. Newman had struck at the king, at least menaced a figure whose power was vested in the Crown. So calculated and furious an attack upon an Imperial Privy Councillor by no more than (as the Diefenbakerites were at pains to say) "an ingrate immigrant" was, to any satrap or corporate magistrate, an attack upon themselves.

No wonder, then, *Renegade*'s author felt the wrath from some "powerful quarters" and the cool indifference of others who henceforth walked wide of him. There is no room for patriots in the court and councils of a kingdom where, after all, patriotism could be suspected only as treason. Newman's fame soon became his notoriety: the true victim of *Renegade in Power* was not Diefenbaker but Newman.

To prolong the metaphor of ringside ambience, as the main event draws nearer, there are now, in the organized chaos at Maple Leaf Gardens, introductions of dignitaries in the crowd — namely the candidates. This ceremony serves to give the varlet's ears a welcome surcease from the amplified energies of the minstrels on stage and to restore the proceedings to the venue of politics. The sound of natural cheers and roars greets the names of Liberal worthies seated among their followers, who represent private cheering sections. There is, the varlet notes, a good-natured sense in the gathering which, taken with its decorum, gives it a familial character. Many of the seats around him are occupied by children with their parents and, in the upper reaches, he had found whole classrooms attended by their teachers. It is, indeed, a good night for the social sciences: doubtless some history in it, perhaps the last appearance of Trudeau or of any party leader in the Gardens when there would be no ice on the floor; the rally would become an artifact in memory, a reminder of the politics of obsolescence.

Jerry Grafstein, unknowingly a subject of the varlet's wonderment over the Liberal campaign, stands outside the media enclosure, a study of managed composure. Grafstein and he had done light partisan turns together on television, usually in moments of election heat, and the varlet had always adopted the tactic of indulging the Liberal warlock, in the knowledge that Grafstein would be finished off by the NDP presence, someone like Stephen Lewis, who could decapitate a man without drawing blood. But now, in the presence of this key political strategist for a party that had none, the varlet takes him on.

"For God's sake, Jerry, when are you guys going to start your campaign?"

"You don't think we've got a campaign?"

"You're dead in the water."

"No, we're taking off," Grafstein says, illustrating his assertion by placing the flat of his hand before the varlet's eyes.

"After tonight," he says, the fingers at the angle of lift-off, "we're going straight up."

"Tonight is a waste of time. You've wasted a week just getting ready for this and there's not a canvasser at any door tonight in the whole of Metro."

"Straight up," he repeats, "from here on."

But not even the proprietor of the party's in-house advertising agency, Red Leaf Communications, can hide the weary resignation in the half-smile. Grafstein bears the visible weight of a pending ordeal out of which would come his likely martyrdom: in the wake of defeat, a storm of recrimination follows, with summary justice for the image-makers. Politicians rarely blame themselves when they lose.

At the end of his forays into and out of the crowd, the varlet encounters Joe Potts, a Liberal devout if ever one could be found, and, he suspects, also something of a philosopher.

"What do you make of all this, Joe?" he asks, gesturing to the galleries.

Potts possesses the only natural voice in the Gardens this night that, without being raised, can be heard above the din.

"Well," he bellows cheerfully, "it probably doesn't mean anything."

Senator Royce Frith, whose luck it is to be chairman of the Liberal campaign in Ontario, now comes to the platform to signal that the moment is at hand. Frith, whose chairmanship has suffered somewhat from lapses into candour about his party's electoral prospects, rises to this occasion with singular merit. He introduces the only man in the house who needs no introduction by sparing him one:

"Fellow Liberals," he says. "The prime minister of Canada, Pierre Elliott Trudeau!"

To rousing cheers, launched from the vestigial hopes of seventeen thousand good Toronto Grits, the prime minister, moving swiftly down a rink's length passage between the crowd, touching an outstretched hand here and there, bounds to the platform. The cheers subside, then rise again — expectation prompting renewed exhortation — as though their fellowship in the heat and tumult of the darkened hall these past two hours has released them from their fears that he would fail them. The varlet, nudged by more sombre premonition, pushes off into existential waters.

Lyndon Johnson, when he had the presidential juice in all his batteries, always began his speeches in a half-audible voice, until he had his listeners straining to hear, hanging breathless on each word. Only then would he give them his resonance. Any man can milk an audience of mindless cheers while it is fresh; the trick is to store its approval for the end, in the final sprint.

"We are engaged in a great battle for our party and our country," Trudeau begins, arms akimbo, fists clenched, a pose for a man walking through fire in the armour of God,

Bob Anderson

"Straight up from here on."

Bob Anderson

"We are engaged in a great battle for our party and
our country and we are winning that battle."

"and we are winning that battle, and I can see here tonight that we're winning it in Toronto!" Hooray!

And then comes Frank Miller. Frank Miller? Yes, Frank Miller emerges wraith-like out of the "gloom and doom" the Tories are talking in this campaign, and here, the prime minister says, fishing a piece of paper from a side pocket of the yellow corduroy suit, is what the Tory provincial minister of finance had to say about Ontario, after returning from a trip to Europe. And, sure enough, Frank Miller thought anything he'd seen abroad was no match for Ontario, there being no place like it. The crowd, unaware of the importance of Frank Miller's true confessions (indeed, a goodly part of it unaware of Frank Miller) but anxious to show its enthusiasm when called upon, sits perplexed and confused of purpose throughout this diversion, and the varlet can sense the ebb of adrenalin in the closed darkness of the house. He searches his memory for another occasion on which he had heard a prime minister quote the words of a provincial cabinet minister; none come to mind.

Provincial ministers are not the fair game of Canadian prime ministers — hardly even of federal Opposition leaders — but never mind that. It is the bankruptcy of material indicated by this reference to Frank Miller, a prime minister reduced to rummaging through a clippings file for something to say to seventeen thousand "Torontonians for Trudeau" (so the rally had been described), a man who seems so dulled and enfeebled by private enervations as to balk at each of the day's hurdles.

In the shadows, behind the prime minister, the candidates are seated in a semi-circle. Whenever the crowd applauds, they join by standing from their chairs. There is, in fact, more applause than occasions for it and, when the speech is over, there is a final, sustained ovation in which there is more than a little compassion and forgiveness. This has not been much of a night for kindling spirits but a better one for testing them.

The varlet studies the closing scene: Trudeau standing

between Sylvia Tyson and Lisa Dal Bello, in the singing of
"O Canada." (Better, he thinks, they had sung "Nearer
My God to Thee.") On the far left of the semi-circle of
candidates, his attention is drawn to Ann Cools, who is
David Crombie's opponent in Rosedale. It becomes clear, in
the closing stanza, that she has not yet learned the words.
Festooned beneath the Gardens' roof are clusters of bal-
loons and these descend over the departing faithful, now
flowing to the exits.

Out there — the vision lurches in the varlet's head —
Keith Davey would be ladling out free cups of Kool-Aid.

X

The people are free, and can be ruled
only so far as they agree to obey.
                    Pierre Elliott Trudeau

When he awoke the morning after, in the American gothic
discomforts of his hotel room, flight was the varlet's first
impulse; to retreat while dignity would still be his company.
In none of the apothecaries of Toronto were there liniments
enough for so many discomforts: a barking cough, palpitations and constrictions, a heavy head and blurred vision. He
had a cold. Furthermore, he had lost his voice. Trudeau was
already in Montreal, that sole surviving allodium of his
party, and the media was, at this hour, flying to attend a
Liberal dinner at the Mount Royal Hotel — the day's only
event on the prime minister's itinerary. The varlet could not
have gone had Coutts and Patterson offered to bear him
there on a stretcher. The company of so many Liberals had
proven too much for him.

Yet, ills of the flesh were slight compared to the fever of
his irresolution. His worrying, fretful vigilance over the

Bob Anderson

When the speech is over, there is a final, sustained ovation in which there is more than a little compassion and forgiveness.

Bob Anderson

The varlet studies the closing scene: Trudeau standing between Sylvia Tyson and Lisa Dal Bello in the singing of "O Canada."

prime minister was inexplicable. His respect for Clark was growing, but grudging. He did not want Clark to do worse, but, at the same time, he wanted Trudeau to do better. To compound his dilemma, a newspaper had asked him to write ten thousand words — a novella! — on his reasons for voting Conservative.(How did they know?)

He had made only a stuttering start on this, composing two lengthy paragraphs on the remedial benefits of the catharsis of change. But no more. And today — as though his spirit needed such attenuation — he must write his weekly column, in which, since time was running out for prophecy, he would forecast Trudeau's defeat.

It was of some consolation that he could write such a column as testament to his objectivity, remorseful though it would be, and that he would also decline the offer to argue the case for Clark. By this convolution of logic, he would at least satisfy himself that he had become very nearly neutral in this partisan contest for power, at some halfway house in his struggle to break old habits.

As to why he should vote Conservative, in ten thousand words or less, he could more easily have written an opinion in the negative. Under that myriad of timber in the Tory platform glowed the dull light of expediency: reinstitution of the death penalty, if only enough hangers could be elected to the next Parliament; constitutional protection for English-language rights in Quebec, but French-language rights elsewhere to be left to the provinces; "flexibility" in the application of the Official Languages Act; a Senate to be appointed by the provinces; medicare to be "studied," and Petro-Canada "sold"; and, of course, Israel's Canadian Embassy to be moved to Jerusalem! Then, too — this caudle for the middle class — tax deductions on mortgage payments (a little something for their purse) and the reduction , over three years, of the civil service by sixty thousand (something for their rage). But had slavery been an issue, the Tories would have fudged it.

Even so, his scorn for the platform did not lessen his appreciation of its purpose. It was Nixonian and Carteresque at once, designed to solicit the support of the silent majority of English-speaking Canadians and, by embracing the Old Testament virtue of fiscal rectitude, to hold out the promise of the latter-day miracle of a balanced budget. The Tory manifesto touched every nerve and massaged every bias in an anxiety-ridden body politic.

Those ragged-assed Canadians who dwelt along the periphery of Canadian politics — the misbegotten linguistic minority of the inarticulate — would wait a long time until osmosis delivered them some dividend from Tory policy. Not since Stanfield had startled Londoners with his visions of negative income tax and guaranteed annual income had any politician attempted to make a case for the poor; in the meantime, mass communications and urbanization had deprived them of their purchasing power in electoral politics, notably their votes on election day.

The thrust of Clark's program for the nation confirmed this new reality in the Canadian demography: the only votes worth buying were now among the middle class and, if there were much left of the homely virtue of sharing, it would be expressed in mortgage interest deductibility on income tax. The varlet, who might be the only Red Tory still above ground, recoiled from the paradox of a party committed at once to restraint and largesse.

No, if the varlet were to drag himself to the polls in this election, it would not be to vote for the Tory platform. If he had an ideology, it was that of a Rowell-Sirois federalist, which, to him, was the belief that the essential function of the federal government was redistributive, and its first objective the achievement of some decent equity in services and benefits. Since wealth was the universal solvent for disparity, federalism could be its only effective agent.

But what of Clark? In the days when the varlet knew him, he had seemed to share this concept. Was he now at odds with his platform? With its liens and codicils to the provinces, the platform seemed a feeble document to a Rowell-Sirois federalist. Did it not appear the same to Clark?

Still, a national party which had so often existed thanks to the grudging support of provincial parties — a hapless political cousin down on his luck — would naturally be a provincial rights party. With counter-federalism become fashionable, this long and dutiful advocacy of the rights of the provinces, dating back to George Drew, was finally in tune with the national mood. There was scarcely a provincial cabinet that had not joined the me-generation, confirming the varlet's sorrowful premise that the country had lost the *idea* of federalism.

That federalism had sunk to such low estate, become so peripheral to the concerns of so many, was the gravamen of his complaint about Trudeau's years in power. But his complaint was heavy with remorse for the fact that the Official Languages Act, as well as the accompanying irritation of hearing so many of the nation's troubles expressed in a French accent, had been the principal cause of federalism's decline. And, while Trudeau would be defeated for cause, the problem for the varlet was that the sting in Clark's mandate would be given by the smouldering resentment in English Canada for the first and only attempt to provide French Canadians with an identity in their federal government.

Bilingualism had been a noble experiment, wretchedly conducted. The varlet himself had paid more than lip service to it; indeed, he stubbornly supported it still. But the insensitivity and arrogance of its proponents and administrators had deprived the program of the popular support it deserved. Perhaps Trudeau himself had given the lead: "If I don't think we can create some form of a bilingual country," he had said to Canadians, "I am no longer interested in working in Ottawa. If I want to work as an English-speaking person, I'll look for a job in another country...."

That he could say this, much less think it, suggested he had no idea, or cared less, how such cavalier presumption would fall upon the ears of the English-speaking majority. But the presumption was a crucial one, for it served notice as to the internal reality of federal bilingualism, which was that the patronage links between the federal government and the unilingual sons and daughters of generations of English Canadians were now to be severed. Could it mean anything else?

Moreover, the medicine of bilingual federalism was always administered with hectoring, scolding accompaniment: "What I'm really trying to show Canadians" — was there another prime minister who thought aloud of himself as having such a duty? — "is that a country whose citizens can't agree on basic rights, including those of language, is on the road to breaking up."

A warning, perhaps, meant to silence protest, though not sufficient to quiet the lurking resentments of those with languages clearly without basic rights. There was nothing wrong with the historic validity upon which his predicate was based, but it was bound to stir the restlessness of the nation's "other ethnic" population.

Such was not the bargain many Canadians thought they had struck with Trudeau, whose earlier affirmation of "One Canada," and his gleeful scorn for the Tory's semantic confusions with "deux nations," contained no hint of this subsequent exclusivity.

The federal élite took on a lofty lingulate identity; civil servants in higher echelons came to be admired, and to admire one another, not for their administrative competence but for their tongues. A new and powerful caste of Brahmins, English civil servants who spoke French, swiftly ascended the vertical mosaic. Once established, they applied the strictures of official bilingualism with the messianic zeal of true converts. Were there an opening in their departments for someone who must walk on water, the Good Lord Himself would have been disqualified unless He were bilingual.

Something was plainly perverse with this new federalism, which would sublimate considerations of personal merit to the demands of a policy on bilingualism. The prime minister, however, was not above deception when denying that the purpose of his policy had any practical application. It was a misconception, he said, "that the Official Languages Act will prevent Canadians who speak only one language from working for the government, the armed forces or the crown corporations, or from being promoted to important government jobs. There is no clause in the Act which states this, or which will have this result."

But it did not work that way. Instead, preferment in the bureaucracy was manipulated by an emboldened cadre of ranking linguists, who could, and did, through a system of winks, nods, smiles, smirks and artful calculation, like tic-tac bookies at Ascot, hire whomever they chose, and the chosen were indubitably in their own ineffable image. The unilingual Québecois was no longer the only citizen not at home in his national capital.

"Of course," the prime minister said, as early warning, "a bilingual state [note!] is more expensive than a unilingual one."

He could not have known how much more expensive the effort would be (although, if expressed in mere dollars, enough would be spent in man-hours and memoranda to finance a space program that could have put Keith Spicer on the moon). But even more costly, because, in the end, too many Canadians would remember the failure of the experiment instead of the folly that ensured its failure.

While the policy grievously diminished federalism, it encouraged a militantly self-conscious ethnocentricity, and for all the nice-nellyism of the media and of the universities (like Berlitz, they sniffed some profit in it), it spawned a new generation of genteel bigots, who, like mushrooms growing in cellars, flourished in Canadian closets. These would soon be heard from.

A steady rain of bilingual edicts drenched the sensibilities of legions of civil servants, soldiers, sailors, airmen and ordinary Canadians. A woman in Kamloops, pushing a cart through a supermarket, was confronted — yes, challenged — by federal policy. Was it accident, the varlet often wondered, that bilingual packages, cartons and cans seemed invariably to be displayed on shelves with French labels facing the Anglophone shopper? Government forms, never inviting to the public, now with their obligatory instructions and directions in both languages, became as cumbersome to manage as road maps.

And all the while, English Canadians heard the lecturing, pontificating voices of their politicians and savants: bilingualism was good, essential, yes, vital. For a while, in the parlours of the upwardly mobile, it was even chic.

Finally, the country could stand it no more. It was not because French had been jammed down the throats of English Canada. Not at all. It *was* in their throats, but also in their noses, in their hair, their eyes, in the folds of their flesh. And having endured it (though they were furtively, secretly outraged by it, even while they remained dutifully supportive), their stoic perseverance went unthanked, even by Trudeau.

Bilingualism was a little like wartime rationing: something to be endured for the common good. But what was missing for most was a sense of involvement; you couldn't save tinfoil for bilingualism, nor was there any end to it, nor a time when victory would be in sight. It was not that it went on too long, but the certainty that it would go on forever, an eternal irritant to afflict generations yet unborn.

Even as "bilingualism and biculturalism" disappeared from the working vocabularies of politicians with English-speaking constituencies, the apparent predominance of French Canadians on television and radio in anything that represented federalism and the nation's problems seemed unavoidable. There was Chrétien, who had succeeded Turner and who looked like the driver of the getaway car, and Lalonde, with his appraising stare, the hawk's beak and the reproving tone; then there was Alphonse Ouimet and Yves Pratte; and then, God help us, René Levesque, Jacques Parizeau — and Jean-Claude Parrot — all French! It had become possible to listen to the CBC News and scarcely hear a clear, thorough, thumping English diphthong. One could quantify the dimensions of the day's crises by counting the "dese" and "dose," the casual damns, hells, my gods and goddams emerging in curls of smoke from the mouths of Frenchmen often in their shirtsleeves. For a decade, all the troubles in Canada had appeared in a French accent: trouble at the Post Office, with the air traffic controllers, with inflation, taxation, and with the unity of the nation.

The persistence and growing pervasiveness of bilingualism had alienated English Canadians from federalism, turning them inwards to more familiar, compatible and nearer political jurisdictions in the provinces. Nothing was more clear, in the recurring federal-provincial conferences, than the isolation of the prime minister, who seemed encircled by more powerful and confident spokesmen for Canadian interests and concerns. The government of Canada had lost its constituency; furthermore, it had lost public sympathy and support for the idea of federalism, and public endorsement would await only the national leader or the party promising less of it. "Strong central government" had become as opprobrious a phrase to English Canadians as it had always been to Québecois.

A majority in a democratic society must be led; it will not be driven for long. By 1979, the English-speaking majority had been drained of its tolerance and, throughout its broad domain, Liberalism being fatefully linked to federalism, the few remaining Liberal governments in the provinces fell from power, while other provincial Liberal parties withered to near obscurity.

Still, there was something admirable, even magnificent, in the man who, for a decade, had been so stubbornly resolute in his purpose. English-speaking Canada had at last firmly set its face against him, the gathered rebuke for a long-festering grievance, but, though he was ravaged by many torments to his pride, some of them unmentionable, there was yet much mettle in him. It would have been a betrayal of the varlet's value system not to acknowledge the substance of the man now standing in the ruins of his good intentions. The substance of men in politics mattered as much as the substance of their policy. Whether to vote for Trudeau, or against, would be a hard choice, if not for the country, at least for himself.

xi

Gide's secret is that he never, in the midst of his doubts, lost the pride of being a man.

Albert Camus

The varlet was not yet to be relieved from the Death Watch, but this being Friday, 11 May, he would soon be standing down. His view from the battlements was made more foreboding by the signals arriving in his morning dispatches.

"Joseph Clark X" was the headline over the lead (and only) editorial in the *Globe and Mail*. Joseph Clark? Well, the occasion called for solemnity, but Charles Joseph Clark might have been even more becoming for editorial investitures. The varlet plunged into the leader writer's prose in search of rationale; it seemed like panning for gold in a swamp.

"We do not agree," said the *Globe and Mail*, "with everything Mr Clark and his party have set their eyes upon."

A plausible disclaimer and, as he read on, possibly an understatement:

"We are not convinced that he should get rid of Petro-Canada....

"... his proposal to also exempt [how often uneasy argument splits infinitives!] interest on mortgages is just another scheme to persuade us that Ottawa knows more about other people's priorities than they do....

"We are confused by Mr Clark's determination to spend more before spending less....

"We cannot say that we disagree with Mr Clark on his Quebec policy. We simply do not understand it."

Nothing, however, on Clark's newest initiative on Jerusalem, other than this oblique absolution: "Mr Clark is a young man whose experience beyond the world of politics is limited." (This would not be an editorial the proprietors of Tory propaganda mills would seize upon for distribution among their far-flung legions beyond the *Globe*'s circulation area.) But not until the last of it did the *Globe* confront the gnawing dilemma of so many of its readers, though it was put in a curious way:

"Would we be taking a chance on Joe Clark?"

Now "Joe" Clark ... the varlet noted the *Globe*'s shift to the familiar, as in *tu*, then shut his eyes before reading further, his mind conjuring appropriate answers that might satisfy the editorialist were he not to find any himself. (From his father, the varlet had learned the habit of reading baseball boxscores by holding his finger over the print so that he could create some slight suspense by reading the progress of the game one inning at a time.) Now, to savour the suspense of this moment, he placed a finger over the remainder of the brief paragraph, reading:

"Of
   course
      we
         would."

Thus far, no better an answer to the question than any of his own.

"That's
   how
      we
         have
            built
               our
                  country."

A faithful reader of *Globe* editorials — an admirer of their style — would know that the paper was capable of subtlety, sarcasm, irony . . . yes, and wit. But was it capable of playing a practical joke on its readers, upon the many impatient partisans among them who had, hours before the first dark beginning minute of this day, rushed out for the bulldog edition to confirm the rumours of the *Globe*'s endorsement of Clark?

The varlet probed for clues. We have built our country by taking a chance on Joe Clark? Only an early morning peevishness could be the source of such literal interpretation —still, in the confusion of much prolixity lay hints of desperation. Was there some small voice behind that editorial trumpet pleading our indulgence?

A skimming of the *Globe*'s archives would yield the testimony of how little this country enjoyed risk-taking. Unless we count the popularity of Loto Canada, or the small fortunes made and lost by robber barons and railroad builders long since deceased, the accumulated venture capital of the nation's history would scarcely purchase General Motors. (Which reminded him of Clark's clarion call: "Canadians must be encouraged to remove their money from their socks and put it into stocks.") No, this country was built upon numerous certainties, not the least of them American power, including purchasing power; it was a country built on the inevitable exploitation of a natural abundance, most of it unearthed by foreign investors and hauled away by them, a reality that would set a later generation of tenured professors complaining of a nation trading its birthright for pottage. We were a nation of bondholders, and for those who wished a flutter, there was always Bell Tel. No country on earth is so governed by pragmatism nor so well served by its Bank Act. The nation's indestructibility is in that genetic caution in the marrow of our bones. Most of us are Scots Presbyterians under the skin.

Such a people are unlikely to know euphoria, the necessary condition for any who would embark upon adventures in which destiny is to be left to chance. Only once had euphoria seized the nation — in the pyrotechnics of its one hundredth anniversary, in the wonders and excitements of Expo '67, when we sensed a world shifting upon its axis and turning now on the fulfilment of Laurier's half-remembered prophecy: the twentieth century will belong to Canada. Epicentre at last!

Did not Charles de Gaulle confirm it? With such Gallic impertinence, it had been the General who conjured elements of danger and challenge enough to ignite the passions of loyalist sentiment. "Vive le Québec libre!" Who has forgotten that hoarse, mischievous, but perfect shout, a *cri de coeur* for a few, a call to arms for many? Then, indeed, there were risks to be run: the country was ready for Trudeau.

Trudeau was the only chance the Canadian electorate had ever taken; a country built on foreign capital and immigrant sweat, and opened up by earlier generations of boat people, does not run many political risks either. In a land drenched in optimism, it required a national seizure of euphoria to be excited by the prospect of being led by a man who was the least likely politician in its history.

The country fell into his arms. Herewith, a sample of the Trudeau wit which swept grown men off their feet. Trudeau is telling a "workshop" crowd at the 1968 Liberal convention that Quebec's Daniel Johnson must oppose Ottawa because he is under the pressure of separatists in his province.

"So are you," a delegate shouts.

"No, you're not very well informed."

"Yes, you are."

"So's your old man."

That was the stuff that broke them up. So snappy a rejoinder that Newman records it in *The Distemper of Our Times* as example of Trudeau's "grace and gaiety." (And in the same book forever misspells the name of Joe Clark.) But after King, St Laurent, Diefenbaker, and Pearson— Trudeau?

So he failed. His was "[a] long record of frustrated hopes, contradictory policy, and squandered wealth," said the *Globe*'s editorial truthfully — but the varlet knew of no Canadian who had so profoundly reshaped Canadian society, as much at least by his style as by his policies.

Men who had been forever drones to convention dared to emulate his dress and affect an altogether novel *savoir faire*. Some, envious of the prime minister's lithe virility, even took up jogging. Others attempted Berlitz. A good deal of the stuffiness went out of politics and protocol. For a long while, the society seemed to have shaken loose from a traditional habit of repression, willing to examine any shibboleth or tribal taboo — divorce, homosexuality, drugs. Even the arts were enlivened! We had never been so near to being an open society. Such a spate of liberality brought a concomitant permissiveness, and a narcissistic individualism. But 1968-78 remains a decade in which the newness of much of our experience gave it the luminous quality of personal adventure, and Trudeau, who so well personified it, provided much of its impetus and style.

Still, the risk had proven greater than the yield: a statement that remained a question to the varlet if not to the *Globe and Mail*. But if the country turned to the young Tory leader, it would scarcely be taking a chance on him. If you were ever in a fight, the safest man around to hold your coat would be Clark.

xii

The varlet hies himself to the Royal York Hotel, site of countless political assignations, trysting place for many a political destiny. There he would find the prime minister who had, thus far on this day, been attending "government business." There was no mystery about Trudeau's luncheon speech: it would be the English version of what he had already said in French the night before, at a dinner in Montreal, which the varlet did not attend since, because of illness, he had been confined to the Toronto Press Club with Larry Zolf, an ideal companion for a man who had lost his voice.

There was a rumour that the prime minister was becoming fractious, demanding to be let loose from his hotel suite and to mingle with the people on the streets below. If it was false, the varlet could not blame Jim Coutts for putting the story out. The feeling was abroad that the prime minister had lost interest in the campaign. The Royal York luncheon would be the only event of the day, as the Montreal dinner had been of yesterday. And this crowd, although smaller than the one in Montreal, was of the same genre — pure Grit, operating under the appropriate cover of "the Confederation Club."

While the prime minister's captive audience dines, the Varlet prowls the mezzanine, finding Toronto Rotary in the convention ballroom — his stomach turning at the prospect of four-hundred-and-fifty plates of chicken and peas, served up with *bonhomie* and giblet gravy. Elsewhere, he notes a seething bustle of Friday affairs: Pepsi Cola Ltd. (Orange); the Canadian Fertility Society; the Canadian Caterpillar Dealers Annual Meeting (more elections); Planned Parenthood (in the Regency Ballroom); Rockwell International....

The head table for this extraordinary session of the Confederation Club proclaims the presence of the day's guest: it has been split into halves to allow the prime minister's elongated microphone, stark and unadorned, to stand between. A young man from the PMO always keeps the dismantled apparatus in a sturdy metal silver box constantly at his feet on the plane. He could tell you the proper height of the microphone from the floor, and his job was to set it up, after testing the acoustics and sound systems in all the halls in which the prime minister was to speak. The prime minister, he said, did not like to speak from behind lecterns since they inhibited the free movement of his hands, and he did not need a lectern anyway, since he spoke without the aid of notes or a text. (The varlet wondered what would become of the young man should the government change.)

With the prime minister's life-support system as a divider, the two head tables resemble teams assembled for a battle on "Family Feud." On closer scrutiny, it appears they have been chosen by random selection, or captured in a dip-net. There is Norman Campbell, who wrote the lyrics for the stage production of "Anne of Green Gables," and Gordon Sinclair (he had that day predicted a Trudeau victory in the *Toronto Star*), Johnny Lombardi, assorted business and financial moguls, a strikingly handsome opera diva, her presence unaccountable, and Donald Macdonald, "Thumper," the next-to-last finance minister of Canada, now returned to the practice of law. (There are more retired Liberal finance ministers extant in Toronto — Walter Gordon, Sharp, Turner and Macdonald — than there are Liberal members in all the legislatures of western Canada. The varlet suspects some root connection to these disparities.)

Among the members of the Confederation Club, and including the head table, Macdonald looks to be the healthiest, happiest man in the room. Private practice has restored some bloom to him, erased the worry from his face and reduced the puffiness. Thumper, in his days in Trudeau's ministry, was known as a "heavy," big enough to be overbearing and with a whiff of Rosedale-Toronto condescension about him. Of course, men do not come out of Trinity College, Osgoode, Harvard and Cambridge, as Macdonald had done, with degrees in humility. And when Thumper describes himself, in his introduction of the guest speaker, as a long-time friend and among the first of the Toronto Liberals to urge Trudeau to seek the leadership, it sounds more authentic than perfunctory. Trudeau's earlier cabinet had been one of the most literate and learned, as

Diefenbaker's probably was one of the least; the difference being that the one was as determinedly rational as the other was intuitive.

There is a sense of fitness, then, in Macdonald's looming presence at this soulful reunion of the party's Toronto faithful. He reminds one of how much cerebral power has been drained from the councils of government, as though a tap had been left running, and how isolated the prime minister has since become, an image now reinforced by his position on the dais, standing behind the lonely microphone, looking into a sea of upturned faces searching his for signs of deliverance.

For an hour he speaks, as he had said he would, and on a subject he admits to be unexciting but, administering the full measure of his gathered resolve, one he means to go on discussing until the campaign is over. The luncheon slowly dissolves into a seminar, the prime minister emerging as an engaging pedant — could anyone else have held an audience so rapt in its attention for so long a time on a subject of such acknowledged dread? Patriation of the constitution is his theme, and the varlet, transfixed by this studiously defiant diversion, can hear the wheezing of his own congested lungs in the silence of the room.

Patriation (a word unique to the Canadian lexicon, like "slap-shot") had been his theme in Montreal, and had been the supposed punchline of his speech at the Gardens, but on this second-reading, at the Royal York, it is mercifully enlivened by occasional diversion, as though to test the quiet of the crowd to determine if it is truly gripped by the subject or merely asleep. When he refers to previous dealing with Levesque, adding "and I intend to deal with him again," his audience pounces on the aside with a burst of applause. Yet, again, he twice mentions his mother, and the varlet can feel a fluttering of hearts in the room, a leap of sentiment in the midst of the solemn march-past of the constitutional history of Canada.

Then, a quotation from Premier Bill Davis is submitted as evidence of Ontario's support for unilateral federal action in patriating the British North America Act: there is still enough politics left in those being lectured, to allow them to savour this morsel of Tory endorsement. It is also the only evidence of pertinent research the varlet has heard produced by the prime minister in the campaign.

Trudeau finishes his discourse on the hour, as though bells could be heard ringing in the corridors, and his audience, relieved of the burden of so much empathy, so long sustained, rises to salute him, its applause building to a sustained ovation. The varlet, standing at the back alongside the journalist from Florida, is astonished to see him joining in the demonstration, beating his palms together in vigorous commendation.

"Wow," he is saying, "that was something."

But George Radwanski, a recent Trudeau biographer, puts it more aptly:

"C'est magnifique, mais est-ce que la guerre?"

There is now a final leg to the varlet's journey with Trudeau, leading to a connection with the Clark campaign. After boarding the jet at Malton, he finds Coutts reading the *Toronto Star* in which the varlet had prophesied doom for the Liberal campaign.

"What is all this crap you're writing?" Coutts asks, looking up from his paper.

The varlet, whose column had mentioned observing Coutts's tears in the Charlottetown meeting, turns the question aside:

"I'm only trying to make you a sympathetic figure, Jim."

It might take some doing. If anyone had been a Teperman's wrecking crew to Trudeau's credibility, it had been Coutts. Too smart for one, but not quite bright enough for two — something Hugh John Flemming had once been heard to say of the varlet — Jim had been given most of the credit for luring Jack Horner out of the Tory caucus and into Trudeau's cabinet. If gratitude counts for much in politics, the Tories owe Coutts at least a senatorship.

Indeed, in a recent conversation with Stanfield, the varlet had felt the force of his former leader's disdain for the cynicism of a man who would make bilingualism the centre-piece of his policy but then recruit the most vociferous opponent of it to his cabinet. As for the varlet, when he had heard that Coutts was romancing Horner, he had — incredible! — tried to persuade Jack to stick.

"You have a lot of clout in the Conservative party," he had told him, "and a big future in it. All the Grits want is to use you."

"Well," Jack had replied, "at least if I go over there, I'll have the satisfaction of kicking a few asses."

Certainly Horner's motives were not the least noble of those involved. The Horner affair had enriched the varlet's perception of Coutts, whom he could now identify as a fiercely relentless partisan, a man whose zest and con-summate adroitness he could respect, even while know-ing how one can be undone by it. Further example was to follow:

"I've got $500 that says we win more seats than your guys," Coutts is now saying to the varlet, having left his seat up front to find him, once the ordinance lights were off.

The wager seems considerable, more than he would put on Secretariat to place in the Canadian International. He says as much to Coutts, offering the advice that, the way things are going, $500 might come in handy even for a man of his abilities.

"And Arnie Patterson has another $500 for your friend MacDonald," Coutts goes on, as though he has not been listening.

"Jim, I don't make book for Finlay MacDonald. All I'm saying to you is that your people have run a terrible campaign."

Bob Anderson

"I've got $500 that says we win more seats than your guys," Coutts was now saying to the varlet.

"We've run an excellent campaign," Coutts says, prim authority in his voice.

It occurs to the varlet that he might be playing the straight man for a show of Coutts's unflinching confidence, performed for the audience in the rear of the plane. This being so, he would not mind collecting a talent fee. He would clarify the position:

"You are betting me, Jim, $500 that the Liberals win more seats in the forthcoming federal election than the Conservatives."

"That's right."

They shake hands on it.

From his window, the varlet can see the nation's capital coming up on the starboard side, rising beneath him in the afternoon sunlight of a ripening spring — an open city awaiting the tread of victorious Tory regiments.

Someone has clipped a newspaper headline (from a story on Uganda) and affixed it to the panelled wall of the aircraft:

"Lifespan of Regime Now Measured in Hours," it reads.

Was there any doubt? The prime minister had made his concession speech in Toronto. In the measured phrasing of his soliloquy on a matter of so little interest, he had acknowledged the inevitability of his defeat. The varlet departs the Death Watch, turning his eyes from the sight of Pierre Trudeau kneeling on the tarmac and sweeping his young sons into his arms.

The Wimp Watch awaits his troubled spirit.

The Wimp Watch

i

The varlet makes a stop-over in Ottawa to see the capital city in the waning days of the eleven-year reign of Pierre Elliott Trudeau. There is, furthermore, some possible therapeutic value in the visit, for, having been in the company of so many Liberals, there is an opportunity to fraternize with a few Conservatives, among them Lowell Murray.

Every successful election campaign must have an "architect," a title bestowed upon the ranking member of the winning party's organization who is most visible to the media. In the Tory campaign of 1979, the designated architect of victory is Lowell Murray, who, in the varlet's estimate, has served a longer sentence in the anterooms of Canadian politics without being repelled by it than anyone else he knows. Murray has stamina.

His endurance is all the more remarkable when you consider where he has spent most of those years: not just within the Tory party, enough of a trial, but seconded, in numbing succession, to E. Davie Fulton, Wallace McCutcheon, E. Davie Fulton again, Robert Stanfield, Richard Hatfield, and finally Joe Clark. He had also run for political office in 1956 but had been unsuccessful in winning a seat in the Nova Scotia legislature. He had worked for the CNR, and before any of these activities, did news and interviews for a Cape Breton TV station. In 1957, during the federal election campaign, he had interviewed John Diefenbaker, which was when the varlet had first set eyes on him. He was then a soft-spoken, boyish-looking, compactly small man, with a direct, quizzical stare and a slow smile, who was obviously very bright; he has not changed.

Lowell Murray has always been uncommonly neat, even fastidious, which is the reflection of a well-ordered, disciplined mind. His principal value to the politicians he has served has been his ability to write — and Murray writes in all the official languages of Canada: English, French, and Bureaucratese. It is an inevitability in the political speech-writing trade that he who puts words in the mouths of politicians will end up putting ideas in their heads, and our boyish-looking, apple-cheeked, clear-eyed architect-friend is no exception. Today, Murray is more valuable as a strategist than as a wordsmith.

"A man has only one good campaign in him," Murray once told a reporter, which meant that after this one of 1979, he would like to quit while still ahead. But the life of a winning campaign manager is a hard one, a little like being the fastest gun in town, and graceful retirement is not easily arranged: either you keep on shooting down impertinent challengers, or you go out feet first.

The architect had a testing apprenticeship. He was Fulton's executive assistant while Davie was minister of justice in the Diefenbaker interregnum, and rejoined him, after the cabal against Diefenbaker collapsed in 1963, in the unreal world of British Columbia politics, where Fulton was poised to lead an invisible Conservative party out of the wilderness. After that certain débâcle, Murray resurfaced in Ottawa in the employ of Senator McCutcheon, the only occasion when the architect had served a tenured politician. Though McCutcheon ran for the leadership at the 1967 Tory convention, so too did Fulton, and Murray, along with Joe Clark, joined in his support.

A puzzle here, as to Murray's affinity for Fulton, who was a politician of uncertain judgement, to say the least, and a difficult, mercurial and bull-headed man to work for, at best. All that Fulton and Murray (and Clark) appeared to have in common was their Catholicism, which does not explain the lengths — and distances — Murray would go to in order to assist a man of such Quixotic inclination. But at

Ted Grant

Lowell Murray has served a longer sentence in the anterooms of Canadian politics without being repelled by it than anyone else the varlet knows.

least it explains something about the architect: he is not one to resist a challenge merely because it is insuperable.

Murray toured with Stanfield during the disastrous 1968 campaign when Trudeau swept the country. After the inevitable retreat overseas, he returned to the Conservative leader's office as his chief adviser; there, for a time, Joe Clark worked under his tutelage. Having by now become a compulsive transient, Murray moved on to Montreal to the peace of private practice, joining the public relations department of Canadian National. But not for long.

Richard Hatfield, the premier of New Brunswick, persuaded him to become his deputy minister, an invitation which confirmed Hatfield's political shrewdness and confessed his administrative shortcomings, both of which are considerable. From 1974 to August 1976, and throughout the campaign in which the Hatfield government was re-elected, Murray wielded enormous power. Some say he ran the government — a careless exaggeration — but what he did do was make the government run.

We have now nearly overtaken the man in his emergence as the architect-apparent of Clark's victory. Leaving Hatfield, Murray managed a year at Queen's University studying public administration, where, intimidated by his background, one of his professors begged him not to attend classes.

At the Tory leadership convention of February 1976, which chose Clark, Lowell Murray, though not a delegate, was in Ottawa with Hatfield, who was busily supporting Flora MacDonald's candidacy. A year later, Murray became Clark's man to put together the organization which the party would take into the federal election campaign.

Now that the taxpayer is helping to fund political parties and their election campaigns, the parties have become more like corporations. Politics is a multi-million dollar business, and raising money has become, to an increasing degree, the achievement of the sure-fire techniques of direct mail; the computer has made the bagman a lesser figure in the system.

But more important, the new money enables the party to buy more people for the organizational cadres, and, while voluntarism is still important, particularly at the constituency level, the central organization is becoming more professional, more numerous, more expensive—and more important.

The greening of Canadian politics, already revolutionized by the impact of television, has brought still more change. The old impoverishments that would drive a party to making-do, to feverish improvisation and to leaving much to chance, are gone, replaced by a rush of affluence which has produced a new world of modalities, structures, systems, print-outs, flow-charts and cash on hand. This new order was made for Lowell Murray, whose cool detachment and fine-honed administrative skills make him the essential manager of a rising political bureaucracy.

It is not that Murray has not suffered, but that he has suffered enough; indeed, he has known some of the longest marches and leanest years in Tory history. So this has been truly a dream campaign, heaven sent and delivered by Hand, much of it preplanned, prepackaged and prepaid, and the certainties have been comforting all along, since the October by-elections. The early blunders of Clark — the "stimulative deficits," and the apparent softness on separatism — were all committed while Murray had been tooling about Ireland waiting for the writ to drop, like Drake bowling on the green at Plymouth. Once he was back in town, and had the show on the road, the mistakes were few — at least the media had not exploited any, which, when you thought about it, would be the only definition there was of a mistake.

The varlet, feeling like a man after his first day on the street coming to meet the cappo, finds Canada's next architect of victory in the rearmost alcove of the Chateau Laurier Grill. In Murray's company are Nancy MacLean, who has shot TV commercials and the campaign travelogues for Stanfield, Davis, Hatfield and Clark, and Allan Gregg, a fledgling analyst-strategist but an astute reader of polls. He is Murray's assistant, and a brash, quick and articulate one. As for MacLean, the truly creative force in the campaign, she has filmed, edited, mixed and measured out the Tory television commercials which have sluiced the Canadian consciousness throughout the campaign. Of all the leaders she has filmed and edited, she will tell you, Clark is the first who can stare into a camera and give you a thirty-second or one-minute commercial from a standing start — and he even writes his own material!

The varlet has not come alone to this scratch dinner, but with Finlay MacDonald and Paul Curley, who is the tour representative at national headquarters. So he is among friends of some years standing, except for Gregg, and if all the drinks they had poured together could be retrieved, they would fill the Chateau swimming pool just down the hall, and if medals were awarded for Tory campaigns, the group assembled around the banquette would look like a gathering of Chelsea pensioners.

Even so, the reunion is tinged with unease. This is the eve of the great debate and, though the briefings and preparations have been exhaustive, there are infinite possibilities beyond their control, including the unknown strategies of the other two adversaries. MacLean and Gregg have examined the studio set for the occasion, and made sure that the lecterns are nailed to the floor, that the water glass has a receptacle, that the chairs cannot be tipped off the podium, and that the camera cannot be treacherously employed. A small mountain of briefing books had been prepared for Clark, who had put them aside to concentrate his thoughts on his own approach, and an American expert had been flown in to give advice on televised debates, which was that Clark should ignore the presence of Trudeau and Broadbent and speak directly to the cameras. Now, there was nothing left to do but worry (although Murray, driving with Clark to the studio tomorrow, would give his leader the ultimate advice on dealing with Trudeau: whatever you do, don't do anything that will show them how much you dislike the son of a bitch).

No, it is not an evening for relaxation; despite the jocular talk, there are hovering anxieties that even strong drink and much common history cannot dissolve. Murray, as diminutive a man as Coutts, slouches in the far corner, his back to the wall, weariness betrayed by a sagging posture and the deliberation of his speech. Front-running brings its own dull pains and fatigue to the race; Murray would have a stiff neck from looking over his shoulder for seven weeks.

Besides, the thought grows upon the varlet that he is no longer one of them and they know it: he is now an alien presence, an interloper in search of source material in a motherlode of secrecy — the highest level of the organizational hierarchy. Bootless to say to this gathering that its secrets are as familiar to him as the face in his own mirror; what could be unknown to him of the lusts of partisans? Even Murray, for all his wisdom and experience, had yet to go through the inevitable aftermath of a winning campaign — anti-climax and protracted bends for the sur-facing ego!

But what needs to be hidden in the vaults of a man's experience in Canadian politics is the inner awareness of its vast irrelevance, so that self-importance may be safeguard-ed. What will come after, for the varlet's table company, will be a daily life of desperate reassertion in a misshapen world of barbiturate sycophancy — lethal to the soul. What they will crave, for their habit, is the constant assurance that Canadian politics is vital, and not merely inevitable, which will be a consolation they can find only among themselves. The reality of Canadian politics is that it is conducted within narrow limits of probability, so that the power of govern-ment is contained well short of adventure and innovation. What remains is the power of governance over the ambitions of others, the small change of preferment and perquisite — old vestments and titles for new men.

The varlet leaves his hosts after a final, lingering after-dinner drink, thanking them, wishing them well, confident they would never appear the same to him again — nor would he to them. A sceptic has not much to offer true believers, and the revelations of politics come not from example but from experience.

As for Murray, the architect of English Canada's coming catharsis, he too eventually goes off into the warm spring night. A policeman, the next morning, will find him asleep on the steps of his apartment house.

ii

> This is a nation where somebody from
> a little corner of the foothills of Alberta,
> without much money behind him, can
> stand in equal opportunity with a mil-
> lionaire's son to become prime minister
> of Canada.
>
> Joe Clark, Timmins, Ontario
> May 1979

The varlet is motoring over the wooded back hills of Queens County, New Brunswick, heading for the Mackay Highway, which will take him to the Saint John (International) Airport and Joe Clark. The early morning air is thick with fog laced by a thin rain.

Not your ordinary Monday, this one, but the beginning of the final week of a wearing, boring, interminable campaign, and the morning after the nationally televised debate between the party leaders. The car radio is alive with comment: a talk show on a Fredericton station, devoted to listeners' opinion about who had won, conveys the earnest sentiments of vox populi.

"Good morning," the male host briskly intones. "This is 'Reaction,' and you're on the air. Who do you think won last night's debate?"

"Well, I watched the whole of the program," says a voice, hinting of grandmotherly hugs and cookie jars in kitchen pantries, "and I thought those other two — Mr Trudeau and Mr Broadbent — just picked on Mr Clark all the time. That's *all* they did. But I thought Mr Clark stood right up to them, just like the little man he is."

The varlet does not share her opinion, although concedes it to be as valid as his own. He had himself thought the millionaire's son had roughed up the young man from the Alberta foothills considerably. Still, he had been half-convinced by an observation of Jeff Simpson, a *Globe and Mail* correspondent of enviable detachment, that it was the collective wisdom of the pollsters (who would know such things) that all the televised political debates in history had thus far served only to reinforce the bias of those who watched them. How great, then, must have been the bias of Mordecai Richler, a man with occasional furies resembling the varlet's own, who was to describe the debate as one between two men, Trudeau and Broadbent, and a boy with a hollow laugh.

No, it was impossible to find an opinion without some bias at its roots. The varlet had watched the debate with Richard Hatfield, who, halfway through, had left the television and gone downstairs to turn on the stereo.

"It's all over," he had said, a model example of Simpson's observation, "Clark wins!"

It would have been a comfort to many viewers, however, if the debates had been followed by some serious discussion and analysis. Many a bias must have remained unenforced — not everyone is like Hatfield — since listeners have been conditioned to suspend their own judgement in events of this kind until some familiar and superior authority tells them what it should be. Had the media been allowed the opportunity for post-debate discussion, it would have helped Trudeau and hurt Clark.

Some three weeks previously, on 27 April, in a meeting between the networks and the parties, the possibility had

Ted Grant

The millionaire's son had roughed up the young
man from the Alberta foothills considerably.

been raised and, curiously, argued against by the Liberals, as this extract from the minutes of the meeting reveals:

> Senator [Keith] Davey (Liberal) raised the subject of post-program analysis by the various networks. Was it their intention to follow the program with panels of journalists discussing what had immediately gone before. "This time," he said, "let's not have panels of journalists coming up and tearing the leaders apart."
>
> Mr [Don] Cameron (CTV) said the Senator had raised a "pretty touchy subject." Senator Davey agreed, but said, "why not just once let the public make up its mind first."
>
> All network spokesmen then pointed out that the meeting was confined to the subject of the pool program under discussion, i.e., the debate, or discussion among the leaders. Each network would decide on its own what treatment might be given to the leaders' program in their other programming. Senator Davey added, with some emphasis, that he was not declaring this a pre-condition for acceptance of the program proposed. However, he did feel strongly about post-program analysis, and wished the networks to consider his position.
>
> Mr [Finlay] MacDonald (PC) and Mr [Robin] Sears (NDP) felt some sympathy toward Senator Davey's views, but likewise did not wish to make this a condition of acceptance of the program proposal.
>
> Mr Cameron, declining on behalf of CTV to give any commitment whatever on this issue, did add that heretofore he had not considered a post-program analysis, and thanked Senator Davey for the suggestion.

However, an instant CTV post-debate poll had shown Trudeau and Broadbent both leading Clark in the audience's perception of winners and losers. But the Tories had also taken a poll, finding to their satisfaction that their man had achieved his objective — he had held his ground.

So, even though the varlet had been discomfited by Clark's uneasy laughter under the pressure of Trudeau's direct questioning of him, and while the Tory leader had, mistakenly, denied that Ontario's Bill Davis had once urged the federal government to unilateral action in patriating the British North America Act, there was apparently nothing decisive in the sum of it.

Ted Grant

A sceptic has not much to offer true believers, and
the revelations of politics come not from example
but from experience.

Trudeau had been the aggressor in his debate with Clark, a tactic of dubious merit in a medium in which images overwhelm the audio senses. "None of them said anything," complains a voice on the open-line show. "All they did was criticize each other." (By now, the radio straw poll is showing Broadbent leading both Clark and Trudeau, 7-6-6, a development suggesting that the bias of Frederictonians was yielding to a sporting objectivity.) The trouble with political debates on television, the varlet had learned from painful experience, is that a clear winner can also emerge as a clear loser. There are consolations in irresolution and split decisions.

Only one caveat could be attached to last night's stalemated non-event: the reinforced bias that decreed Clark's survival of it might not be as strong as a countervailing one, which was that Trudeau might have shown enough fire in the debate to ignite the dampened spirits of his party, reinforcing bias with ardour, and lending the weightless factor of momentum to the variants in the latest polls. Such was the varlet's hunch, however slender.

Too early, then, for useful conjecture; better to await a sampling of the atmosphere around Clark today — the mood of his crowds and the static in his entourage. Besides, there were more immediate questions: after the varlet's initial voyage with Trudeau, what would it be like, joining this tour of a Tory leader, to travel in the back of the bus? An original experience, at least, like riding in a bathysphere.

Part of his wariness on this leg of his mission would be in his meeting old friends aboard Charter 087, some who pre-dated the Diefenbaker years, all of whom were seeking some fresh identity in future scenarios. The varlet would also see the revised, alloyed version of Joe Clark, the prime minister-apparent, who was less familiar to him than the young politician who had been a protégé. The man who emerged from the pages of David Humphreys's strenuous biography — the first ever book to be written about Clark — had been unrecognizable, even disfigured. (Humphreys would make a fine revisionist historian for the new régime!) Had the varlet not known another Joe Clark, he would have shared John Diefenbaker's contempt of him.

The burden of his doubt about the plasticized politician in the book was the heavier for the caricatures of him in the media. The Toronto *Sun*, which supported Clark, had nonetheless called him "a nerd," and, to the journalists on the campaign, he was "the wimp." The flowering of Clark as the nation's leader was all but obscured by the nettles of his detractors.

In his book on Clark, Humphreys had quoted his hero as saying, "Anyone who can bring the Conservative party together can bring the country together." The varlet admired the syllogistic ring but doubted the first premise.

iii

I am their leader. I must follow them.
Andrew Bonar Law

The jet aircraft has altered campaign politics as much as it has changed the precepts of transportation. Options and possibilities escalate as speed and range increase. The jet campaign has also spawned a new genre of organization men: the logicians, managers, wagonmasters and advance men who plot the leader's itinerary, direct the movements of his flying capsule, provide the in-flight ambience, summon the cars and buses at the airports, book the hotels, hire the halls, stage-manage the leader's arrivals and departures, attend to the needs and monitor the morale of the media, and otherwise "make it happen" — a recurrent expression in their idiom.

The men who find this role in politics — and they are all men — are invariably young, in their thirties, out of the entrepreneurial community, resolutely cordial in their sales personalities, fiercely proud of their place, and convinced of their importance in the overall scheme of things. They are not much interested in the politics of campaigns, and, although most of them are occupational conservatives, their satisfaction comes from an intense involvement in the mechanics of electioneering.

That they are serious men going about serious business is apparent in their mien and reconfirmed by their self-evaluation of "work definitions and development" when the campaign is over. For an illustrated tour of a day in the life of one of these men, our guide is "the Wagonmaster" of Clark's 1979 campaign himself, describing "a sample day" in a post-campaign memorandum:

0645 — [Wagonmaster] Wake-up call by hotel.
      — [Assistant Wagonmaster] Wake-up call by hotel.
      — W. calls A.W. — calls W. to ensure each is awakened.
      — Review division of room list wake-up responsibility of W.-A.W. and content of our wake-up call — e.g. "Good morning Mr Mansbridge — get out of that bed — do you want people to think you are sick? — baggage in lobby at 0745 — green eggs and ham in the Continental Room at $3.00 from 0715 on. We leave at 0815. See you later."
0700 — Wake-up calls to all press by hotel.
0705 — W. & A.W. begin second wake-up calls.
0730 — W. proceeds to Continental Room to supervise breakfast and collect $3.00 from each consumer.
      — A.W. proceeds to baggage drop area in lobby to oversee baggage arrival and truck loading — always loaded in separate vehicle to precede buses to aircraft by 30 minutes — always deposited in main lobby — both staff and press — no bags delivered to or picked up from rooms — to avoid misplacement (or loss) of bags.
0805 — Terminate breakfast and begin bus loading.
0815 — Buses leave for airport.

0830   — Buses arrive at airport, to load aircraft directly from ramp.
        — A.W. does head count.
        — W. reviews passenger manifest prepared *after* take off of flight immediately preceding this flight, and alters where appropriate. All baggage loaded, head count checks with manifest — air crew ready — GO!! (10 minutes from bus unloaded til aircraft engine started — on average.)

0845   — Charter 087 departs for London, Ontario. En route to London, W. discusses, with purser, menu and wine service from Windsor that evening en route to Fort McMurray, Alberta. Final departure time is coordinated with air crew. W. & purser control *together* all access to flight deck en route by any passenger.

0915   — Charter 087 arrives at London airport.
        — All photographic media deplane first. W. remains at door to signal waiting photographers that Mr Clark is about to deplane so that they may begin "shooting" at the appropriate moment. W. ensures that Mr Clark's final appearance is acceptable.

0925   — Buses are loaded and, when ready, depart for Strathroy (10 minutes average time for deplaning and departure).

1000   — Buses at Lincoln Square, Strathroy. Mainstreeting begins.
        — W. & A.W. proceed to coffee and donut stand during mainstreeting — buy 7 dozen donuts and 60 coffees (cream and sugar separate) — board same on buses.

1025   — Mr Clark speaks.

1050   — Mr Clark terminates speech.
        — W. & A.W. direct press to phones arranged for filing. If none arranged and filing is required, W. & A.W. will have visited shopkeepers during speech and arranged availability of phones on gratis basis and will direct media accordingly.
        — Mr Clark mingles.

1115   — Buses are loaded.

1120   — Buses depart for Windsor.

1300   — Buses arrive at Windsor Periwinkle Square.

1315   — Mr Clark speaks.

1330   — Mr Clark terminates speech and retires to Windsor Arms Hotel next door for lunch and rest.
        — Media also proceed to hotel where a hospitality suite and lunch room await. If no specific arrangements for phone have been made, W. & A.W. enquire at hotel desk for 6-10 rooms for

press use of phone only — 10-15 minutes — leave room unused otherwise — hopefully no charge for rooms.

— Beer, sandwiches and coffee arranged in hospitality suite.

— A.W. monitors hotel and press arrangements.

— W. proceeds to Brewers Retail and purchases 8 dozen cans of Labatts 50 and Blue. 48 cans soda pop, 4 styrofoam coolers and 5 bags of ice are purchased as well at the Dominion Store.

— All are taken to the buses and boarded.

1500 — Buses are boarded by tour.

1505 — Buses proceed to Wallaceburg.

— Cold beer and pop are offered en route.

1630 — Buses arrive at Wallaceburg, Beatty Hotel.

— Mr Clark rests, writes speech and dines.

— Press hospitality suite — beer and cheeses are available.

— Media wish to organize a pick-up baseball game after more filing in hotel.

— W. & A.W. locate bats, balls, gloves and ball park.

1730 — Ball game begins.

1830 — Ball game terminates.

1900 — Press bus leaves hotel.

1915 — Press bus arrives Robarts Auditorium for set up.

— Ensure positioning of buses and drivers for speedy departure.

— Adequacy of space in front of podium for cameras — press tables at side of podium close to unimike — adequacy of and location of telephones — all are reviewed by W. & A.W.

— Mr Clark's route of entry is determined, and T.V. and "still" cameramen are advised.

— Arrange cars and drivers to drive T.V. and "still" film and people to stations.

1935 — Mr Clark arrives.

1945 — Mr Clark enters.

— The advance man should guide Mr Clark and Tour Manager to entrance of hall and describe routing to podium. Cameras and W. & A.W. will be waiting. The advance man should trail the procession, and W. & A.W. will guide the retreating cameramen along the route. The Tour Manager and advance person should ensure that Mr Clark walks slowly and follows the cameramen. Advance persons should be stationed at critical corner turns to ensure that the entourage negotiates the turn. For T.V. effect, no en masse aisle clearing should be conducted: simply a general routing intention should be made known to the multitudes gathered, and overall path opened. W. & A.W. will do the rest — in the terms of opening and guiding through crowds.

— In Spruce Grove, 6 persons tried to precede Mr Clark and "knife" through 10 T.V. cameras and 20 still photographers — W. & A.W. had more trouble trying to guide cameramen past our own advance people than past a prearranged routing. When we got to the front of the crowded hall, all of a sudden the advance people found they had no place to go and indeed clogged the direct access to the stage. There is a better way, and proper coordinated preparation by "on tour" plus "advance" personnel is required.

1950   — Mr Clark speaks.

— During his speeches, it is very important to monitor separation of people and media near or in front of podium to ensure no upset occurs — one or more getting in the way of another or others must be quietly prevented.

— If heckling occurs from persons gathered at front — referee and prevent flareups.

— No overt quieting of a heckler should occur and certainly not in close proximity of T.V. and still cameras.

2020   — Mr Clark finishes speech.
        — Route "filing" media to phones.
        — Ensure that buses are ready for departure.
        — Assist T.V. crews in take downs and routing out.
        — Give T.V. film to pre-arranged drivers.

2055   — Board buses.

2100   — Buses depart.

2120   — Buses arrive at Windsor airport. W. ensures that band brings guitar and banjo on board (to commence sing-song) for this long late-nite flight (after long day).

2130   — Charter 087 departs for Fort McMurray. En route, gourmet wine service quickly handled by (and originally purchased by) W. & A.W. with meal. W. & A.W. also facilitate liqueur distribution due to crowded aisles. Sing-song is started and all have "merry old time." Mr Clark joins in sing-song and contributes to "pretty heavy" high-profile flight. This is an intense psychological happening and can be used to parallel programmed speech and tour targets for accelerative impact on the national media, if not on the leader himself (and providing he has coordinated and programmed speech material in conjunction therewith).

2330　— Charter 087 arrives Fort McMurray.

— Buses are boarded.

— Separate truck boards baggage for delivery to lobby of hotel.

2340　— Buses depart for Peter Pond Motel.

— W. & A.W. will have received pre-registered and pre-packaged room keys together with 4 copies of numbers *and* name-keyed room lists.

— En route all members of media will receive a room key. (Often names on advance list are different than when first transmitted and W. & A.W. simply reassign rooms and alter room list accordingly — while handing revised copy of room list to advance man for transmittal to hotel for inter-room accuracy.)

2355　— Buses arrive at Peter Pond Motel.

— All media may proceed directly to rooms after picking up their bags deposited directly in front lobby — all bags are always kept together — properly name-tagged and each media bag has 3 fluorescent red stickers attached and each staff bag has 3 fluorescent green stickers attached.

0030　— All bags have been picked up — any last minute room alterations taken care of — under W.'s & A.W.'s direction.

0035　— W. & A.W. proceed to meet Tour Manager and advance persons to review, amend, and make tomorrow's itinerary come together in a way acceptable to all. Phone calls ahead to other advance persons are made by W. or Tour Manager, as may be appropriate to cover tomorrow's events.

0130　— Bed.

UNSPOKEN WARNING TO
WAGONMASTER AND ASSISTANT WAGONMASTER

If at any time during the day you think you have "covered every base" — think again — because you're sure to have overlooked something!!

MOTTO

Always try to run the lives of the people on the tour as if each of those lives was your own — feed it, humour it and encourage it in all you do.

iv

The Clark tour has been late leaving Ottawa, and it lands in Saint John behind schedule. The day's program calls for a shopping plaza rally at noon in Saint John and an evening rally in Yarmouth, N.S., both centres of Liberal constituencies the Tories hope to win. The early weather report for Yarmouth was discouraging — ground zero visibility — so Clark's staff and party headquarters are exploring alternative sites for the evening's media event.

The varlet, now a part of the critical mass in the Tory leader's tour, senses a change in his environment. How different from the Trudeau tour! There is no sense of brooding unease in this entourage; instead an atmosphere of lively curiosity, as though its members are attending a portable pageant of continuing surprise.

For illustration, spontaneity attends the thought: as the cavalcade of cars and buses proceeds from the airport to Saint John, Clark sees a gathering of schoolchildren at the roadside, and orders an unscheduled stop — even though they are running late — so that he can meet them. (Had Trudeau done the same, he would not have been allowed near them until they had been frisked.)

Is there some festering concern in Clark over the debate? His conversation with the children of Loch Lomond Elementary School, held well within media earshot, turns on the debate. How many watched it, he asks? Many had. He is as relaxed as he knows how to be, and one of the children feeds him a useful line: "Mommy and Daddy sent me to bed early. They said I was too young to watch."

A millionaire's son need not enjoy all the advantages for a future career in politics; Clark, whose father was publisher of the *High River Times*, knows something of the biorhythms in journalism as well as in the journalists. On this sodden morning, in the anti-climactic lull following the previous evening's debate, Clark employs his practiced eye

Ted Grant

Clark employs his practiced eye for making sure he
will be on the six o'clock news.

for film and photo opportunities and his knack for making sure he will be on the six o'clock news. Besides, the varlet dares suspect Clark might know that Trudeau, during his visit to Saint John, had spent an hour in a prearranged visit to a local school.

As to the debate, the consensus developing among the media on the bus is that Clark has cleared the last hurdle, and nothing lies ahead of him but ultimate validation in the grand assize next Monday, final proof of all the opinion polls and their own predictions. Doug Fisher, too impassive and independent a man to be swayed by the consensus of his colleagues, thinks Broadbent had scored the most points — "which doesn't necessarily mean anything" — and that Clark had taken the most heat, yet emerged unsinged. No one on the bus thinks Clark did badly, but no one thinks he won either.

The subject keeps coming up in any conversation with the Clark people. When pressed for his own view, the varlet gives out a hastily improvised reply that stresses Simpson's Law of Reinforced Bias and the opinions of the Fredericton grandmother.

The Clark event in Saint John is an advance man's caprice. It is staged on the mezzanine floor of an indoor shopping mall, Brunswick Square, and the speakers' platform has been established hard against the mezzanine balustrade, so that the orators at this noon-day shoppers' rally will speak directly into the well, to a loosely gathered crowd around the well and across from it, except for that part which is below them, and largely invisible. The general effect is that the speakers appear to be addressing an audience that has unaccountably fallen through the floor.

While Clark's performing minstrels proclaim the imminence of a happening, the suggestion that it might also be newsworthy is strengthened by the presence of cameras and a blaze of hot lights. The advantages and disadvantages of staging a political meeting in the midst of an indoor shopping mall are evident: there are perhaps five hundred people present but no focal point for them to gather at, even if they wish to, so that, while this meeting is well attended, it is by no means certain how many really have come.

Television program scheduling and the swiftness of jet travel encourage the use of random audiences, and the touring leader now goes wherever his handlers — like beaters in a jungle bush — tell him a crowd might be found. This is neither fail-safe nor foolproof (as will soon be proven), but when it works, as more often than not it does, it satisfies the minimal demands of technology upon election campaigns.

The high content of banality in political speeches, as well as their length, make them unwieldy for the purposes of television. A viewing audience accustomed to seeing mystery solved, justice done and love requited within the time-frame of thirty minutes (less commercials) cannot sit still for the snail's pace of election campaigns. In fact, it cannot endure the drone of a single voice, or focus upon a politician's face, for longer than a few seconds in a newscast that busily shunts the viewer's mind from wars and other disasters to the demise of celebrities and the latest cancers induced into rats.

Political campaigns are a menace to the visual excitements offered by television's global reach, provoking only ennui, too-familiar figures in their ritual performances — as lively as a Latin mass — and in which the end or resolution of it all is not measured in minutes, but in weeks, years or eternities. Thus, the gaggle of shoppers caught up in the train of Clark's procession, led by the wailing of the Heather Legion Pipe Band, have not come willingly to hear the Tory leader, nor has he come to address them; but they have become his crowd, and a service to the needs of television news that can decently produce his commercial endorsement of himself on a newscast only if it is delivered with the sanction of a visible number of onlookers, whose presence is proof that something is happening.

The local orchestrators of the Saint John rally have assembled nine of New Brunswick's ten Tory federal candidates, the premier, Richard Hatfield, a local provincial cabinet minister, Gerald Merrithew, and — the varlet's heart leaps for joy — George Hees! While he had feared this might be a typical Maritime contest of endurance between the assembled orators and the milling crowd, he would wait a long time to hear Hees. George possessed a formidable capacity for unconscionable insincerity that had once repelled the varlet, but that he now found endearing.

When Clark joins the platform guests, he promptly puts himself in charge. The man who only hours before had taken the best shots of Trudeau and Broadbent is not prepared to lean against the gusts of Tory oratory any longer than it suits him, which is not long at all. Part of the leader's cerebral equipment is his media clock, which tells him the deadlines of Western afternoon dailies and the time-frames within which the network film crews must operate. Bypassing the planned introduction by Hatfield, Clark seizes the microphone and gives his speech.

While Clark speaks, the varlet wanders, sampling the expressions of the listeners. Shopkeepers, resigned to this interruption of their business and wearing masks of imperturbability, idle in doorways; shoppers pick their way warily through the standing crowd, clutching handbags and parcels firmly, as though this might be a congress of pickpockets: incredible, the varlet thinks, how many feel themselves threatened in the company of politicians.

Clark's speech on this day turns on energy, following the lamentation (a strain upon the varlet's imagination) that "the prime minister had to go to Mexico on bended knee" to seek oil to replace the dwindling sources elsewhere. The varlet feels himself sinking in the tar sands of Alberta as the Tory-leader briskly dismisses the possibility of buying foreign crude when "two new projects here [in Canada] would produce seven and one-half times as much oil" as nine billion dollars would buy in a decade from the Mexicans.

Yes, and there would be a pipeline from Sarnia to Montreal; a gas pipeline from Quebec through the Maritimes; the development of coal and tidal power in the Atlantic provinces; and, for the coastal provinces, "the same right" to the underwater resources off their shores as Alberta and Saskatchewan had to their resources underground. This last, the varlet thinks, the neat analogy of a tidy mind. As for Petro-Canada, Clark says it will carry on finding new energy resources, but as a private company.

If anyone has come to Brunswick Square to lunch on Tory policy, he can now skip his dinner. Clark's repast offers second helpings of nourishing conservative staples: long-term "tax contracts" for business and industry in the region; tax credits for small business and businessmen; a general incitement to all Canadians to "raise their expectations." The varlet senses a sated audience, eager to leave the table.

But compared to this feast of policy, how great was Trudeau's impoverishment! Who could blame the prime minister for delivering his lecture on patriation in the safe confines of Liberal clubhouses?

Clark, who had encountered some early heckling from high-school students on their noon recess, has overwhelmed his listeners with his commanding pace and assurance. There is little response left in them when he finishes, and the hand-clapping that follows his speech expresses nearly equal parts of relief and appreciation. Like a good belch.

The Tory leader has been wise to put himself first, since what follows are the ancient rites of established custom, to which none adhere with greater zeal than Maritimers, including the lengthy introductions of nine candidates and a speech from one of them, Eric Ferguson, the Tory standard-bearer in Saint John.

It had occurred long ago to the varlet, when puzzling about the noticeable lack of homely virtues in himself, that the reason for it was only because God had stuffed so much of them into men like Ferguson. The Tory candidate is a manifestly virtuous man, a large and looming, upright figure of a man, with a clear eye, a bright smile and a strong if slightly alto voice. His candidacy bears faithful witness to the times: retired as the city's police chief to enter politics, Ferguson is a law-and-order man, an ardent supporter of capital punishment, a foe of abortion, and worried about marijuana. The varlet is struck by the thought that at least some of those within a few paces of Ferguson, as he speaks, could have been themselves arrested and booked by him, given the right combination of happenstance.

The retired chief's virtue on this occasion is his brevity; perhaps he has sensed that Clark has used up the crowd. But he does deliver a rapid-fire eulogy of his leader — a man no less a pillar of respectability than himself, although half his size — and, to the varlet's bemusement, also comes to Clark's defence in the matter of last night's debate: "Don't be put off," he shouts into the well, "by those two boys who were trying to bully our leader."

What could this be about? The varlet knows sweetness and innocence when he sees it, and Ferguson is a highly visible man, with no more con in him than a cherub would have. Have his supporters been put off by the debate? In a city like Saint John, where political gossip spreads with the speed of flames in a tenement fire, has the word been passed that Clark had been bullied? Ferguson, whose early lead is said to be slipping, might be the first casualty of the debate.

But now — at last — the chairman calls upon George Hees. An after-dinner mint!

He is about a month before his sixty-ninth birthday, but the old Argo and caucus cheerleader can still make the weight of many a man half his years. Some politicians discharge the nervous energy of restless ambition, others the unguents of flattery and dull pleasantry. Hees dispenses ebullience. He has made glad-handing and the hustler's charm a high political art — an example, if not the proof, that nothing wears as well in politics as affability. The handsome face is leathered now, the moustache thicker and grey,

the complexion ruddy, but the eyes are sharp — as close together as always — and the voice compressed in the same
familiar sing-song that so suits the litany of the perfect
excess of his rhetoric:

"You know," Hees shouts, taking all into his confidence,
"*our* party has had some *great* leaders over the years — but *I*
wanna tell ya' — *Joe* Clark is *second* to none of them!
[Cheers.] An' *I* wanna' *tell* ya' — he's one *helluva* lot better
than Trudeau!" [Louder cheers.]

First down, now, and goal to go:

"I never saw a man with a *sharper* brain — he listens to all
of *us* — *knows* whose advice to *take* and whose advice *not* to
take without hurting *any* feelings — and *when* the people of
Canada *elect* a Clark government — you're gonna' see *jobs*,
you're gonna' see *unity* — you're gonna' see the *kind* of
country it should be. And *you're* gonna' see — after a *few*
months of office — that the *people* will be saying '*this man
Clark* is the *best* prime minister this country has *had* in *fifty
years!*'"

Hees scores with the crowd, and brings half-sheepish,
admiring smiles to the faces of the pols standing behind him;
nobody can spread the stuff like ole George.

The premier of New Brunswick, designated by the
program planners to introduce the national leader, is now
called upon to give the benediction. Joe Clark, Hatfield tells
the thinning congregation, "is the only leader who can work
with the provinces to make this country work." He is not
nearly as convincing as Hees had been.

V

Finlay MacDonald — "The Grey Fox" and the varlet's close
friend during the Diefenbaker-Stanfield years — is also
travelling with Clark. He has been working out of Ottawa, a

Ted Grant

"*Our* party has had some *great* leaders over the years — but *I* wanna tell ya' — *Joe* Clark is *second* to none of them!"

media adviser to Lowell Murray, the national campaign chairman, and had represented the party in the negotiations for the television debates. The owner-operator of a Canadian radio news service in Florida during the winter tourist season, MacDonald is still deeply tanned.

Before joining the Clark campaign, the varlet had learned that his coming had created anxious tremors among the Wagonmaster and his aides. It is possible that MacDonald has also joined the tour on this day to serve as ice-breaker, buffer, or custodian. Whatever, the varlet is glad of Mac-Donald's company, even while recognizing him in a new dimension — a Clark man.

Together, they repair to the dining room of the Admiral Beatty Hotel, an old, oak-beamed, darkly panelled, heavily carpeted room with sturdy silverware, white tablecloths and a reliable bill of fare. His longstanding relationship with MacDonald has known recent strains, but these are tactfully submerged as they review the excitements in the passing parade of political events. Nor is there much purpose in either of them acknowledging a history in which they are both captives. The elliptical silences between them are poignant, a far cry from the days when banter, cheerful insult and an unreserved candour bespoke a limitless trust. The varlet has the feeling that, were he to offer his true opinion of last night's debate to his friend, it would be embarrassing to both of them.

Between a Bloody Mary and a second martini — the hard day's work of the campaign now half done — they are joined by Hees, bringing effervescence and anecdote to the table:

"One day, after question period in the House, I came out in the Members' lobby and I saw young Perrin Beatty. 'Perrin,' I said to him, 'I thought you were just outstanding in question period. Just great!'

"Well, you know, Perrin looked at me and said, 'But, George, I never said a *thing* during question period.'

"And then I thought, migod, I've got the wrong guy. So I said to him, 'That's right, Perrin, and that's just what I mean. You really know when to keep your mouth shut!' "

A woman comes over to the table to congratulate Hees on his speech at the rally.

"Now listen," he tells her, a light grip on her elbow, "the next time you drive up to Toronto and you're coming along the 401, I want you to stop by and see us. Just drop in, no need to call. Love ta' see ya' an-n-n-n-y time!"

Politics is irony, and little else. The varlet marshalls the complex permutations of history to support his thesis. He will put them to the reader:

In February 1963, on the eve of the defeat of Diefenbaker's government, George Hees, with Davie Fulton, had called upon the prime minister at his official residence (some sheets to the wind, according to Diefenbaker) and asked him to resign his office, promising a judgeship as compensation.

Rudely rebuffed, Hees had then led the charge against the prime minister in caucus, once the government had fallen.

Routed by the wrath of his colleagues, Hees had emerged from caucus on his leader's arm, temporarily chastened: "We're going to knock hell out of the Grits!" George had proclaimed in his renewed declaration of solidarity.

A day later, Hees resigned from the cabinet, refusing even to be a candidate, while Fulton withdrew to British Columbia, to become the leader of the provincial Tory party or, as Diefenbaker put it to the varlet, "to sit on his ass in Salmon Arm."

As for MacDonald, the varlet's other companion at the table in the Admiral Beatty Hotel, he had, on the very day of Hees's resignation sixteen years ago, in protest at such treacherous betrayal of the party and its leader, volunteered his own services as the party's candidate in Halifax. No matter that he lost — "he had stood!"

And what of Clark, then the fledgling president of the Tory student organization? He was studiously attending the provincial aspirations of Fulton in British Columbia, in the company of Fulton's adjutant, Lowell Murray.

And, of course, though the voters confirmed the good sense of Parliament, and the Diefenbaker government was no more, the varlet, to his credit — and here a tremolo of violin to cover this self-serving interjection — had been Diefenbaker's campaign manager throughout this ordeal of defection and duplicity.

But if the reader had then been spirited away for the sixteen intervening years, sequestered in some distant constellation, would he not be astonished on his return to know that:

Joe Clark has become the leader of this party;

Lowell Murray is *his* adjutant;

Davie Fulton has been forgotten;

George Hees has been forgiven;

but Finlay MacDonald is suspect!

Of course, Hees had meanwhile done his penance — two years as president of the Montreal Stock Exchange — and had returned, after Diefenbaker's limp embrace, to win a seat in the general election of 1965. And so did Fulton, his two years as provincial Tory leader in B.C. enough of a sentence.

But then, in the climactic party meeting of 1966, where the festering sore of the party's leadership issue was finally lanced, the varlet's call for reassessment had been supported by Fulton (though plainly disconcerted by the varlet's sudden pre-eminence), and supported by his friend, Finlay MacDonald, and by Joe Clark certainly, and by Murray, with ardour. (Hees had been prominently neutral; he was, his friends confessed, down to his last insurrection.)

A striking lesson in the rudiments of politics, the varlet thinks, seeing George Hees in such glowing political health, and in good standing in his party, restored in part, one might suspect, by his years, which have reduced the reach of his ambition so that he is now beyond either fear or envy. And there is still usefulness in him; like an aging football star, he has utility as a spot performer of considerable experience, and as a crowd-pleaser who helps build the gate. Even so, the miracle of his restoration among the Diefenbaker loyalists — and among those who pretended to be — was the achievement of his indefatigable, irrepressible affability.

As for MacDonald, who had stuck in 1963 when Hees had bolted, and who had stood in 1966 when Hees had ducked, the varlet knows him to be a marked man in the party. His modest ambition to be a senator, should Clark win, would be challenged by the vociferous vetoes of legions of vengeful Tories, many of them, though by no means all, in his own province of Nova Scotia. All this had become a mild infection in the varlet's friendship with MacDonald, the cause of the slight distance between them. Both of them knew that the varlet's enemies would seek to visit their vengeance on his closest friends.

This would be a fossil's bone to pick with Clark. If the Tory party could forgive Hees for his role in bringing down the Diefenbaker government, could it not do as much for MacDonald for his role in giving Clark his opportunity?

vi

The varlet had become an expense item in the Clark campaign: MacDonald had bought his lunch. As they climb on board the bus for the airport, the word is that the Yarmouth visit has been scrubbed because of the weather. Instead, they will be going to Newfoundland and to the constituency of Humber-Port au Port-St Barbe, a seat won from the Tories by the NDP in last October's by-elections. The decision seems to suggest that the election campaign has been deferred until tomorrow, in the interest of a scenic tour.

As the varlet boards the aircraft, the first person he encounters is Clark's highly visible bodyguard, a giant of a man with a naked head, prominent in all the photos taken of Clark in crowds, who resembles the advance guard of the Turkish Occupation, lacking only a scimitar. He does not appear as one to be trifled with, but the varlet, eager to introduce himself to the personnel of Charter 087 with an appropriate note of levity, promptly seizes the giant's paw.

"Congratulations," he says to him, "on being the most photographed man in Canada." He is rewarded by what might be a smile.

The second person he meets is Clark, standing nearby, seemingly amused by the jest. They shake hands and greet each other — warmly, the varlet thinks. An ice floe might not have melted in the currents between them, but still, he can detect no wariness or apprehension.

It strikes him, thinking ahead to Clark's likely destiny, that he will be among six or seven dozen who will claim that there had been a time when Joe Clark had been like a son to him. Now there was just a hint of the royal jelly in the Tory leader — any man knows when so many others begin to defer to him that something is up — and, even apart from the red-rimmed eyes that reveal the depths of his strained fatigue, he looks older, older than he appears in his campaign commercials. The young politician is taking on years, as though some force in nature were hastily outfitting him for his role.

The varlet bears his reflections to a seat in the middle of the plane, where he will be able to monitor both ends of this operation. A mood has settled among the passengers, a shared sense of suppressed exhilaration, as might be felt by men who have risen early to stand in darkness and watch the break of dawn upon an unfamiliar landscape.

As the aircraft taxis to take-off position, the engines' whine settles into the roar of full-thrust, and the media in the back erupt into a mule-skinners' chorus of shouts and whistles:

"Heee-yah . . . heee-yah . . . giddap . . . giddap . . . Heee-yah!
C'mon, c'mon . . . heee-yah!"

To these accompanying exhortations, Charter 087 hurtles
down the runway until finally — to a round of grateful applause — it lifts into the air. The journalists in the back of
the plane will not soon forget the flameout over Oshawa.

Newfoundland is two hours and some minutes distant
and, as the aircraft breaks through the cloud-layer, the
Wagonmaster and his crew open the dispensary and the
travellers name their potions. The varlet accepts his vodka
martini and awaits developments. Behind him, he hears the
intermittent clatter of a typewriter, unmistakably the sound
of a two-fingered operator, and the rasping shriek of a
jockeyed tape-recorder. Fotheringham was right: the varlet
is the only man on the tour whose deadline is once a year.
(Had he been required to file on this day, his lead would
have been George Hees.) Opportunities are available for
public relations.

He watches Clark easing his way along the aisle, a V-neck
pullover, which has replaced the jacket of his dark suit with
its thin pinstripes, accenting his informality. The tension in
Clark is somewhere along his forearms, between wrists and
elbows, and he holds his head well back, as though expecting to be surprised. No more surprised than anyone else, the
varlet reckons, thinking of the millions who have under-
estimated his political skills, and the several Liberals who
have been waiting for him to add fresh incident to his reputation for misadventure. No public man has ever been
stalked as Clark has been, so that every waxed floor, curb,
step, set of stairs or swinging door on his route brings the
suspense of myriad apprehensions and anticipation, while
friend and foe alike hold their breath. Were he to drown in a
bowl of soup tonight, all would mourn him but recall that he
was never much of a swimmer.

In the back of the campaign buses, most of the conversation has been about Clark, a fine, needling, contemptuous
talk. Of his awkward gait, they will say that it's not that he

leads with the wrong foot, but with the wrong arm; that a lady in Rockcliffe has been delegated to tutor him in table-manners, introducing him to salad forks and finger bowls; that he is shallow in conversation; that during a tour of a museum overseas, he had said nothing in response to his guide but "I see" twenty-nine times.

During the varlet's travels with Trudeau, a writer had returned from the phone to announce: "I have a report from the Wimp Watch."

"What is it?"

"Clark is standing on the Red River dykes in Manitoba and he points to a road which disappears under the water. You got the picture?"

"Got it."

"Clark says to this farmer, 'That's a road.' The farmer says, 'Yes, sir, that's a road.' "

"Anything else?"

"That's it for today, fellows."

Irreverence is the new mask of fashion for the journalist, replacing the veiled respect that once acknowledged the symbiosis of his relationship with politicians. Even so, it was expressed differently, and impersonally, in the media's attitudes to Trudeau. They could now, since he was losing, return his arrogance with more of their own. That he studiously avoided personal contact with them, in the closing weeks of the campaign, suited them as much as him; he was becoming less a public man and more a curiosity — the Emperor seen removing his clothes.

As for Clark, he was making himself increasingly accessible, in ways and manners of his choosing. There seemed even a characteristic calculation to it: if you didn't seek him out, he would soon come to you.

This new-found self-possession was the hard-earned profit of a fierce discipline. If he were still uncertain or afraid, and sensibly aware of the risks to him of spontaneity, he had learned to hide it. Instead, he had developed a knack of apparent spontaneity, injecting himself into situations for which he had carefully rehearsed himself. All the while the media had been mocking him, they had also been instructing him. He had not only matured in the campaign, but surmounted his inexperience and naiveté: only after he had become prime minister would others notice it.

It must have occurred to him, as it did to the varlet, that the media's contempt was not so personal as it was generational. He was of their age and too much one of them: they shared with Clark a common history, a life's experience as brief and unremarkable as their own. What they glimpsed in Trudeau or Stanfield, they might have seen only in their fathers, and the rest was mystery, in a past they never knew. But they knew Joe Clark only too well. There were dozens like him in every student body: guys who didn't go out for sports, settled for passing grades, busied themselves with the small beer of student politics, and covered their shyness with the prides and perks of campus office-holders. True, most of them were chasing footballs, pucks and girls, while Clark was flirting with politics — enough to set him aside from the others, yet not enough to distinguish him.

To his peers in the back of the plane, his coming to the leadership of his party was the lavish gift of luck, and they were unready even now to take him seriously. He was still a somewhat comic figure, acting out the triumphant closing moments of his fantasies — Thurber's J. Walter Mitty commanding the politics of Canada. Nothing in their own lives had prepared them for Joe Clark as prime minister, any more than any of them could expect that next week they would be tapped for the job as publisher of the *Globe and Mail*.

For the older members in the Press Gallery, Clark's age was less of a problem. (Doug Fisher, Charles Lynch and Bill Wilson came to mind as among those who could write of Clark free of hangups about his years, his inexperience, or his social awkwardness.) Notwithstanding the varlet's veneration for the elder statesmen of the trade, he shared the unease and confusion of those who were of Clark's generation, although not their doubts. He had enough of his own. The tensions between Clark and the journalists of his generation were the challenge to the ambient, hustling cheerfulness of the Wagonmaster and his help. To them, the game between the media and their man had to be played with skill and finesse. Early in the campaign, the Wagonmaster had noted a column by Tony Westell in the *Toronto Star*:

> Meanwhile, the reporters who covered Clark's foreign trip and were much criticized for their fault-finding, are confident the Tory leader in this campaign will confirm their judgment that he is shallow, clumsy and awkward in personal relations. His every stumble will be described, his every word written down and used in evidence.
>
> How the Tories plan to deal with this press scrutiny and persuade the media to project a positive image of Clark remains to be seen.

The Wagonmaster (a flash-forward here), in his post-election memorandum, sets out the response of the tour organizers to Westell's question:

> The writer was concerned that Mr Clark *should trust us* —his tour people — to "deliver the logistical goods" as it were and to concentrate *his* efforts on consistent and well planned speech writing (principally designed to attack Trudeau —keeping the attention away from him) and let us deliver the "credible" image projection.
>
> He did and we did.
>
> In the prior two campaigns, I learned that, above all, the members of the national press gallery, like other mature media members, are *human*. Treat them as *intelligent, human* beings and you win their favoured disposition. Make things *look* good, appear to work efficiently and you'll win their written favour.
>
> It meant watching our every logistical move with the intensity of a hawk while laying on the *intelligent* and *human* press treatment without overtly appearing over anxious.
>
> My experience has been that there is always a time to appear decisive and authoritative while treating them otherwise constantly as equals, a fine line between staff *and* press mentalities must be occupied by those of us charged with dealing with the press. We permitted no one other than the Assistant Wagonmaster and myself to have continuing direct

contact with them. Locals or our own advance persons were quickly advised whenever it presented itself. One slipped word or false step and it could have been front page news the next morning.

With all of this in mind, we left Doug Ball behind in Thunder Bay the first night of the campaign on our return to Toronto (he having not left his office in time to catch our advanced departure) — I'm sure it did not "even the score" for his 1974 football photo [of the infamous Stanfield fumble] — but may have been an early demonstration of "true blue justice."

The second night on a planned departure from Toronto, the Ottawa airport closed due to fog. Our buses arrived at the airport at 10:10 p.m. to discover this and we were so advised. The A.W. and I reversed our steps to the Bristol Place with tour in hand and phoned the Holiday Inn. The A.W. went to the Holiday Inn, received the keys first and registered later. All members of the tour were in their respective rooms in one hotel or the other by 11:00 p.m. in time to watch the CTV news or CBC National News. Baggage was available for all in the respective lobbies of the two hotels at 11:15 p.m.

A lot of doubt in the minds of the media was removed that night.

From that time on, rigid discipline, good humour, food and wine (or beer) were to work in favour of the task at hand for the Wagonmaster and his Assistant.

The press pens stayed in check and Mr Clark began to appear credible. His speech writing and delivery improved consistently in a new visible projection of confidence enveloping us all.

Night time press hospitality suites (fully stocked) were used intermittently — but not blatantly. Late evening gourmet dining in various groups (but not cliques) was encouraged.

Two baseball games and the Assistant Wagonmaster's hard anticipatory work at organizing post-game fun, chinese food buffets, beer and barbeques were not overt —but effective modes of attitudinal stimulation. At one point in one of the games, the A.W. came up to me at my position of 3rd base to inform me quietly about post-game arrangements — where upon the coach of the "Bad News Bores" at 3rd base commented to us "don't you guys ever stop?" — we smiled and replied "Never!" and resumed the ball game.

"Beer on buses and food to cover missed lunches due to filing, etc. were always provided — we tried to live their life formula and, in that understanding, asked them to understand us in the job we had to do — they did.

Nothing infuriates the press more than to be invited along to do their job on a national campaign tour, to be presented with reportable news (hopefully coloured by the treatment and logistical favour they are shown) and then to experience the frustration of not being accorded time by us to file their stories (and occasionally not being supplied with adequate numbers of telephones so to do.)

Filing time allowances in planned daily itineraries were sadly lacking in the early days of the tour. We could hardly expect them to understand us in our jobs if we couldn't accord the same spirit of understanding and cooperation in return.

The improvisational requirements placed upon us early in the campaign were intense in these regards — and we "made it happen" until we were finally able to get the message through to the tour office to ensure adequate filing and phones. In the future however this is an area that *can* easily be mishandled — we must be ever attentive.

In the pressurized capsule of Charter 087, those in the service of the leader know the supreme importance of their function. "One slipped word or false step" — disaster! Travelling with Clark was different: not the cool, remote hauteur of the Trudeau plane — a walk-in freezer! — but something else, more like the feel of a flying massage parlour.

The varlet accepts a further libation from the strolling Wagonmaster, something for his ague, as Clark folds himself in a seat beside him.

"How long do you think you can stay with us?"

A question, indeed, the varlet has been asking himself! He responds by explaining his ailments, which are self-evident in his strangled voice, the interruption of fits of coughing, and the need to blow his nose. (Had he a gauze mask, he would have worn it out of solicitude for the leader.) Besides, as he has noted in the itinerary, the bus would stop finally at Spruce Grove, Alberta, which was some distance from his polling booth in Cambridge, N.B., where he was determined to vote on election day before proceeding to Toronto to participate in the CBC's election-night coverage. Aware that he had converted a simple question into a fret of logistics worthy of Tour Group, he aborts his careening answer to ask a question:

"How are you feeling after the debate?"

He feels fine, Clark says, as though he has already made a cursory search for broken bones; but there had been a let-down, of course, afterwards. He was "a little tired today."

But had he been nervous about it beforehand?

"No," Clark says, "I really wasn't. I thought I'd do all right. But, you know, the only thing that really bothered me — just before the thing started — was when I suddenly realized how nervous my own people were. I had the feeling they thought I might fall off my chair, or throw up, or something like that. And that bothered me some."

As for the debate itself, he felt the format could have been improved. He didn't think the questions had been as pertinent as they might have been (Peter Desbarats had asked the leaders about their stand on marijuana, which had interrupted the debate for several minutes), and he felt he had been cut off a couple of times from completing his answers. But when it was over, everyone seemed to think he had done all right.

It may have been this opening conversation that put some further unease between them. The varlet offers Clark no assurance of his own about the debate, though he privately admires the leader's calm, laconic appraisal of it. They switch the talk to Trudeau, and he gives Clark his best guess as to the present position of the Liberal campaign: dead in the water. It is also his best effort at ingratiation.

And yes, there are remnants of his affection for Clark and an approaching awe of his fortune's leap from High River to the steps of Sussex Drive. But there was a glimmer of the new Clark in the alabastrine model with labels attached by his hagiographer. Humphreys has written of his subject:

A pragmatist? Its a label Clark himself wouldn't reject. . . . Ordinary? Clark has frequently been called ordinary, scornfully by detractors, approvingly by supporters... Of all the labels, populist is most apt.

So, your ordinary, pragmatic populist! But read on, for these few brief words of deification:

And it was the populist who won the leadership without the support of any important political figures or alliances.

Such may not be the virtue in Clark's leadership of his party, or the country, but the problem. The man who won the leadership without the help of any important political ally or alliance must then have had to stuff the ballot boxes to do it. And of course he didn't; he won because Flora MacDonald went to him on the third ballot, as did Sinclair Stevens, as did nearly all the Red Tories, there being nowhere else to go: an army of sudden converts to pragmatism marching *against* populism. Had Flora MacDonald been her mother's *son, he* would be riding Charter 087 this very day. What greater luck could any man have had than Clark?

But a politician who is indebted only to his luck might end up by owing everyone. Nor is it that Clark has too many sides to him, as his biographer asserts, but perhaps too many pieces of him, distributed among the consortia of Tory powers in the land. It may be possible for a prime minister to be a Western populist, an ordinary man (of simple tastes) in the Maritimes, a pragmatist in central Canada, and a Red Tory in his bedroom — but for how long?

The varlet, with the country, had already suffered under one populist too many, and it would be another generation before the Conservative party would be clear of it. Populism was the shell-game of demagogues, a way of paying off the rubes in the coin of rhetoric.

An aide comes to summon Clark from his visitation. Watching him work his way back to his place on the aircraft, the varlet, in a rush of recollection, remembers when he himself was not the varlet, and the man returning to his seat was not this Joe Clark.

vii

Over the years of Diefenbaker's ascendancy and decline, my Toronto office — otherwise and ostensibly an advertising agency — became a clearing house, talent bank, hiring hall and recruiting office for the Tory party; even a confessional (not merely in jest had Duff Roblin once called me "the lay pope of conservatism"). From there, forces were deployed to fight provincial campaigns in Newfoundland, Nova Scotia, New Brunswick, Prince Edward Island and Manitoba. In the inner offices were the architects, artisans and mechanics who had developed the media strategies and scenarios of five federal campaigns. There was a daily flood of mail, calls, messages and signals to and from all parts of the country; as Diefenbaker's grasp upon the party grew weaker, and the factions within it grew bolder, the traffic intensified in volume and urgency.

Following the defeat of the Diefenbaker government in 1963, I determined my own future purpose and course. My purpose was to do whatever I could to ensure that Diefenbaker continued to lead the party through another election, assuming that was his wish (and I had every reason to believe it was); in pursuit of that objective, I needed allies within the party. I was then chairman — a title I had myself invented and that Diefenbaker had conferred on me — of the national organization committee. In the wake of the government's fall from power, there were three emergent factions in the party: those who wanted Diefenbaker out, at any cost; those who wanted him to remain, at whatever price; and those who weren't saying, or had not made up their minds. The president of the Student Federation could belong to any of them. But if the Chief were to survive, and the party remain tranquil, the young Conservatives would need to be mollified. They were, as I well knew, the most restless and outspoken of Diefenbaker's critics.

Scarcely two weeks after the election, the president of the

PCSF, Joe Clark, wrote me, in my capacity as chairman of the party organization. The letter struck me then as remarkable, coming from the leader of a group in the party that I considered fractious:

April 24, 1963

Dear Mr Camp:

I understand your Committee will soon meet to discuss the future directions of our party organizations. For your information in considering the Student Federation, I set down views I think concurred in by my executive and most students of experience in the Federation.

We should provide the party with recruits, publicity on the campuses, and, ideally, fresh and constructive criticism of policy; we should provide the campus an opportunity for objective discussion of national policy and participation in its formation. Recruitment and publicity have been sparsely achieved; the other aims, barely at all. There are reasons, chief among them (1) the apparent tendency of the national party to regard the PCSF as ornamental rather than functional; (2) the difficulty of organizing without a model in a broad various country; and (3) the preference of most students for the hoop-la sauce, and not the policy substance, of politics. None of these fundamental problems is insurmountable. In light of our party's present weakness, both among students and within the cities and areas of community influence to which the university graduates gravitate, I think they demand attention. Here are specific proposals:

(A) The party should give priority to an approach to young Canadians. Regarding students, national headquarters should play a more active and consistent role in the arrangement and co-ordination of speaking tours to the campuses, and perhaps the preparation of working papers for use as a basis of student discussion groups. Party leaders should meet more frequently with youth groups, in public meetings and less formal gatherings, and should encourage students to study policy and speak out; the present part attitude encourages acquiescence and stifles discussion.

(B) The Federation can itself encourage policy discussion, and extend our recruitment actively into areas previously ignored. I think it possible to put individual club activities on a more regular and attractive basis, and to make each club a more effective spokesman of, and within, the party.

(C) Essential is a change in emphasis from party publicity and recruitment to political education and participation in policy discussion. Our present emphasis merely puts the party name on campus, and gives people who are Conservatives some cause to meet. It is on the model of a constituency social club, whose function is merely to hold the faithful together. But the challenges of a campus differ from the problems of a constituency. To get value for the PCSF we must concentrate upon that quality which makes the campus peculiar — a desire to learn and discuss. If this desire does not animate the majority of university students, it is important to the minority who, by nature, will have extraordinary influence. This minority may not take membership in a student political organization. But to a party which shows interest in, and respect for, its views and aspirations, it will reciprocate with interest and respect. That is a gain more significant than any so far won. A new emphasis could involve (a) university speaking tours by MPs and Senators; (b) "special theme" seminars requiring prior preparation and including addresses by authorities; (c) formal indication of official interest in student ideas, by Kingston-type conferences, or projects of the kind initiated in Britain by the Honourable R.A. Butler (by which the Young Conservatives each year study and report upon an area of government policy, first Youth Opportunities in Britain, then the Commonwealth, now Taxation.)

I believe the relative failure of the Student Federation and the YPC is only in part due to the size of our nation and the apparent political disinterest of young Canadians. Much more significant has been our own unwillingness to create virile youth organizations. Most young people get into politics because they have something to say or want something to do; we have provided neither forum nor activity. Where one or both have been provided — in the British Young Conservatives, in certain American political youth organizations, in non-partisan Canadian student seminars — the response has been encouraging.

Your Committee can determine whether we continue in the old style or turn to the new. I believe the latter course can be most fruitful to the party, and assures you of the enthusiastic co-operation of the PCSF executive should you embark upon it.

I will take this opportunity to extend our thanks and congratulations for your inspired management of the General Election campaign.
With very best regards.

Yours faithfully,

Joe Clark
National President
Progressive Conservative
Student Federation

It was, as I said in reply, "a most thoughtful and constructive document," adding: "I am in substantial agreement with the points you raise as regards the future direction of your organization."

Unmistakably, Clark was a serious young man (he was twenty-three) and serious about his office. For me, this was refreshing, since so many of his age in the organization were, as we came to describe them, "veteran youth leaders" — largely satisfied with the sinecure of their office and resolute in their determination to do nothing but cling to it. Furthermore, Clark was not only a dutiful correspondent but a lively one.

At the outset of our relationship, I did not glimpse in him the shape of a putative prime minister. But, among the random shapes and sizes of Tory political fledglings, Clark stood apart. He was different.

While many youthful politicians take their early involvement seriously, as did Clark, he possessed a rare and leavening sense of humour. He was caustic, irreverent and, at times, irritatingly flippant. Among the Varlet Papers, Clark's letters are nearly unique for their light shafts and needles of wit. But most of his correspondence bears the imprint of thought and care; he had a sense of history and, even then, a precocious glimmer of some personal destiny.

There was another characteristic of his which ought to have been an augury; if not, then an unerring trait in the preselective process of destiny's children: there was nothing in him of excess.

His wit served him as a censor against the offences of pomposity, sentimentality or pretension. No one had ever seen him drunk. He did not smoke, nor was he boisterous or loudly profane. In any company of student Tories, or even in the councils of their elders, a young man of such moderate disposition and disciplined habit would be soon prominent, even eminent.

viii

In the months following the 1963 election, Diefenbaker and I exchanged letters which expressed genuine loyalty and support for his leadership on my part, and gratitude and admiration on his. Though I resigned as chairman of the organization committee, I made it clear that I was not doing so out of any lack of confidence in him.

It seemed to me, then, that there could be nothing between us, from here on, but mutual amity, even affection. And, while I held no official position in the party, I resumed my activities as peacemaker and as a listener. I was also acquiring some ornamental value to the young Tories, who believed they detected in me a measure of idealism and intellect with which they could identify. They were far removed from the intense partisanship which now began to cast a sinister glow upon federal politics; the adversary role of opposition, which Diefenbaker personified, made them uneasy. Among the caucus members, Heath Macquarrie, Gordon Fairweather, Alvin Hamilton and Leon Balcer were student favourites. Some of the others appeared to them as either irrelevant or merely embarrassing. They were a great deal more interested in Walter Gordon's economic nationalism than in the comedic disaster of his first budget as Pearson's finance minister. And they did not give a damn for scandals, real or alleged.

Clark inspired and organized a tour of Western universities for me in the presumed interest of presenting a con-
trasting face of conservatism. As a reminder of the uneven
results of this journey, one of the students I had met along
the way later wrote me:

You may recall having spent an hour in a classroom at the University of
B.C. with Howard Green, Peter Hyndman, and another fellow during
your tour of Western Canada . . . I was the other person present.

But the overall results were not so meagre, at least
according to Clark:

You will be interested that the reaction I received from friends who
heard you in undergraduate classes was surprise that "such an urbane,
intelligent man is in the Conservative party." This is both a compliment
deserved, and indication of the views students hold of our party . . . Next
time I will arrive at the beginning of the meeting.

In reply, after thanking him for his flattering comments, I
dealt with the substance of our mutual concern:

I fully realize the failure of our Party to create a favorable environment
for on-campus activity and recruitment. We have had a reputation,
deserved or not, of scorning intellect and being bereft of thought and
philosophy. This image will not be changed overnight. This is not to say,
however, that the consideration of ways and means by which we might
improve this situation may be delayed.

Within a week, I wrote further on the subject, suggesting,
as well, increased support for his organization. Clark's reply
is that of someone already capable of rare precision of
thought, and with a working vocabulary to accommodate it.

Herein (a lawyer's word) my observations on your observations of
December 5.
　　We have indeed an anti-, or at least non-, intellectual image, perpetu-
ated by the popular caricature of Mr Diefenbaker as a creature and cap-

tive of the past; by the unchallenging propaganda nature of our publications; by the absence of such indicia of progressive policies as a Kingston Conference or a Troubled Canada; by the association of "Conservatism" with the blind retention of the old; by misinformation about our policies as government; these things at least.

Liberal Party popularity on campuses springs from a union of opposite forces — one, the progressivism you mention as being accepted as inherent in "Liberalism"; the other the attraction of association with the Establishment. The polarity of these sources can be the undoing of Liberal strength among students. I regret that your Winnipeg reference to the Establishment has not been systematically followed up. We should heed the lesson of 1958 that students — of quality, in quantity — will respond to an attack upon established ways when that is mated with imaginative alternatives.

You suggest the campus Conservative "does not accept present day Conservatism as either conclusive or binding"; more accurate, I think, to say he has no idea of the nature of present day Conservatism. We must put bridges and adjustment grants, and social justice into context and, for recruiting purposes at least, extract and make known the operating principles of Canadian Progressive Conservatism.

Your emphasis on quality, not quantity, I welcome. The Senior Party's curious concern for Model Parliament results has encouraged a Model Parliament monomania within the PCSF. Our executives now try to restore sanity by emphasizing seminars, resolutions, policy research. The formation and attitudes of the new Caucus Committee on Youth are great help. But more such encouragement must come.

The idea of bringing individual students to Ottawa is excellent, but should proceed only on an organized and educational, not social, basis. Perhaps we could go a step beyond. How feasible would be establishment of a Progressive Conservative school which would (a) teach Party policy and philosophy to selected students in a two week course each early-Fall and (b) stimulate, co-ordinate and publish — and endow where necessary — academic studies of Progressive Conservatism?

And I like the idea of more money for students.

We are striking a committee of students experienced in the Federation to examine the present and possible functions of the Federation. This will meet in Ottawa January 31, immediately before our annual meeting, and I will inform you of any conclusions there reached.

During the Christmas holidays of 1963, I made a fateful decision — one that would alter my own life so much, that, given foresight, I might have decided otherwise. As for Clark, the decision would ultimately affect him even more. If there are benchmarks in one man's passage, this one will be visible to surveyors of the Canadian Tory party until a millennium. I decided to seek the presidency of the party's National Association; I had no doubts that I would get it.

Having made up my mind, I first wrote Egan Chambers, the incumbent president, whom I knew was seeking a second term, and informed him. I assured him no personal criticism should be implied from my candidacy, but I told him that I thought I could do a better job than he of holding the party together until the next election, which, given the minority circumstances of Parliament, might not be far off.

I liked Chambers, considered him a friend and an effective president. But I knew that Diefenbaker mistrusted him, as did a number of Diefenbaker's caucus supporters. As a candidate in the last election, Chambers had taken his own position, as distinct from the leader's, on the nuclear arms issue, which, since he was also the national president, had created some excitement in the press and consternation in the party. Furthermore, Chambers was from Montreal — a wilderness for the Tory party — which, perforce, left him as out of the mainstream of internal party activity as would be a Créditiste leader who lived in the Yukon.

I was determined to encourage the return of the many prodigals who had left the party — and Diefenbaker — during the abortive mutiny in the winter of '63 and the subsequent fall from power. These included George Hees, whose name had been arbitrarily struck from the national executive, to which he was, by the constitution, a life member; Doug Harkness, a proud and decent man consigned to Coventry; Eddie Goodman, who had been purged from the Ontario Tory executive; John Bassett, whose goodwill and media holdings were of more importance than his brief defection; Davie Fulton, languishing in exile in Salmon Arm,

B.C; and George Hogan, a personal friend and client, who had been an outcast since his public disagreement with Diefenbaker during the Cuban missile crisis.

This repatriation of such essential Conservatives I believed I could achieve, knowing that Diefenbaker would not and Chambers could not.

At any rate, it was neither a mindless nor a casual decision. Interesting, nevertheless, how many worthy public motives and purposes can be summoned to substantiate private ambition. Not only would I, as national president, heal the party; I would restore Diefenbaker to his estranged friends. Or so I thought.

Early in January 1964, I wrote and called a good number of those who would be delegates to the February meeting, including the president of the Progressive Conservative Student Federation:

Dear Joe:
Possibly you know by now that the announcement has been made [sic] that I will stand for the office of President of the Senior Association. I would, of course, greatly value your personal support.

Clark replied immediately, writing in his own hand:

I am pleased to have your note and confirmation that you are a candidate. Certainly you have my personal support. Probably, if it's desired, we can arrange a brief appearance before the students in convention for you, Egan, and any other declared candidates. I wish you well, and look forward to seeing you in February.

While I welcomed his personal support, I was also mindful of the tone of his now familiar rectitude, and beginning to suspect that the young politician least liked the necessity of making a choice — the instinct for collegiality already discernible. He had the makings of a model chairman.

Clark's response to my plea for support, however, was more pleasing than that of Robert Stanfield, when I telephoned him in Halifax: "I don't know why you'd want to do a damn-fool thing like that," he said, which may have been the very best advice anyone has ever given me.

The launch, however, was a salubrious one: on the eve of the balloting at the annual meeting, Egan withdrew from the contest and I became the party's unanimous choice. With all the tumult and furor to follow in the train of that event, I can remember little of the annual meeting itself, and certainly nothing comes to mind of Clark, or whether, as a candidate, I appeared before his group.

But a week after the meeting, I heard from him:

The Camp magic is already drawing the young into the front lines.

Mike A. . . . is looking for work until law school opens in the Fall, and would like to serve the Party in some capacity. I know Mike only from the brief time we were classmates together, by his keen interest in Party affairs here, and by the success of his work in non-political student organizations. If there is work available, I would not hesitate in recommending him.

While on this subject, I would like to work this summer in eastern Canada, (that is, the near east), and would appreciate your help in landing a summer job in Toronto or Ottawa.

Again my congratulations on your election. I, and all the students who know you, look forward to the work of your presidency.

In reply, I proposed a project of my own: "working in a small number of students in Party Headquarters in the summer months," once I had examined the "essential implications of finance."

The response was essential Clark, as I was coming to know him:

Such a summer-work program would certainly have value to the students selected, provided they were meaningfully occupied. Perhaps they could be assigned long-range work in our Research department, or assigned co-ordinating responsibilities for a particular province, as is Bill Macadam now in Stuart Fleming's office. Their value to the Party would derive chiefly from the national point of view they would carry to their homes, and the familiarity with people and procedures they'd take to campus. Selection might best be done by PCSF regional vice-presidents, in consultation with pertinent provincial officials, and in accord with criteria as to activity in the Party, year of study, and maybe even capacity.

Both Peter [Hyndman] and I, who had this experience, by chance, benefited personally, and have managed to pass some of the benefit along.

I had no interest in assigning youthful, temporary employees to "long-range" research but rather, as I wrote, "in exposing them to the very practical aspects which govern political organization."

Besides, I had other plans. In the long periods of time spent at national headquarters, I had become impressed with the accumlating litter of paper, abandoned files, clippings and various sorts of obsolete party propaganda. Some of the offices upstairs in the old building on Laurier Avenue served no other purpose than as repositories for such stuff, while downstairs there appeared to be a glacial movement of material from the front offices to the back, where, inevitably, it became trash and was hauled away. Besides that, there was a garage in the rear of the property which contained, I was told, the mouldering artifacts of Bracken House, the party's national office since John Bracken had been the party's leader.

On my first day as national president, I met with John Meisel through the auspices — of course — of Flora MacDonald. Meisel, a professor at Queen's University and a pre-eminent Canadian political scientist, implored me to retain every scrap of paper relating to my function as president — "even your doodles," he said. He impressed upon me the potential value of all party documents and correspondence to future political scientists and historians. It was this conversation with Meisel that led to my proposal to Clark:

I am . . . very anxious to establish at Headquarters an Archives Section. Unless we do this, a lot of the Party papers and documents relating to the history of the Party's organization are going to be lost or destroyed. I would hope to get on with this project this year and it might be, under the direction of some knowledgeable authority, work undertaken by students assaying and sorting out the material that exists.

Clark wrote to say that he now agreed. As well, he dealt with other questions I had raised about the project — who and how much. There were never any loose ends:

The Canadian Union of Students has this year run a program similar in principle to our Students-at-HQ project. CUS pays roughly $3,000 per year, $60 per week. Although that is substantially below what could otherwise be earned by students of the talent we seek, it would probably be adequate in the circumstances. The summer period is generally from mid-May to the end of August or mid-September. While I suspect most of the following already have summers planned, I recommend, in order, Art Donahoe, 456 Francklyn, Halifax; Graham Scott, 236 Hyman Street, London; Tom Chambers, 6530 Marine Crescent, Vancouver 14; Brian Hay of McMaster (HQ has address); Doug Rishor, 3600 St. Famille, Montreal 18; Paul Niedermayer, c/o St. Mary's University, Halifax; Doug McReady, Riverfront Road, R.R. #2, Amherstburg, Ontario; Mike Vineberg, 32 Summit Crescent, Montreal; and Irvine Gaul, 179 Durocher, Hull.
    Bien à vous.

I had forgotten Clark's earlier request of me that I scout Toronto for the possibility of summer employment. Late in February, he reminded me of it:

Dalton:
    Flora mentioned last weekend that you are hiring to fill permanent vacancies in your agency. I'm in search of Eastern summer work, and wonder if you might have opening for me on that temporary basis. Please understand that I don't want to presume upon either our offices or your good nature, but would be most interested if there is good use to which you could put me.
    . . . My specialty's the bucolic, but I can learn.

By then, I could tell him that:

... it may well be I shall need some sort of assistance, as you suggest, in
this office during the summer and I can think of no one more suitable
than yourself.
My questions are: what do you mean by temporary? What kind of
salary are you looking for? When do you have to make up your mind?

He replied:

I have your note of the 3. By temporary I mean from early May to the
end of August; I can be in Toronto for May 4. I would require a salary of
from $85 to $100 per week, and would like to know what's available
before March is spent.

Obviously, the student politician was in search of experience and not income. "I think your salary requirements are
very high," I wrote him, "but I believe them to be in line with
your talents."
The job, I told him, would involve providing assistance
"in the mass of detail relating to my activities in the Party, to
say nothing of the [Fredericton] Conference and events to
come, in addition to the business of running this Agency."
Clark replied, "I would accept, and look forward to, the
arrangements outlined in your letter."

ix

My first major initiative as national president of the
Progressive Conservative Association was "The National
Conference on Canadian Goals" to be held at Fredericton
that summer. I saw the conference as a means of diverting
the party from its obsessive preoccupation with the leadership question, its recent experience of defeat, and the endless
feuding of its many factions. Further, it would be a means of
satisfying at least some of the activists in the party, particularly those among the young who craved some intellectual

nourishment in their staple diet of partisanship. And finally, as a unifying force, it would only be helpful if the like-minded, forward-looking Tories were brought together in common fellowship, if only to assure them that their intellectual curiosity was respectable in a party with, as Clark had said, a "non-intellectual image."

In May, Clark moved into a corner office in my Toronto agency, where he applied his considerable aptitude for detail to the logistics for the conference. I do not recall that he ever required much help from me, or anyone else. He was a self-starter, and he saw things through. And while persevering in this activity, he continued to attend to his responsibilities as PCSF president. A memorandum to a colleague (a copy of which he sent to me) on the subject of a proposed format for a new young Tory publication once again attests to the encyclopaedic range of his interests:

... The front page would always be in the nature of a cover with a picture or cartoon, an indication of contents, and little or no written material. The eighth page would contain the "Sea to Sea" column, a factual digest of events in Parliament, and Association news. The rest of each issue would be composed of two-page articles, illustrated by pictures, graphs, etc., and designed to be pertinent, objective, and informative.

It is proposed that the first edition, whose appearance will coincide with the re-opening of universities, contain one article on modern Conservatism; one entitled "A Look at Latin America," including an examination of what's there and what's happening in Latin America, and Canada's interest; and an article on education, to include reference to swelling school and university populations, new curriculum requirements and teaching methods, the "Brain Drain," the increasing phenomenon of the educated unemployed, and perhaps a projection of other education changes to come.

Other topics suggested to be considered include individual rights; foreign aid, and our Commonwealth policy; automation; "science, Government, and research"; trade and diplomatic relations with Communist China; changing patterns of Canadian trade; the changing political power centers in Canada; the balance of Federal-Provincial powers; "subsidized culture," including discussion of our pursuit of a "national identity"; Canada's resource frontiers; Canada's Olympics participation; the implications of the Columbia agreement; problems of urban development; poverty in Canada, especially among farmers of the East; faults and reforms in Parliament; welfare in the modern state; leisure and recreation; foreign ownership in Canada; and "the new Europe."

My personal relations with Clark were cordial, informal and easy. The idiosyncratic glints I saw in him were occasionally irritating, but, given both his years and his abilities, he was entitled to them. A hand-writing analyst would have been intrigued by the highly stylized signature — more a graphic than a name — which he put on his correspondence. (One letter from him bears the puzzled query of my secretary: "Clark?") A stranger might have guessed him to be pompous.

He was not then a good listener, and he gave the impression of seeming offended when one told him something he already thought he knew. I once complained to my colleague and confidant, Norman Atkins, of Clark's habit, when we were in conversation, of finishing my sentences for me, or punctuating them by vigorously nodding his head and saying, repeatedly, "Uhuh, uhuh, uhuh." I asked Atkins to speak to him about it; years later I had come to doubt that he ever did.

I knew nothing of his personal life, who his friends were, male or female, and I knew less of his political opinions than I thought I did at the time. While he was invariably agreeable and sympathetic whenever we discussed serious internal problems of the party, and even though he appeared to be supportive, his own views on such matters were more assumed than expressed; it is only now that I recognize his exemplary caution.

There were a number of his contemporaries — Brian Mulroney, Michael Meighen, Nathan Nurgitz, Larry Lang to name a few — who were better company and whose social graces were more marked. Clark concealed his lack of sophistication beneath a cloak of gravity. He was still very much from High River — "just a boy from Okotoks," he sometimes said, in mock self-deprecation — and it might well have been his frustrating pursuit of elusive academic qualifications (about which we knew nothing) that would account for his shy and secretive side. He spent his twenty-fifth birthday working in Toronto on the Fredericton Conference; something of an enigma to his associates around him but, all the same, a fellow who was plainly making his own way.

That the conference was ever held was nothing less than an act of will. Everything that could have been done to obstruct or prevent it was tried. The caucus in Ottawa was contemptuous of it; Diefenbaker, I knew, was extremely wary; Leon Balcer, the designated "Quebec Lieutenant" of the day, whose co-operation I earnestly sought in recruiting suitable delegates from his province, gave none; finally, and ominously, Beverley Matthews, the Toronto corporation lawyer, who, as bagman for the party, alone had the keys to its treasury, at first declined to support the conference.

I promptly appointed a finance committee to raise the necessary funds, $35,000, and informed Matthews of my determination to get it on my own. He capitulated immediately. (After the conference, to my chagrin, he deducted an equivalent amount from the operating budget of the party's headquarters, a stint painfully felt. In all my tests and triumphs, small or large, in politics, I could never outwit a party bagman.)

The basic organization of the conference and the supporting logistical planning were left almost entirely to Clark and Norman Atkins. Early on, they had submitted a plan to the conference committee which was agreed to, and after that Clark wrote hundreds of letters, inviting the delegates, confirming their acceptance, collecting their conference fees, and informing them of transportation arrangements, while Atkins, on the ground in Fredericton, was to look after their requirements on arrival. Flora MacDonald, then at party headquarters, supervised the preparation of material, the distribution of position papers, and the verbatim reports on the proceedings. Lowell Murray was responsible for media relations. The conference did not lack for organizational competence.

Otherwise, it was an exercise in spontaneity and revelation. Marshall McLuhan, the keynote speaker and not yet the international guru he would become, made a first impression upon the delegates which could only be described as stunning; Diefenbaker appeared briefly and delivered one of the best speeches I had ever heard from him; Marc Lalonde warned against any weakening of the federal powers; W. L. Morton raised the spectre of separation — a subject few of his listeners had heard before — and went on to say that, if necessary, it should be resisted by force of arms. And the French lieutenant, Leon Balcer, left early, before the subject of Quebec's role in Confederation arose, describing the conference as "a waste of time." This last was the only sour note in the harmonious and cheerful proceedings, during which, even where there was profound disagreement, civility and humour were always present.

The Fredericton Conference covered a lot of ground, from McLuhan's global village to the lurid possibility of fratricide. It proposed no policy and set no goals; as McLuhan himself had said, goals are obsolete in a rapidly changing technology. (I think that's what he said.) In all it had been an intellectually stimulating experience.

Afterwards, many in the party came to speak of "the spirit of Fredericton," which was that of looking to the future, forgetting the quarrels of the past and enduring with patience the trials of the present. Some even thought we had reached a turning-point in affairs of the party; they were wrong.

Clark returned to the Toronto office to attend to the administrative loose ends of the conference. He had not lost any of his wit at Fredericton and seemed to have gained significant amounts of assertiveness:

(1) . . . An informal meeting of my executive just after the annual meeting recommended that action in high schools should be taken jointly by the four national organizations, with the Women's Association providing meeting places, maybe chaperones, maybe tea, the Y.P.C. and especially the students actively contacting high school students and involving them in regular or special programs, and the senior association providing speakers, money, etc. I have no idea how many high schools exist in Canada, but certainly there are a great many students who should be approached if it was decided this was a valuable or proper thing to do. I have personal reservations about the propriety of intensive recruiting in the high schools, but necessity speaks louder than propriety.

(2) You will remember the Clokey affair. Attached is a copy of my letter to him, which refers to the possibility of research by the Ontario Y.P.C. I have not pursued this further but think that one of Del O'Brien's committees might be capable of drawing value from the submissions. Otherwise the documents might be sent to Alan Smith, whom you recall is working with Alvin Hamilton and some of his apostles (I think there are twelve) in Ottawa.

(3)Attached also is a copy of Alec Langford's letter. His response to your invitation suggested that he smelled some kind of anti-Toronto, anti-Diefenbaker plot in the location of the Conference in Fredericton. He also suggested that we were discriminating against people who have children.

(4) We had a special rate of $120.00 for the Dick Bells and the Eddie Dunlops, since in both cases husbands and wives came as delegates. As matters developed at Fredericton every wife who wanted to, attended sessions. Should we reimburse the Bells and the Dunlops? Mrs Bell pointed out this discrepancy to me in Fredericton.

After he had returned to Edmonton, Clark wrote further reflections on the conference. He was broadening his perspective, but his outlook continued to be leavened by a sense of irony and the familiar irreverence:

Sorry to be so late in writing, but most of my home-coming has been a long and losing battle with the 'flu, penalty either for coming back or for leaving in the first place. Anyway, I am now healed, and looking to my responsibilities.

I have read the excerpted news and personal reports concerning the

Conference, and think sending them out was an excellent idea. Unfortunately, there is also a broader audience which is, and should not be, effectively ignorant of Fredericton, and it comprises people who live in places like Edmonton where Conference news coverage was unexceptional. Perhaps these people are beyond us now, but you might think it worth while trying to trace them. There do exist lists of various categories of people — professors, doctors, lawyers, architects, etc. — with their addresses, and there might be value in thus broadcasting your statement of the Conference purpose, and synopses of some of the better attributable reports of its success. Even if that idea is too wild to consider, attention should turn to spreading the story of our good works to these influential groups who now know nothing of them.

While I agree that Fredericton Conferences shouldn't become habitual, certainly there should be some more regular relation between academics and the Party (or, pardon me, the Association). One approach which might work would be the establishment of an informal council of academic advisers, to members of which we could go for advice on particular short- or long-range problems. The very fact of the council's existence would improve the "party image," and there might be MPs eager for such help; if not, then at least no crusading Association president need again go wanting for speech ideas.

As to the December meeting, one item that should go on an agenda is that of High Schools, and what we're going to do about them. This is a problem we tend to shove to the background as unimportant but, even without a reduced voting age, concerns a recruiting area of great potential. I think it also offers unusual opportunities for co-operation among the various levels of the Association, and that is an end to encourage, in itself. Unless this seems too petty, the question of publications and propaganda might also be raised; the students have this year dipped into our non-existent budget to pay for pamphlets, and especially a new broadsheet series called On The Record which reports upon positive PC proposals in Parliament, which I think would more properly be financed by other Party sources. We've taken the initiative because we can't recruit without some kind of material which offsets the "anti" image we have from the House. Not only can't recruit; we're having trouble activating admitted Conservatives. The attitude of students, and the effectiveness of our student organization, is of course another problem area, but I think there's little point in discussing it unless some solutions are in sight, and at this point I have none. However, members of my own national executive are meeting in Ottawa the

Friday night, and after that I will perhaps know better of our effectiveness across the country, and maybe even have a fresh Manifesto, or Chart for the Future, or something.

I'd appreciate advice in advance of the likelihood of an annual meeting in January or February of the senior Association, as that will influence the decision we take. In its present state, our budget won't allow an annual meeting but, if the general Association was also to meet, we might find a transfusion.

When I last saw you, I suggested one project [your] Mafia might consider would be in the area of "political education" or establishing citizen groups only affiliated with the Party or Association. As I understand it, this combination, adding up to non-partisan partisanship, is the instrument Romney uses with such effect. Citizen groups are traditionally a rural and prairie phenomenon, but today the cities might be ready for them. If the suburbs in the USA are conservative Republican, why wouldn't George Hogan with a mortarboard burn up Don Mills? Suburban "colleges on conservatism" might take hold. Or "panels on Progressivism."

I gather your procession through the prairies has been set aside; if not, and if you and/or Hogan have time to visit campuses, that would be a boon. And if you are going to be in Alberta you should look up Peter Lougheed, a lawyer in Elveden House in Calgary. He was one of those invited late to Fredericton, and couldn't come, but he is also interested in the provincial leadership here, and is described to me as both serious about the proportions of that charge, and able. A grandson of the late Senator Lougheed (whom you read about in *my book* on Bennett), he is 35, has made money and his own high reputation as an oil lawyer, and is actively supported by your great and good friend George Clokey (during his occasions in the Party.) I've never met Lougheed, but respect some of those who tout him highly. (The leading alternative for provincial leadership, rumour says, is Doc Hugh Horner, which might be a relief to Ottawa, but . . .)

Don't know what insurrectionist talk is going on in the East (though the word "axis" seems back in the newspaper vocabulary) but there seems little of it here. As nearly as I can gauge, there is in most of PC Edmonton a sort of reluctant loyalty to the Chief and, even in confines, there seems none of the outspoken criticism one finds in central Canada. There isn't what I would call "enthusiasm," but there is a willingness to work, probably a wish that he'd gracefully retire, but not an inclination to rock a boat. I've no broad sampling of reaction to his present stand upon the flag, but my impression is that people generally oppose his stand, and those who support it do so only because he has taken it.

Enough of this happy news — I'm due in a class on parties and pressure groups, which so far this year has done nothing but bewilder me.

X

Meanwhile, in Parliament, the debate over a new Canadian flag — "Pearson's Pennant" — dragged on and on. Although feelings about the flag, in the Tory party, were largely generational — the young for a new flag, the old for the old Ensign, and the rest of us indifferent — it was also becoming, unhappily, a litmus test of loyalty to the national leader.

The "Spirit of Fredericton" began to evaporate in the heat of events. The rank-and-file of the party, particularly its younger members, and those who were sensitive to the party's seemingly eternal problems with Quebec, became increasingly concerned and restive. Added to these discomforts was the continuing exposure of a number of "scandals," many of which seemed to involve French Canadians. That much of this was politically legitimate material for an Opposition party was inarguable, but that so much of it related to French-Canadian politicians was unfortunate.

It worried Clark, who wrote me in mid-December:

Is there a chance of seeming statesmen by declaring: "It is important that these findings not be used to frame an indictment of the French Canadians, but rather of the Liberal hierarchy, French and English, who countenanced corruption"? Or does that paint with too broad a stroke?

Surely, for balance, there must have been some Englishman tapping the till in those old Young Liberal days.

The note provoked me: my response was unnecessarily cynical:

It is important that these findings not be used to frame an indictment of the French Canadians, but rather of the Liberal hierarchy, French and English, who countenanced corruption.

Not only that, but our Party is making available certain volunteers who have kindly agreed to come forward. I trust this meets with your approval and will satisfy your exacting Canadianism.

But I was still determined to see Diefenbaker through the flag debate and, as national president, to support him. Besides, I had learned enough about politics to realize that, were the shoe on the other foot, the Liberals would not have been at all restrained in their muckraking, even if most of those involved had been members of the Royal Household.

Nevertheless, as indicated by Clark's attitude, and that of many others, it was becoming plain that a considerable gulf was forming between the parliamentary party and the National Association. I went to Ottawa to convey my unease directly to Diefenbaker, and to some of those in the caucus whom I knew to be the hardliners on both sides of the flag issue — George Nowlan, Gordon Churchill and Leon Balcer — and to explore the possibility of compromise.

I was not prepared for the bitterness and recalcitrance I found among those I had long considered to be reasonable, sensible people. Particularly, I recall a heated conversation in George Nowlan's office, climaxed by a wild shout from a member of the House of Commons staff: "Why do we always have to give in to the fucking French!"

I was all the more impressed by the fact that the author of the sentiment was a lady, and distressed that Nowlan had merely shrugged his shoulders and smiled at me. "You see what you're up against, old man," he had said.

In a speech before a university audience in Hamilton, I was moved to say, "I have always wanted a distinctive Canadian flag. The time has come for me, even if it's a flour sack; when they raise it, I'll salute it."

All this culminated in a sudden challenge by Balcer to Diefenbaker's leadership, joined by all of his Quebec caucus colleagues, notably Théo Ricard, Jacques Flynn and Heward Grafftey. If I was dismayed by their action, I had to admire their unanimity. It was the first time I had known any of them to agree with Balcer on anything.

Citing the "spirit of Fredericton" as inspiration, Balcer wrote me on behalf of his group, demanding that I call the national executive "in order to fix a date for a national convention to decide upon the leadership of the party." This headlong assault on Diefenbaker's leadership by the Quebec caucus necessarily required many to make the hard decision as to whether they should, by their response to it, defy the Quebec wing of the party or antagonize the Chief. There was very little ground in between.

Clark, writing from Edmonton, was only one of many looking for that kind of turf; his note was not typed on the stationery of the PCSF, but under his own letterhead.

"My people" in Quebec (i.e. our eleven students) are clamouring for a public PCSF statement encouraging Balcer to stay. I've declined, on the ground that internal persuasion is more effective, and that Mr Dalton Camp is undoubtedly in frequent conversation with his good friend Mr Balcer.

As Clark surely knew, I would make no attempt at "internal persuasion" with a man as intransigent as Balcer. Anyway, we were not dealing with the man but with an institution — the leader and spokesman for the Quebec caucus — and with a wretched Tory legacy in French Canada. Nevertheless, when polled by the national president, Clark was among those who agreed to Balcer's demand that the national executive meet.

Even then, he was alert to the damage inflicted upon his party by its parliamentary wing, and, unquestionably, he also saw the party as two separate forces — those in Parliament and those outside it. More than most, Clark was dismayed by the obstructive, negative course the caucus had embarked upon in the prolonged flag debate, in the exposés of "scandals," and in its reaction to the Quiet Revolution in Quebec.

Cynics would say that one could always tell a Tory politician with national aspirations if he were learning French or pleading for understanding of French Canada. Whatever his motivation, Clark was at his most outspoken in his advocacy of a more tolerant and accommodating position for the party in matters which touched upon national unity and the role of Quebec in Confederation.

In March, on behalf of his student organization, he wrote to the chairman of the Tory caucus, Michael Starr, sending a copy to me. The tone of the letter was uncharacteristically firm, even tough, while the substance of it expressed an outlook shared by the party's progressive wing. No one of us could have said it better:

Members of the National Executive of the Progressive Conservative Student Federation met in Montreal last weekend and, among other things, discussed the question of the attitude of the Progressive Conservative Party towards the "opting out" legislation. I think our views may be of interest to Caucus.

Since our views are necessarily based upon public reports, and are hampered somewhat by our distance from Ottawa, we are not competent to comment upon the detail of proposals which are before Caucus, or may go before the House. However, we are in a position — perhaps a position more reliable than is yours, in the heat of the House — to comment upon the public reaction that would arise, and is arising, to proposals already aired in the public press.

To our view, the "opting out" proposal is only one aspect of a much broader question which concerns the separate fields of relations between the federal and provincial governments, and relations between Canada's two founding races. By its nature, as an interim measure, this particular aspect has not the actual significance of measures which might follow. However, it has a substantial tactical significance, because our reaction to this measure will determine the credibility of the later, more important, positions we assume. It is our clear and unanimous view that the Progressive Conservative Party today owns the unenviable reputation of being automatically opposed to measures which would seem to advance the interests of French Canada. Apart from the damage it does to our effectiveness as an instrument of national unity, this reputation virtually destroys our effect as an instrument of national understanding.

To us, as the young Canadians who will live longest in whatever kind of Canada emerges from these debates, the principal need now is for an atmosphere of understanding and of cordiality. We believe that great issues are at stake, to which enduring solutions can be achieved only if all sides of all questions are considered with frankness and fairness and freedom from prejudice. The opportunity to achieve and sustain that atmosphere lies now, with you, in Caucus. To our view, you must take account of the unhappy reputation of prejudice we now bear, and then take action to shuck it off; a large step towards freedom from that reputation would be achieved if you would let this interim measure pass, and then make positive proposals which would advance both understanding and unity.

On basic issues, the Caucus and the students generally agree. Most students agree that the central government in Canada must be strong, and we believe that that strength need not discord with special provisions to meet the special requirements of French Canada. We emphatically agree that measures respecting Federal-Provincial or French-English relations must be framed in the context of the whole question and the whole country, and no longer approached piecemeal. And we see great merit in the proposal for a Constitutional Conference, and a persuasive precedent for the preparation of such a Conference in the striking of a special legislative committee by the Progressive Conservative government of Ontario.

Our recommendation, then, is that we seize this opportunity to re-assert our inclination and capacity to serve as an instrument of national understanding and unity. If we do not, we run the danger of speaking forever on this issue to the deaf. Moreover, from our conversations, on and off the campus, with students and with older citizens, we conclude that if we fail to divest this uninvited cloak of prejudice, that failure will go hard against us at the polls. I, of course, am a Westerner, and know only the reactions here, but I am assured by my colleagues that, in every section, our appearance of prejudice loses far more votes than it wins. Those are the reactions not only of the young, but also of adults who have voted for us in the past but now suspect we are no longer a national party.

Of course, final decision rests with you. But this is one of those issues

on which the view of Caucus may not accord with the view of Party
members and Party supporters across the land. If we are to realize this
Party unity, which we all sincerely seek, the Caucus must give weight to
the considered views of other Progressive Conservatives.

Clark also sent copies of his letter to three other members
of caucus, Walter Dinsdale, Heath Macquarrie and Alvin
Hamilton. Still, it was curious that he had not written,
instead, to the party leader, which would have been the
normal course.

Despite the continuing ferment in the party, Clark
persisted in the admirable struggle to lead his own
organization in more positive directions. The PCSF had
resolved to stage a simultaneous number of "Confederation
Banquets," and Clark proposed that I be among the
speakers, who were to include Diefenbaker, Ontario
Premier John Robarts, Premier Duff Roblin of Manitoba,
Robert Stanfield of Nova Scotia, Davie Fulton, and Leon
Balcer, who was then half-in and half-out of the party.

"I have not spoken to Alvin Hamilton," Clark wrote, "as
to others he might nominate as speakers since I do not think
we have that many cities."

Even so, there were difficulties, as he later reported:

... Leon Balcer is still the biggest name we could have participate in our
Confederation Banquets. As you might suspect, my inclination is to
keep open our invitation to him.

In the end, Marcel Faribault came in Balcer's stead, and
Wally McCutcheon took the place of Roblin. It was to
Clark's credit that he managed to mount such an ambitious
enterprise in a party that was in growing disarray and far
too busy with factional manouevre to concern itself with
ceremonial observance.

xi

After the 1965 federal election, Clark wrote to commiserate on my defeat in Eglinton and was the first to say that he "earnestly hoped" I would run again for the presidency of the National Association. His summation of the election contained hints of the turmoil within himself:

What struck me most during the campaign was the cynicism and sense of disappointment which burdened the students I taught and talked to at U. of A. And what struck me most when it was over, and all seemed so unnecessary, was the sense of being betrayed that I found among the academic "moderates." These are people who felt a real kinship to Pearson, and that may have been the linchpin of their Liberalism, and now their spokesman has succumbed — abjectly and ineptly — to The System. More so than before, our unpopularity among at least these two groups is tied to a man and a style, whereas the Liberals are more generally distasteful. But, if they have farther to go, they would also appear to have more of the men and more of the means to re-establish themselves. I think that fact imposes upon us an urgent obligation to make the party congenial to these and other key groups estranged by the image of Main Street and the still-persisting suspicion of a reactionary influence from Bay Street.

In the new year, the fateful one of 1966 in which the leadership question would be resolved, Clark began to turn to Alberta politics, and the provincial party under the new leadership of Peter Lougheed:

"We in Alberta," he wrote in January, "meet our first major test next weekend, with the first annual meeting since Peter's election (as leader). We've managed to slip both a bazaar and Bob Dylan into the agenda, so the meeting at least won't be traditional."

He reported on the meeting with undisguised satisfaction, even before it was over, writing on hotel stationery:

We've a live one in Alberta — this convention is the best I've attended anywhere, in terms of enthusiasm, unity, maybe even talent . . . the banquet was the largest in the history of the Palliser. Even George Hees was great, for our purposes — delivered an enthusiastic revision of "Campaigning to Win," which he now calls "Conservative Philosophy."

He was also meticulous in reporting matters he knew would be of interest, however slight:

One discordant note was the *private* remark of [the president of the women's association] to the effect that you've not written or talked to her since the election. One of these is enough.

"It is now likely," he informed me early in December, "that the National Students Meeting will be held in Ottawa, on February 10th, 11th, and 12th, 1966, at the Talisman Motor Hotel, and I hope that it won't interfere with your Hanoi ambitions."

Indeed, I had a strong desire to go to Vietnam and see that tragedy at first hand — perhaps to escape from the brushfire wars breaking out in the Tory party as well. But the impulse was swept away by events. At the PCSF meeting in Ottawa, I learned from Wally McCutcheon that a new national director for the party, James Johnston, had been approved by Diefenbaker. I smelled a rat. However, I held the firm conviction that the office of national director was the exclusive prerogative of the national leader, just as I believed the choice of the national president was in the right of the National Association.

McCutcheon, somewhat mysteriously, expressed his concern over the continued presence of Flora MacDonald at headquarters, saying "we can't have more than one person in charge there." I replied that Flora had diligently and faithfully served every person who had previously been in charge of the national office, including Allister Grosart, Richard Thrasher and myself, adding that I thought her assistance would be essential to any national director if the office was to be run efficiently. I tactfully suggested to Johnston that he proceed with caution in his new responsibilities and reminded him that the National Association considered her services to be invaluable. He appeared to have heard me.

A few weeks later I left for a holiday in the Bahamas, having been promised by Johnston that no decisions would be made affecting the National Association in my absence. The day after I arrived at Eleuthera, I was summoned from the beach to respond to an overseas call: it was from Norman Atkins in Toronto. Flora had been fired.

This betrayal forced me to the realization that I was at war with Diefenbaker, and I spent the remainder of the holiday considering my position and possible courses of action.

When I returned home, I found that the storm which had broken over the firing of Flora MacDonald was continuing to gather velocity. I was inundated with mail and persistent calls reflecting the indignant outrage of party members throughout the country. I could sense, in this mounting chorus, a shift in focus from the injustice done to Flora to the issue of Diefenbaker's leadership. As for Johnston, his name went unmentioned, since no one knew who he was. But everyone knew Flora would not have been sacked unless the leader had approved of it. Nothing Diefenbaker had done so diminished him in the eyes of his party. For a man who had so often preached loyalty, it seemed an unworthy act. It was, for many, the last straw.

One of the first letters I received on the subject came from Clark, who wrote me when I was still in the Caribbean. Reading it then, on my return to Toronto, I was touched by it:

I know you may be a little upset because nobody in the party ever tells you anything, and am sorry to continue the practice of sending something second hand. But Newman's article on Flora's firing drew a letter from a girl who is a friend of mine and a constituent of Eglinton, and these are excerpts:

"... over the last few months it has been my silent conclusion that Diefenbaker is a hindrance to this country's progress, and anachronistic (although I do accept your word and others'

that he has sterling qualities — good parliamentarian rhetori-
cian, articulate, a memory that devours everything relevant,
prophet, idealistic, etc. .) He is still leading one of our two major
parties (simply) because his authority is so rooted that he has
made the party fabric his own design. He has toned down his
colleagues' designs, drawn over them, ripped them out, made
them weavers not designers . . . though you all say 'we are doing
what we can quietly and effectively and building a strong party
for the future,' I think that until you rid yourselves of this self-
interested demagogue you will not gain . . . respect . . . I don't
understand the weakness of the individuals who kow tow to
Diefenbaker today; they may be nostalgic and nod that there is
no one of his calibre to fill the gap and the party would be rent in
pieces, but I could only answer that this is the easy way out . . . I
don't think that any of you will admit in the end that his faults
today outweigh his virtues. If you can show me the way to understand all this, I would be very appreciative. He is a
courageous man and what is needed to fight him is greater
courage. You have courage and so do others in your party; why
not muster together a greater courage? Please answer if you
will."

Of all the communications I received on this sorry business, the letter from Clark was the most striking and
memorable. And it was at this juncture in my relationship
with him that I came to realize his considerable influence on
my own thoughts. I assumed that he endorsed the opinions
expressed by his correspondent, or he would have indicated
otherwise. I also knew that Clark, unlike many others, was
too young to be led to any conclusion in this issue by
personal ambition; he was first a party man.

Curiously, I cannot remember Joe Clark at that tumultu-
ous annual meeting of the party in Ottawa that effectively
marked the end of Diefenbaker's leadership and the agoniz-
ing, bitter tensions and frustrations which had been so des-
tructive to both the country and the party. If he was there, I
cannot recall him. If he was absent, it is further testimony to
his providential good fortune.

Indeed, I have been unable to place Clark in any of the

crises that were to come later. A man with an appetite for confrontation would have had his bellyful of it in the months and years to follow. It is only with hindsight that one can appreciate how prudent a man Clark was, and how invisible he became in the prolonged internal struggle for position and power in a party, which, in so brief a time, he would suddenly emerge to lead. Those who nurse similar ambitions would do well to write, in large letters, the object lesson in his example: DISCRETION!

The true enemy of the ambitious in politics is politics itself: profit accrues to those who stay above the fight, or walk wide of it. In this conscious strategy of detachment and disengagement, Clark bears some likeness to the early Diefenbaker, who was a loner both in caucus and in the party, whose instincts told him when to be present in events of the day and when to be absent, and who never belonged to any faction or group other than his own. It is, however, surprising to find so much shrewdness so early in Clark, but not, when one thinks of it, so surprising in a man who would become prime minister. Still, if there were schools for politics in which these lessons could be learned — and too many graduates — there would not be any parties left for them to lead. But the fact remains that, like the Liberal leaders, nearly all the leaders of the Tory party since Borden and Meighen were of the party, but not too much in it.

Before the year was out, I heard from Clark again, no longer the student president, now writing under the letterhead of the Department of Political Science at the University of Alberta in Edmonton. It was, as I had come to expect of him, thoughtful, constructive, with the familiar flashes of wit. More than many I knew, Clark saw things very much as I had seen them, and glimpsed the future of our party in a similar light:

This may sound like a job application which, despite happy memories, it is not.

It seems to me there would be merit in the National Executive considering the convening of another Fredericton Conference. While the recent news from Caucus is ambiguous, it seems hardly likely that the struggle is finished between the Association and the majority in the parliamentary group. Two Caucus tactics seem logical — first, the maintenance of Mr Diefenbaker's leadership for as long a time as possible; second, an effort to meliorate the present image of Caucus, as a first step towards restoring the influence of that group. Both tactics could prejudice the stronger role for the Association which many of us seek, and both could have the effect of again discouraging that sizable number of intelligent potential Conservatives who have sensed a reformation. (I suppose, "sensed a Renaissance."). A new Fredericton would (1) indicate the kind of positive role an Association can play, and thus belie the interpretation that the November exercise was merely negative and vengeful; (2) fill the gap between November 1966 and January 1968; and (3) provide a focus for the energies and idealism which suddenly became accessible, and must be held.

I fully realize that the Party agenda for next year is already crowded, both with potential elections and with the jockeying of the prospective candidates for the succession. But those events *need not* consume all the time of all of us, and *will not* either excite or satisfy the potential new Conservatives, whom we could lose with a lull.

I'll look forward to hearing from you when you've the time, and will always be grateful for the initiative you took this Fall.

xii

A few months later, in June 1967, Clark wrote to a friend:

We came within inches of the upset of the election but didn't quite have time or momentum enough. Polled 4900-plus to his 5200-plus, which isn't bad for a shoestring assault on Mr Speaker by an upstart non-resident. My troops are elated, and I'm thinking of running for national leader.

Larry Lang also almost won. The Issue beat him. A narrow little mayor in his constituency . . . filed as an Independent Conservative, because he didn't like Larry's stand at Ottawa — "This is Diefenbaker country." [He] polled 500 votes, and Larry lost by 400, to the Social Credit.

The young politician had been blooded. He had contested an Edmonton seat against the entrenched forces of Ernest Manning's Social Credit government, and had narrowly lost.

"Another statistic of some interest to me:" he wrote, "my vote total was 13th highest in the province, higher than all but six of the elected Social Creditors (including, sadly, my opponent); and some kind of redistribution is around the corner."

In the careers of most of the best politicians there is the incident of defeat. The poorer ones mourn over it, the good ones learn from it — indeed, take consolation from it! Defeat, more than anything, is a test of one's ego; for the tender, it is a private rebuff, for those with sinew, a public challenge. Clark's defeat in Edmonton, as though he needed it, merely whet his appetite for electoral politics.

Ten years after this first incursion, he would be thinking — seriously — of running for national leader. Twelve years later, in May 1979, only a failure of nerve or judgement, or a fall from a public platform, could prevent him from becoming prime minister. He had, in the interim, enjoyed a textbook apprenticeship: as national president of the Progressive Conservative Student Federation; with a stint in the backrooms of provincial politics; an unsuccessful provincial candidacy; as ambitious acolyte in the offices of the federal leader of the Opposition; then as a successful candidate for the House of Commons. All along, he had been the beneficiary of the slight esteem of his peers, but, despite that (more likely because of it), he had developed, in the trench warfare of internal party politics, a skill and caution, and a sense of timing, that most of them lacked.

xiii

Newfoundland produced the weather for this improvised stop on Clark's campaign itinerary, soaking it in damp and shrouding it in fog. The Tour steps off the aircraft in the darkening late afternoon, piles into two nondescript buses, and lumbers through an unrelievedly desolate landscape of stunted conifers and black-faced rock, for so long a time that the caravan is obliged to make a rest-room stop at the only habitation thus far seen along the route. The rest-room being a single toilet, the media recede into the hovering mists: pack journalism at its apogee.

The varlet wonders what Trudeau would have done, had he been weathered out of his evening event. He would have returned to Ottawa and slept in his own bed. But not Clark. Being shut out of Yarmouth is simply another logistical problem for Tour Group, and Corner Brook is the solution — a committee decision if ever there was one — since Corner Brook is in a constituency the Tories cannot win, where Clark is neither needed nor sought after, and as far from Toronto, the final stop at the end of the day, as the geography of eastern Canada would allow. A town nearly as far from its airport as Calgary is from Edmonton.

Baffled by the workings of the minds of Tour Group, the varlet asks its director, "Why are we going to Corner Brook?"

"Because it's there," he replies, with a nervous laugh.

In truth, Clark is running out of places to go. And Tory research has found a curious pattern surfacing in its data, which suggests the possibility that wherever Clark goes, voter support dips in the wake of his departure. (They have found the same phenomenon with Trudeau.) The constituency organizers are not exactly clamouring for the Tory leader's presence; getting out a crowd for him is hard work and a distraction from the basic chores of constituency campaigning. Clark is not a draw in western Canada, and they wouldn't need him if he were. In Ontario, where the prime purpose of any meeting is to show off a crowd to the media, there are not that many sure-fire Tory power centres — even the Hamilton rally had fizzled, in a hall that swallowed the crowd (and Clark had burned the telephone wires to national headquarters afterwards).

The trick had always been to underexpose Clark, and, while maintaining the illusion of pace and drive in the campaign (made easier by Trudeau, who was running like a turtle), to keep the leader off the ground and in his capsule for as many hours as possible. There is a nice paradox in jet-age politicking: the further you flew, the less you had to do, but a man flying from Windsor to Fort McMurray looks like he's running hell-bent for election.

Best of all, you could contain the media. When they weren't on the plane, they were in the bus; when they weren't on the bus, they were covering an event; after the event, they had to file, and after that, they were back in the bus, returning to the plane. At the end of a long day, the Wagonmaster handed them their room-keys, and saw them off to bed. A bevy of Havergal boarders would be under no more diligent surveillance.

Corner Brook is a mill town, but it may be amongst the prettiest, with a vernal lushness about it after the rain. The hotel that accommodates the visitors is also the scene of Clark's evening meeting. There is enough time before the rally to visit the bar and then the dining room, a bright, spacious place, with bay windows overlooking a thick carpet of lawn and beds of flowers in luxurious bloom, and where the *cod au gratin* and fish chowder meet the varlet's exacting standards. He is hard-pressed, in these genteel surroundings, to identify the territory as belonging to the NDP; out of earshot of the Wagonmaster, however, the local Tory wheels had assured him that it was and would remain so.

"We haven't got a chance," they had said, without trace of rancour. But the diversion of Clark's tour to Corner Brook has given them something to do in a lost cause, and they thought they would produce a decent crowd, having spent the afternoon on the telephone beseeching the faithful.

When the crowd arrives, filling a modest-sized function room (that resembles an amphitheatre) opening onto the corridor, the varlet stands at the back, while Clark, already in full flight, attends to the needs of the media, this time adding fish to his policy mélange — a little something for provincial consumption. The candidate, a man named George Hutchings, gives his leader his rapt attention, while Brian Peckford, Canada's newest and youngest premier, sits gazing up at the ceiling, as though imagining what else might fall upon Corner Brook with the day's rain, besides this flock of mainland tourists.

The varlet feels a nudge from a fellow standee who whispers, "Not a bad turnout for five hours' notice."

Nor is it. A well-dressed, polite, bemused audience, unaware of its functional utility in the Tour's scheme of things, and plainly unattuned to the taut economies of Clark's campaign speeches. A people whose ear for political oratory has been conditioned by the marathon perorations of Joseph Smallwood are perplexed by the cautions and restraints of mainlanders. Besides which, the Tories of Newfoundland are a breed apart, a demographic profile turned upside down; it is the only province in Canada in which the party's tradition is anti-Confederation, and where the Irish Catholic vote is preponderantly Conservative. It is also the most difficult province in Canada — yes, including Quebec — in which to elect Tories to Parliament.

None of this matters, however, to the minds at Mission Control, Ottawa. Their leader has been kept out of harm's reach for yet another day, and this fleeting glimpse of him afforded the Tories of Corner Brook is not sufficient to reveal to them a man who is elevating the art of politics to a science. While there is no magic in Clark, the varlet is learning, there is much method. The last to know this will be the Liberals.

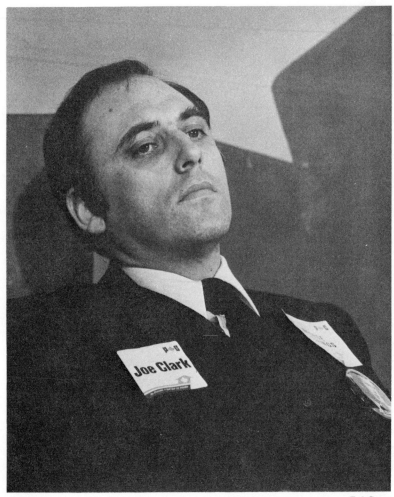

Ted Grant

Brian Peckford sits gazing up at the ceiling, as
though imagining what else might fall upon Corner
Brook with the day's rain besides this flock of mainland tourists.

The enervations of the day overwhelm the varlet as he re-enters the bus: one needs the disposition of a test pilot and the arse of a cowboy to endure modern life on the campaign trail. It is dark now, the rain has resumed, and the passengers are wrapped in the discomforts of a springless, stinking vehicle, manufactured, some years past, for the short runs of city streets. The varlet accepts a can of pop from the Wagonmaster, lights a cigarette, and coughs deeply in the closed darkness. The bus has two speeds: one groans, the other shrieks.

Clark, sitting opposite him across the aisle, is winding down after his exertions.

"You know," he says to the varlet, "you're the fellow who introduced me to Sinc Stevens."

While busily searching his memory for the occasion, the varlet replies, with an *ignotum per ignotius:* "Well, Senator Dave Walker introduced *me* to Sinc Stevens. Walker told me Sinc was Canada's next E. P. Taylor. And Stevens was a good friend and supporter of mine for a long time; at least until he ran for the leadership and made a speech in which he identified the three greatest problems facing the country. One was inflation, the second was unemployment, and I was the third. I never knew what the hell I ever did to Stevens to warrant that."

Which reminds the varlet, further, of the day, early in the campaign of 1974, when Finlay MacDonald, then Stanfield's troubleshooter, had telephoned Stevens to ask him not to run. At that time, Sinc was to the financial community what Leonard Jones, in Moncton, was to the Liberal champions of bilingualism — poison. MacDonald, the third party to the conversation on the bus, recalls Stevens's reaction to his call: "He told me to go to hell."

By such errant misadventure is the politician warned against the excess of scruple. Stevens, a better broker in political properties than he ever was on Bay Street, is now a few days away from membership in the Privy Council, while Jones, who had won Moncton anyway as an Independent after Stanfield had removed him from the Tory ticket, has already retired. Nothing so well serves a political career as procrastination, nor will anything betray it sooner than impulse. Given procrastination's gift of time, Jones would have surely been at home in Clark's caucus after Horner had been recruited by the Liberals. As for Stevens, the financial community had tempered their judgement of him — they only did not want him as minister of finance, a caveat Clark had allowed them.

As the Wagonmaster's convoy lumbers through the night, the Tory leader continues to make light conversation, as if seizing the opportunity, in the close darkness of this howling machine, to exercise his captive self. He makes a rueful comment on the brooding omnipresence of Diefenbaker. (With a week to go in the campaign, the old man is still prowling the deep, and doubtless has a few torpedoes left in the tubes!) "No ordinary Joe can lead this country," he had told Jean Pelletier of *La Presse* early in the campaign. (Had he been reading Humphreys's biography?) "I would guess I haven't heard the last from him yet," Clark says, and quickly changes the subject.

"I remember when I first came down here," he goes on, chuckling to himself, "I had to make a speech to a crowd of people after they had already heard from John Crosbie and Jim McGrath. That's hard enough for anyone to do, but I gave a bonehead, pompous, prepared speech that even embarrassed me. I've never forgotten it either."

This was the man for whom the varlet felt a considerable nostalgic affection, and a far cry from the pliable man of infinite calculation and timidity unwittingly exposed by his biographer: "Clark had considered making a direct pitch for support from Quebec delegates," wrote Humphreys, describing the scene in which Clark is preparing his convention nomination speech.

> Clark proposed a reference to his strong support for Michael Meighen as the national president of the party: "Thus the party got its first fully bilingual national president, a Quebecer."

Innocuous enough, you might think, to pass muster with Len Jones, and pass unnoticed by millions in the media audience. (Perhaps even inaccurate, as well; had not Leon Balcer been a party president bilingual enough to be considered as the Confederation Dinner orator in Vancouver?) But wait: "The phrase was killed," Humphreys recounts,

> after the strenuous objections of Allan McKinnon, MP for Victoria. He pointed out that Meighen's opponent, Donald Matthews of London, had had strong support throughout the West. Clark's identification with the struggle for the presidency would do him more harm than good. A potentially damaging reference was dropped.

And note how history has been suborned to the dull gloss of expedient revision: more than giving Meighen "strong support" in his successful run for the presidency, Clark had chaired the organization committee, canvassed the caucus for Meighen support (and found little), even helped with his nomination speech — acts of commitment now consigned to some secret closet of unmentionables, even though Meighen had made an excellent president and remained devoutly loyal to Clark. But how many more such impulses of the Tory leader would be hostage to the sour malevolence of his united party? The varlet knew the answer — more than enough, he feared, to submerge the true nature and spirit of the man.

Finlay MacDonald — how appropriate! — had often said, "An adult is anyone prepared to accept the consequences of his own actions." Are politicians, even with their power lusts, somehow exempt? Sparta alone would know the stoicism of Stanfield's most devoted followers, who endured the spites of that good man's detractors while he bowed his neck and bent his back to accommodate militants and recalcitrants in his caucus. In the end, in the deadly post mortem of the 1974 election, they achieved his resignation by confronting him with a churl's sullen silence, and he departed, in appropriate dignity, never understanding their contempt for him, much less its genesis.

In truth, he had never led them so much as they had driven him, but he, too, had imagined that he could unite his caucus by capitulating to its demands for vengeance upon those who had held the brightest hopes for his leadership and worked the hardest to attain it.

And now Clark. Like Stanfield, not the choice of his caucus but of his party, and setting out, in the footsteps of his predecessor, with the same brave faith in collegial leadership — save only more so, for this is a true child of consensus. Stanfield was a man of patrician bent, with a massive patience born of self-assurance, who believed if he listened long enough, he would finally have his way. Consensus was the first article of Clark's faith, and compromise his dogma; he had learned not to voice opinions of his own.

The varlet's lugubrious spirits lift at the sight of lights ahead — Stephenville airport emerges from the murk and he can see the aircraft parked on the strip. The media board Charter 087 with the weary relief of dorymen returning to the mother ship.

xiv

Finally, the organizational contentment
of the national press was the responsi-
bility of the writer.
From the Wagonmaster's Ode

The French-language media occupy the centre seats on both sides of the plane's aisle on the Clark tour, as they had done with Trudeau. They ride together on the same bus, and the English-language media board a second bus first, before the overflow and latecomers fill the French-language bus. On takeoff, the francophones often burst into song, a note of defiance in their voices. They laugh a lot among themselves, and too loudly. Their favourite song is the separatist anthem: it sounds as a lament to their claustrophobia.

The engines hum at cruising speed as the Wagonmaster nurtures the organizational contentments of his charges. Clark, despite the rigours of today and yesterday's burden of fatigue, continues to campaign. At thirty thousand feet, there are errands to be run and signals given. The Tory leader, again in his pullover, a slight exploratory smile on his face, moves slowly to the francophone enclave. In one hand he carries a campaign-issue bilingual songbook (courtesy of Imperial Oil!) and in the other a glass of amber liquid that the varlet guesses might be apple juice. He then proceeds to lead the French-speaking media in song.

There is a deft fitness about this gesture. The varlet suspects the leader is no more at home in some parts of Canada — Newfoundland being one, Toronto another — than the members of the chorus he is now directing, nor comfortable where they are most at home. Were alienation an experience to be taught, they could learn from Clark, who, as much as he clings to his High River heritage, dared not even contest the Tory nomination in his own home riding, even though he was the party's national leader. Like Mackenzie King, Clark would become prime minister without a constituency of his own, never mind a fiefdom.

The ghost of Marcel Faribault attends the varlet's reveries: *deux nations* even on the Wagonmaster's manifest! Poor Faribault, maligned by friend and foe alike for giving unintended expression to a reality that was the dread of the practicing politician in English-speaking Canada. And in that heap of scorn, the exquisite insult of being lectured on French semantics by unilingual Wasps. *Deux nations* meant two nations — could it mean anything else? As when Premier Jean Lesage had addressed himself to the Ottawa federalists with the words, "Je demande," English Cana-

Ted Grant

He proceeds to lead the French-speaking media in song.

dians knew they were being confronted by peremptory orders. Among the hardships imposed upon the French in Canada is that they must accept responsibility for the English translation of the meaning of their words. If only Faribault had said *deux peuple*!

All the dictionaries in all the *bibliothèques* in Quebec were no match for Diefenbaker's direct translation. He not only understood what Faribault had said but also what he was up to — a sly linguistic plot against One Canada, by a trick of the tongue inserting deadly heresy into fundamental Conservatism. French kiss of death! But there were also internal ironies in this calculated confusion: in 1963 Diefenbaker had tried and failed to recruit Faribault (then the highly respected president of a Montreal trust company) to his party; afterwards, he would explain that, in fact, he had rejected Faribault because the man had a price.

Imagine! Faribault, too, had wanted a trust fund.

The varlet, recalling the mawkish plea of Diefenbaker at the leadership convention at which Stanfield was chosen, that the party not accept the doctrine of two nations — something that had never occurred to anyone present — can still hear the huge applause, a thunderous volley of hypocrisy, as though no tribute could be enough for a man who had warned them of the consequences of self-immolation. It had been yet another day of politics in which a seasoned Tory could better call himself a Vomitory.

There had been a thin file of them — Balcer, Faribault, then Wagner — as Quebec subalterns to anglophone leaders, the last one as luckless as his predecessors, even though more promising.

Brian Mulroney had arranged the varlet's meeting with Claude Wagner, then a Quebec judge, and being wooed as Stanfield's next French lieutenant, to fill the shoes of the luckless Faribault. It was a role, the varlet had thought, then and ever since, inspired by chronic Tory frustration and despair over the party's fortunes in Quebec; it was doomed to repeated failure. If Cartier had lived forever — as he did in the rhetoric of Conservative orators — it might have been different. But the example of Cartier was a singular one; after him came Leon Balcer, who became a Liberal, then Faribault, a man of ruinous good intentions, who became a liability, and now, presumably, Wagner, who had been a Liberal and whose fate, should he become a Tory, seemed sadly preordained.

But, acting on Stanfield's request, the varlet had flown to Montreal in 1972 to appraise Wagner's potential and, more important, to try to assuage the doubts of some Conservatives, notably MPs David and Flora MacDonald, and Richard Hatfield, the premier of New Brunswick. "See what you think of him," had been the varlet's simple brief.

Wagner was believed to be anathema to Red Tory, liberal, Liberal and, indeed, separatist opinion. He had acquired a reputation as a "hanging judge," a law-and-order devout, and it was a significant part of his political curriculum vitae that, as the responsible minister of the Lesage government, he had ordered the police to use their clubs on demonstrators on the occasion of the last visit of the Queen to Quebec.

The varlet also knew of him that he had been elevated to the bench as compensation for his defeat, a narrow one, at a Liberal leadership convention that had been rigorously stacked against him. But what he did not know was that many hands had been busy, even as the meeting with Wagner was arranged, to smooth his entry into the party: following worthy precedent in Liberal practice, a purse was being got up to compensate Wagner for his loss of income and security should he leave the bench and surrender himself to the dubious fortunes of Tory politics.

Among those courting the judge, none was more assiduous than Mulroney, perhaps the brightest and ablest Tory in all of Quebec, but whose political misfortune was to be born in Baie Comeau, to live in Montreal, and to be of pure Irish descent — thus condemned to opportunities and options far more slender than his promise.

After the varlet had checked into the Queen Elizabeth Hotel, Mulroney had brought Wagner to his room, had made the introductions and had then withdrawn.

It had been the varlet's first impression of Wagner that he was nearly mod in his dress — a stylishly cut tweed suit with a rust coloured fleck — and that there was also a cosmetic touch of orange, hinting at vanity, in his thick, short stand of hair. But he exuded charm and, if there were any wariness in him, it was well concealed. The varlet had poured him a scotch and water, and their conversation had begun with Stanfield. Wagner was impressed by Stanfield's personal qualities and believed he had great appeal for the people of Quebec.

When they were into their second scotch, the varlet had posed the question he had carried with him from Toronto: "Tell me," he had asked, "how did you get your law-and-order reputation?"

The quick, disarming smile indicated Wagner's welcome of the subject. It was, he replied, a reputation given him by his political opponents, something that came out of the Queen's visit to Quebec in October 1964.

Sensing footnotes to history — and that the man had a story to tell — the varlet had asked him about the royal visit, as though this would all be news to him.

Which, as he was told of it, it was. Wagner's further answer had been graphic, illustrated by gesture, mime and the artistry of a born historian. Riveted, the varlet had soon become an audience.

In 1963, with the knowledge and approval of his cabinet, Jean Lesage, the premier of Quebec, had invited the Queen to Quebec City in celebration of the centenary of the Quebec Conference. But as the time of the royal visit drew near, a few in the cabinet had second thoughts, and at least one of them, René Levesque, had expressed his views publicly. These were changing times in Quebec, and the Quiet Revolution was becoming less so. Lesage, recalled Wagner, began to lose his nerve, his fears mounting daily that some incident, or something worse, would mar the visit.

As for Wagner, he had only just been elected and had not been long enough in his portfolio of attorney general — a matter of days — to know what, if any, security precautions had been arranged by his predecessor, who, awaiting appointment to the bench, had repaired to Florida.

So that when Lesage summoned his attorney general, on the eve of the Queen's arrival, Wagner found the premier so agitated that "he was shaking like a leaf." Lesage poured out his concerns, stressing the damage that could be done to the government and to Quebec should anything go wrong. So saying, he gave Wagner full authority, and responsibility, for seeing to it that nothing would. Wagner, it became clear, was the Queen's first, maybe only, protector.

"I want you to see," Wagner had quoted Lesage as instructing him, "that no one touches so much as a hair on her head."

But the highlight of the interview was to come:

"But at least," Lesage had said, "we have the car."

"The car?"

"We have a car ready. It is bullet-proof. We had it made."

It was true: a bullet-proof, armour-plated $75,000 car — a windowed tank — had been made ready for the visit, to transport the Queen from the royal barge to the Citadel. Wagner later found it, secreted in a government garage.

"There will be no bullet-proof car," Wagner had told Lesage. "And there will be no trouble. I will see to it."

Which he did, he recalled, calling in the chiefs of the provincial police and giving them his orders — no one was to touch so much as a hair on Her Majesty's head.

But of course, when the Queen was being driven through the streets of Quebec City, there had been a waiting crowd of demonstrators, who were asked to disperse.

"When they didn't," Wagner had said, with a shrug, "we dispersed them. There were a few who resisted and some of them took a few lumps. But that was all. The Queen never even saw them."

Afterwards, the royal visit safely concluded, there had been an outpouring of protest from some of the media and, of course, from the separatists and their sympathizers. Later, in cabinet, René Levesque had proposed a judicial inquiry into police brutality, a suggestion that appealed to Lesage, who was now "running in the other direction."

"But I told them that, as attorney general, I would not permit an investigation. If there were one, I would resign. And I said to Lesage that the Queen had come to Quebec and left — and no one had touched a hair on her head."

And that's how Claude Wagner came by his law-and-order reputation! Impressed by this narrative, the varlet could only say to him that if he did venture again into politics, and into the Tory party, he hoped that he would have the occasion to tell that story in Winnipeg; indeed, anywhere in Canada where the deposits of Tory candidates were presumed safe.

The varlet had said as much to Stanfield, admitting that he had, to his surprise, been both impressed and charmed by Wagner. Palpably a stronger man than Balcer, more supple and far less innocent than Faribault. How could he miss?

But he did. Among the hardships endured by French-speaking Quebecers in any Conservative caucus, the first must be the loneliness. Given the early leaps and bounds of Wagner's political career — a by-election winner one day, a Liberal minister the next, and, not long after, very nearly the party's leader — he knew he had allies and a broad base of public support. Now Stanfield's right-hand man in the Commons, chieftain of whatever there was of his party in Quebec (but, as he knew, that would be up to him), and granted the shadow cabinet role of foreign affairs critic (the ideal umbrella for a putative national leader), he had all he could ask for, except friends. Stanfield, sensing the isolation of his Quebec lieutenant, dispatched Hugh Segal from his own office to attend him, but even the best and brightest of the new boys in the leader's office was no compensation for the fact that Wagner was, by definition, the spokesman in caucus for no one but himself and for a non-existent party outside of it.

And then there was the dower, the dark malignancy in the depths of his pride, about which he could not bring himself to tell the truth, lest it be believed that money had been a condition of his decision to re-enter politics. That, too, isolated him from the others.

Even so, he was not an easy man to live with, as difficult for Stanfield as for Lesage, and impossible for Clark, who was relieved of the burden of trying when Trudeau appointed Wagner to the Senate.

The varlet, who never spoke to him again after they parted company in the Queen Elizabeth, thereafter observed him from a distance, becoming increasingly aware of his moody, withdrawn, unpredictable intransigence. There was more than a little resemblance to Diefenbaker, who was at his best on public platforms and before crowds, and at his ease only in the company of trusted cronies and sycophants. Wagner, alas, had too few of the latter. Still, he could not keep his eyes from the vision of things unseen, of sinister influences in the party, cabals in secret rooms, conspiring against him. To the varlet's surprise, he himself became personified as one of them, during Wagner's leadership campaign. It seemed an unkind cut, coming from the lips of a man for whom, at the very moment of his utterance, the varlet had felt only a strong compassion and sympathy.

Indeed, indignation would be too weak a word for the varlet's helpless rage when the Wagner trust fund became an issue in the leadership contest, an issue pumped up by Tories, and worse, English-speaking Tories. Of course! But imagine the inducement to paranoia these opportunists and tattlers would provide for a man already certain he had been used, his presence in the party symbolic, his rank a token one. Would the Liberals have done as much to Pearson? Would the Tories have done as much if Wagner had come from Saskatoon? Would they have done as much to any man known to have friends and allies within the party who knew the arts of retaliation?

But no, he was a loner to the last, and the support that grew around him on the second and third ballots to make his election a near thing were from Horner, Hellyer and the Diefenbakerites, whose motivation ranged from contempt for Clark to mere mischief. A few, like Segal, supported him out of affection, some others were drawn to him because of his suspected ideological tilt to the right, and others still because "it was time for the party to be led by a French Canadian." He could never shake off his token value to the party.

Even so, his was the most eloquent speech to the convention and, when he lost to Clark on the final ballot, his concession was moving and graceful, and for that moment, at least, it appeared he might yet fulfil the promise of his role. But afterwards, he lapsed again into diffidence and despair, undoing the good he had done for himself at the convention. He was, as were Balcer and Faribault, seriously flawed, as though any politician of promise who would venture from Quebec into the Tory party must have some blighted imperfection to begin with, which makes misadventure inevitable. Or again, it may be that and, as well, some pernicious force in the party that disfigures these men and destroys them.

But then, even on so morbid a note, the varlet's recollections are relieved by a blessedly cheerful distraction: *les chansons*, under Clark's direction, are interrupted by the Wagonmaster, who enters from the galley bearing a cake flickering with candles, a surprise, at first suggesting an apparition. It is the birthday of Alfie Moreau, and the occasion prompts a boisterous chorus of *Il a gagné ses épaulettes*. As portions of cake are dispensed throughout the plane, there are renewed requests for mini-bottles of wine. The leader raises his glass in toast to the celebrant: there is something about this ritual observance that reminds the varlet of a ship's company taking communion. In the watchful eyes of the Wagon-master there are glints of secret satisfactions.

"Consistent and determined application of people and principle," the Wagonmaster wrote later, and with his own emphasis, "from the beginning to the *very* end is critical to success (an enormous tendency and danger was to let up a few days too soon as the end approaches — *detailed precision, self-discipline,* and *constant good humour* are essential — no matter what the circumstances and no matter how virtually fatigued some of us were — and we were!)"

With Clark returned to his forward seat, there is speculation in the back of the aircraft as to what everyone had witnessed. Agreed that it was more than an act of ingratiation, doubtless not one of spontaneity either, but, as someone suggests, it might have been Clark's way of saying to the French-language media that, even though his Quebec support will be pitifully slight, and, while he recognizes their unease with the prospect of an anglophone prime minister and government, he would make himself accessible to them, would go out of his way to ensure against their isolation, as he has demonstrated aboard Charter 087. To the varlet, it is an appropriate gesture coming from the man he used to know.

A curious country, becoming more so in the stubbornly protracted pretence of One Nation, many a bigot's meta-phor for the primacy of English. And how curious a cam-paign, that it would be waged with serious purpose only in English, and only in English Canada. Each of the parties had yielded to the hard realities of their polls, leaving the voters of Quebec as either taken for granted or given up as lost. The token forays of the leaders into that province merely confirmed the monolith as unshakeable or impene-trable. For Clark, Broadbent and — yes — Trudeau, it was necessary only to be seen in Quebec, but important not to be seen more often than necessary.

Although in English Canada the Tory television commer-

Ted Grant

Il a gagné ses épaulettes.

Ted Grant

"Consistent and determined application of people and principle."
The Wagonmaster

cials were a judicious mix of party policy, Clark and Clark's team, laced with some tart and telling reminders of Trudeau's record (adding some of Pearson's for cumulative effect), the French-language commercials were startlingly offensive.

Writing in the Montreal *Gazette*, Ian MacDonald described them as "the most insulting and politically stupid advertising that has ever gone out over Quebec's airwaves," adding, "Once again, the Tories have shown an alarming ignorance of Quebec."

In that other solitude of English Canada, had the rankest Tory partisan seen his party's television campaign in Quebec, even *he* might have flinched. As strategy, the Quebec campaign reeked of scorched earth and bore the imprint of a cold, contemptuous fury. (And yet another tangled knot in the varlet's confusion: Clark surely had known and approved!)

The most the Québecois might have gleaned of the Tories' intentions would have been that they would put the prime minister in the dock, find him "coupable" and send him to jail: viewers heard the clanging of a cell door. Anglophones, on the other hand, were lured by offers of mortgage deductibility, jobs and lower taxes: *deux nations*, as Diefenbaker understood it, exalted in the media plan!

As for the six million in the audience for "the Great Debate" — the campaign's climactic hour and its only moment of drama — the seats had all been reserved for English-speaking viewers. Fabien Roy, whose Créditiste party would outpoll the Conservatives in Quebec, could not participate because of his inadequacy in technology's official language — a denial of the broadcast ethic of even-handed treatment of the parties. No, the promised excitements of the debate (and the pride of producers) triumphed over such untidy considerations as the dubious right of a publicly owned utility to mount a political spectacular as though one of the political parties did not exist.

Such affront and injustice to so significant a minority —

and a Quebec one at that — passed unnoticed in the stampede of producers to provide English Canadians with similar political divertissements as those enjoyed by Americans. (Are not the systems the same?) And even though a man might know barely enough about politics to be able to mark his own ballot, he could mount a formidable case to support the presumption that the debate did injury, as well as give offence, to the Créditiste cause in the election. And if Fabien Roy had never before heard of the two-nations phobia of the anglophones, he might now wonder how they could so cheerfully practise what they pretended to abhor.

XV

Canadians sin at the Holiday Inn.
advt.

The essentials of Canadian politics are few: the system needs enough good men to make it work and enough fools to make it interesting. Of all the parties, none is more interesting than the Progressive Conservative Party of Canada.

On Tuesday, 15 May, gremlins and gerbils mounted Clark's bandwagon, the leader's entourage came down with a case of doubts, and the dour weather the leader had found in the Maritimes began to follow him. It was the worst day of his campaign.

Not only had the weather changed — it was raining hard as the day began in Toronto — but there seemed to be some light seismic rumbles in the city as well. Monday's consensus on the debate, that Clark had done the necessary and survived it, did not last longer than the morning after; by

Tuesday, in the lobby and corridors of Toronto's Constellation Hotel, a new consensus concluded that he had lost it. Liberal canvassers, going door-to-door, reported a near-miraculous improvement in voter response.

The Toronto media, at last given a bone to gnaw, had pressed Bill Davis to say whether Trudeau had had it right — and thus Clark had had it wrong — when he had quoted the premier's position on unilateral patriation of the constitution.

"We believe," the premier had indeed said, less than four months before, "that the time has come in 1979 . . . to take, without further debate, the decisive step of patriating our constitution . . . we are proposing, on behalf of the government of Ontario, that the government of Canada . . . request the British Parliament to terminate its power to legislate with regard to our constitution . . . in other words, we should bring the constitution home to Canada."

The options for Davis, in response to the media's calls, were few: it would be impossible to deny it, even difficult to bury it in obfuscation. The best course, in Clark's interest, was to make himself unavailable, which he did.

Trudeau had suddenly begun to campaign, as though the debate had refreshed his confidence in himself and reactivated his disdain for Clark. He had even gone mainstreeting in Ottawa, along Sparks Street Mall, and the Grits were buying a television network in preparation for his visit to British Columbia. Furthermore, Petro-Canada had been a party to a gas find in the high Arctic, a timely happenstance suggesting divine intervention.

After six weeks of fumbling for a handle to the campaign, the prime minister seemed close to having a grip on it in these last days. It had finally struck him, somewhere in the course of the debate perhaps, that he had made a serious error in strategy — that rather than wait for Clark to make a mistake, he should have realized that Clark *was* the mistake.

The varlet kept random notes of his odyssey (not all of which he could later read), gathered up campaign litter to stow in his flight bag as memento, and stuffed his pockets with the columns of Richard Gwyn and Geoffrey Stevens to remind him of the matters of true import that otherwise he would be certain to forget. But, for the last Tuesday of the long campaign, he retrieved little other than its essence.

The Tories' Toronto rally was intended to be a peaking period-piece in the campaign, something luminously upbeat for the campaign diaries of the networks, which would record a sun-dappled sea of upturned faces, a lensfull of bright young men and women turned out of the banks, brokerage houses, legal firms and the pricey stores, their eyes fixed upon the new star of plaza politics — who would be Joe Clark — and viewers "from sea to sea to sea" would be able to see for themselves that Trudeaumania had turned its coat in Toronto. The varlet, studying the overcast sky and noting the pavements already drying as the tour bus carries him from the airport strip into the city, feels a quickened sense of anticipation for this event. No one has told him, even as the bus disgorges its passengers, that plans have been changed.

The Tory leader emerges from the elevator into the lobby of the Royal York Hotel, to be greeted by some of his Metro candidates, his tour band, Flora MacDonald, and a press of cheering partisans armed with placards.

"By golly, we're going to win this thing!" Flora tells the varlet.

Briefly warmed by her enthusiasm, he follows the leader through the lobby, down the stairs and into the long tunnel leading to the Toronto-Dominion Centre. As the band strikes up a marching air, he moves well out in front of Clark, lest he be thought a member of the entourage. There is at the outset a brisk flow of pedestrian traffic, as many going as coming, but when the varlet enters one of the centre's four underground shopping malls, he can see ahead of him a mass of humanity, congealing at the intersection. Within moments, he is engulfed in a jostling, shoving, wall-to-wall mob. And it is only now that he realizes that the organizers have moved the outdoor rally indoors, and underground.

Not all of this mob are Tories; some are shoppers, others are on their lunch hour, but none of them can move. Although the varlet has been in many a captive audience, this is his first experience in a trapped one, and, though he has never before suffered claustrophobia, there is now enough of it in the heavy air to panic a mole. He can feel water coursing down his back, the escaping juices of his repressed anxiety, and, among many unnerving aspects to being thus imprisoned in Clark's crowd, is that Clark himself has disappeared in it. There is not *one* band playing, but two, imposing on every ear a cacophony that tears at composure and assaults the senses.

Triumphant over the bands are the shouts of the partisans in the crowd — would that they had been the first to be suffocated! — chanting, "Go, Joe, go! Go, Joe, go!" The lengths to which insensitivity can be carried before it constitutes battery might be usefully tested in such instances. The varlet, however great his immediate discomforts, is a volunteer to this ordeal. He has, indeed, loped along the corridors, like a bull following a Judas goat to the abattoir, mindless of naught but his own momentum. Nor would he have wanted to miss it — should he survive it — for its educative value alone would be worth his miseries. Were there limits to which the public might be exploited, herded, entrapped — yes, entombed! — so that politicians might provide the media with its fix? In the example surrounding him, in which the varlet can see a part of the crowd, and feel the heat from all of it, there appear to be none. It confirms a growing dark suspicion: there is a madness loose in all this business, something beyond the control of the systems-managers. Politics has disappeared in the maw of its own technology: the varlet can smell the sour breath of Orwellian prophecy.

Finally, Clark's head emerges from a thicket of waving placards. "I would ask you," he says, over cheers, shouts,

Ted Grant

Although the varlet has been in many a captive
audience, this is his first experience in a trapped
one.

boos and grunts, "I would ask those of you with signs to lower them, so others in the audience can feel the full force of my charisma."

A voice bellows, "Get off your knees!"

To the relief of all, Clark's speech is brief, beginning with prediction — "Trudeau is a prime minister for only seven more days" — and ending with homily, a desire to build Canada on its "strength and diversity." No man could have made a better speech in an underground tunnel to an audience, a good part of which had not come to hear it. His brevity might also have saved lives. Even the hecklers are quieted since they find nothing Clark has said to be objectionable, although, at the end, they boo strength and diversity just for the hell of it.

The varlet, his senses pummelled enough, extricates himself from the scrum of bodies around him and finds an exit, and, above the stairs, clear sky. A coal miner emerging into daylight after a bump could not be much more relieved. Others who follow him, a hint of desperation in them still as they hurry up the steps, vocalize their frustration:

"Yecch!" a young woman says, "Every time I see him, he's worse!"

Having survived the perils of Clark's Toronto rally, the varlet is inordinately happy to rejoin his comrades in the back of the bus. He is told that the decision to move the event underground was made by Tour Command in Ottawa, only after being advised by Environment Canada that the rains would likely continue, with the possibility of thunder showers, which meant not only the likelihood of a sparse, damp crowd but some risk to the leader's life, standing in the midst of all that high-voltage sound system with lightning flashing around him. The fact that the rain has stopped and the rally could have been held out-of-doors casts no reflection upon the wisdom of the decision. There was no virtue in wiring Joe Clark to the amp-metres of heaven.

It is a long way from downtown Toronto to the outskirts of

Cambridge and the Cambridge Holiday Inn. In some of the
lulls, rolling through the redundant countryside of southern
Ontario, the CBC's Carol MacIvor plays her tape, which
consists of a hundred edited snips of Joe Clark saying thank
you: "Thank you thank you thank you very much thank you
very very much thank you very much very much thank you."
It never fails to break up the journalists. The Wagonmaster
endures this irreverence with the fixed smile of a man at a
smoker listening to a yarn about his girl from an old beau.
(Ms MacIvor will later be chided for her artistry by her
superiors, who have read the polls.)

The marquee outside the Cambridge Holiday Inn reads:
WELCOME JOE CLARK AND MAUREEN McTEER.

In a room outfitted with a bar and piles of sandwiches, the
media gather to be given their room-keys. Mysteriously, the
varlet is assigned a room registered in the name of Geoff
Stevens: he has the feeling the Wagonmaster has designated
him as a non-person, to be held incommunicado in the name
of the *Globe and Mail*'s associate editor, who is back in
Toronto. He decides to go along with this game, hoping
some local prominence will call Stevens in his room, and he
will then say he is too drunk to talk sensibly to anyone and
hang up. (Alas, no one does.)

An afternoon at a motel — this one located in surroundings nearly bucolic — offers limited distractions. The
Wagonmaster is seen cruising the lobby with ball and bat,
looking like a day-camp counsellor, and there is an agitated
air of urgency about Clark's staff on the upper floors as its
members bustle from room to room, behind whose doors
one can hear the clatter of typewriters and the clacking of
the photocopier.

Some of this tension upstairs may have been induced by
the reporters below, who are talking about "momentum"
and the Tories losing it, of Clark's "icing the puck" in the
closing hours of the campaign, and of the events of the
morning in Toronto, agreed to be a disaster. The varlet himself had not liked the feel of Toronto — never mind the rally

— and his earlier assumption that the city state would swing one way or the other and determine the result of the election seems unlikely now. Besides, he still has not found a taxi-driver who would be voting for Clark. There must be, he thinks, a good deal of Toronto still left in him — he too was of half a mind.

The Cambridge rally is a regional one, in the heart of the Ontario panhandle, embracing key ridings in Kitchener and Waterloo. When the media buses arrive, the crowd is already in place and being entertained by rousing airs — "United we stand, dee-vided we fall" — while prancing drum-majorettes do their stuff along the front of the platform. If there is a Middle Canada, it is here in this vortex of sound, colour and rock-ribbed, anglo-saxon angst. This is a crowd with a ripple of muscle and stout heart in it, whose approval of the Tory ticket — John Reimer, Chris Speyer, Perrin Beatty ("definitely cabinet material," says his intro-ducer) and Walter McLean — is registered in the exploding thunder from pounding palms the size of Schneider hams.

Sitting at the press table, the varlet hears the mayoress of Kitchener, who has presented the candidates, promise that "a surprise guest" will also be introduced later — a note of suspense in this undiluted atmosphere of simple, no-non-sense politics. Mulling this, he feels a firm hand on his shoulder, then a voice in his ear. "We've got that fucking frog this time!" the voice exults. "By Jesus, we've got 'im for sure!"

The varlet resurrects the name from memory — no small feat — and hastily rises from his chair to elevate the conversation above other ears. Yes, he knows him — a small, fine irony here — as a local scion and a man who had, more than a quarter of a century ago, parachuted into France on D-Day to help liberate Europe from the abomi-nation of German fascism. By what perverted process could such cheerful malevolence have become distilled in the breast of a hero? Not to say such sentiment would be repre-sentative of Waterloo, Kitchener and Cambridge, but for a

man with normal hearing who had sat in enough bars, or
talked to strangers in airport lounges and hotel lobbies, the
venom would be familiar. Yes, it would be the nub of grievance for a small army of detractors — Trudeau was a frog!

"See you later," the man promises. "We'll have a drink."

"Sure," the varlet tells him, covering the lie with his
hacking cough.

Applause escorts the mystery guest as he makes his way to
the platform: the premier of Ontario has come to Cambridge to introduce Joe Clark one more time.

Ambling up the long aisle, Bill Davis bears with him the
equivalent talents of the best relief pitcher in baseball. If
Clark is tiring and his lead endangered, this is a man for the
last innings — a fireman for the Tory cause. Ontario's
premier is a man of deceptive motion whose delivery seems
easy to hit until you take your first riffle. He would be, in the
parlance of the trade, a junk pitcher, with no blinding speed,
but a good change-up, a slider and a knuckler that soars and
dips like a butterfly. He is hard to hit because he doesn't give
you anything to swing at; coming in from the bull-pen in
relief of Clark, Davis has the cat's grace and nonchalance of
one who has been around, who is used to taking charge, and
for whom this occasion is merely another game in a long
season.

Bill Davis's passions are few but enough, and faithfully
attended: his family, his country, his province, the Tory
party, football, the brief winter respite in Florida (and, as
someone remarked, not necessarily in that order). At heart a
traditionalist, in spirit an activist, at the soul's core he is a
loyalist. The times of budget attrition and restraint have
tempered the reformist impulse in him, but in the simmering
tensions of national politics, the premier of Ontario remains
an identifiable, uncomplicated federalist.

It had been Trudeau's grievous blunder, early in the
campaign, to attack Davis, in the lump sum of his abuse
directed at all the premiers, when he could have used him as
a foil to get at Clark. As to policy: Davis and the prime

Ted Grant

Ambling up the long aisle, Bill Davis bears with him
the equivalent talents of the best relief pitcher in
baseball.

minister are more allies than adversaries, if only Trudeau had the wit to see it. In truth, Ontario's premier would rather keep Petro-Canada than see Alberta's dominance in the energy field further magnified. He is wary of Clark's mortgage deductibility scheme, which will be largely financed by Ontario taxpayers, and, on the record, holds opposite views on the subject of patriation.

No paradox in all this would suggest itself to Bill Davis as he stumps Ontario in support of Joe Clark. The party loyalist in him would lead him to do so in the clear light of no other conceivable alternative, and in the conviction that election platforms are always subject to the subsequent accommodation of reasonable, responsible men. Besides, no party can come to power in Ottawa without a generous helping of Ontario's ninety-five seats, even though it might sweep Alberta.

The appearance of Davis stirs the curiosity of the media, jaded and weary from fifty-seven days of tedium: has he come to clear up the contradiction between his federal leader and himself on the issue of patriation? Every hand has a pencil poised or a finger on the button of a tape recorder; at last, there might be some sport in this wearing business.

The premier plucks a text from inside his suit-coat and squares his shoulders to the crowd. The voice that has mixed a thousand soporifics in the vials of politics works its chemistry, holding its listeners silent lest they miss a turn in the maze of his speech, while every vowel lies flattened under the weight of his monotone — sentences and paragraphs smoothed into this magic elixir of homogenous goodwill. There is not a grain of malice in the man.

But more, William Davis, "Premier Bill," is not a sedative to drug the senses, but a voice of soothing calm and reassurance — a blessed, long-held note of reassurance. Were a man to be wracked with torments on a sleepless cot, his mind writhing in the coils of subliminal anxiety, the varlet would give him this advice — *think of Bill Davis.* Put your mind to him, the sensible, amiable, loyal spirit in him, the corporate decencies of the solid Wasp Canadian Progressive Conservative Red Tory leader of the keystone province of Ontario; if you meditate on Davis, you will know a transcendental experience and find rest.

But let us return to the metaphor of baseball — Davis, the relief artist — and watch him now in these late innings of the campaign of '79. His first pitch is for majority government! Yes, a premier cursed by two minority parliaments knows whereof he speaks. While this spectral offering bemuses us, there is the next delivery: a passing reference to the debate — that Trudeau and Broadbent had "tried in vain" to get to Clark, but had failed.

It is obvious to the media that Davis is closing in on the matter of their interest, that he will now answer all the calls to his office at Queen's Park. Was Trudeau right and Clark wrong?

"You know, ladies and gentlemen," Davis says, winding up once more, "the prime minister I thought demonstrated questionable judgement the other evening when he . . ." Yes, when he what?

Honest to God! Returning on the bus, after the meeting, and during the night, and the next day, everyone *knew* Davis had said something about the patriation issue, about Trudeau's challenge to Clark over Ontario's position — but no one knew for sure *what* he had said. It had just floated up there in that easy preamble, looking as big as a basketball, so that you could have counted the stitches on it, and then it had sailed by. Had he changed the subject? (Later, the varlet would call Queen's Park to ask: "What did he say?" No one knew.)

Having retired the side, Bill Davis presents Clark to the crowd as "the next prime minister of Canada!" It sounds, for once at least, more prophetic than trite, the likelihood of it emphasized by the deep-throated roar that follows; so emphatic an ovation that Clark, at the podium in his black suit, looks suddenly frail and vulnerable standing before the force of it. People who can cheer like that, the varlet thinks, already have a taste of the morrow's triumphs.

In response to his ovation, the Tory leader flashes his Nixonian sign — the four-fingered wave — and the varlet wrenches himself from the blissful contemplation of the peculiar mastery of William Davis to attend the business at hand.

Clark makes a good, forceful, sound speech, flawed only by an inexplicably reckless diversion to the exotic question about the amount of Petro-Canada's holdings in the consortium which, as Trudeau has just revealed, had found gas in the high Arctic. It seems to be, Clark says, working the figure down by stages from half an interest, "5.4 per cent" (which turns out to be incorrect and inconsequential), and the Tory leader strenuously objects to the prime minister announcing the find before the stock exchanges had closed.

It would need an exhaustive search of those in attendance at the Cambridge rally to find one who was alert to the pertinence of this banter, but the dutiful crowd gives it their attention — although a recital of the Dow Jones closing averages would have done as well — because the man before them represents the agent of change, which is the true sum of all they want from him.

Apart from that, it is a composed performance, strengthened by inarguable logic. When he comes to the heart of it — Trudeau — one of his audience volunteers his agreement: "Throw him in jail!" (Has he seen the commercials in Quebec?)

"You can't have a one-man band, or a one-man government, in a country like Canada," Clark says. That being so, none of the two thousand or more within his hearing believe the Tory leader capable of so unCanadian an ambition.

Bused back to the Holiday Inn, where the tour would spend the night, the varlet samples a variety of its diversions: the Wagonmaster's sandwich tray, the coffee shoppe, and the disco; despite the talk of Tory slippage, lost momentum and manifest jitters, no one doubts a Clark victory next

Tuesday, the only remaining subject for speculation being the numbers. (Before this last week was out, the Wagon-master would poll the press and then average its predictions. When the election results were in, the press was one seat out in its calculations — proof of the internal wisdom of pack journalism.) This imminent reality took some getting used to, and the period for adjustment would be longer for some than others. But it was an effort everyone felt obliged to make.

At breakfast the next day, the varlet notes the ardent attendance of certain media luminaries upon Bill Neville, a man not previously spoiled by such rapt attentions, as though he had overnight plumbed the meaning of the universe. The room seems filled with tight, compressed squeaks of sound — like osculation. Where better to begin a honeymoon than at the Cambridge Holiday Inn?

xvi

The Clark tour wheels into London under a bright midday sun, passing rows of tidy houses along the quiet, shaded streets. As in Toronto, there is a lively sign war here between the parties, being waged on the well-watered lawns; the campaign in London appears to be a three-way fight.

There are other resemblances to Toronto, for this is a city with nearly all that Hogtown has, only much less of it, but including a procreative mix of industry and commerce — beer, machinery, gombeen houses, and insurance — enough old money to provide a social order and enough new wealth to give the place a booster image.

John Robarts came from here (out of Banff, Alberta, of all places), and, over the ten good years he had been premier of Ontario, it was merely enough for a man to be from London to give him access at Queen's Park. It could be said that Robarts had done as much for the city as had the brothers Labatt. As for Clark, this is a city tailored to his campaign rhetoric: it is a community steeped in self-assurance, and a solid strata of its population are the true devouts of free enterprise. Many of these have gathered in a corner parking lot in the centre of downtown London to hear the gospel preached, a solid middle-class, middle-aged, agreeable crowd in business suits, waiting patiently through the warmup routines of Clark's band.

Val Sears, the varlet's seat companion, looks out on the crowd from the window of the bus: "There they are," he says, "one thousand insurance salesmen!"

On closer inspection, they could be a thousand actuaries, brokers, bankers or hotel managers, but a lunch-pail crowd they are not. As leavening, however, there is a cluster of boisterous young hecklers in the centre of the crowd (a recurrent problem of noon-hour rallies is their allure for schoolchildren) and their brave, somehow eerie, chants of "Tru-deau, Tru-deau" enliven the scene. The varlet works the outer fringes, and finds himself being interviewed about the television debate. No one seems sure about it and a good part of the uncertainty lies in the disappointment that a program of such inordinate length could conclude in such irresolution. People are not accustomed to watching so suspenseful a contest without knowing the result of it at the end.

Clark, his wife beside him, approaches from the City Centre Holiday Inn, a half-block away, bringing more crowd with him. An incongruity this, for there would be nothing apparent to a tourist stumbling on the scene to inform him that the couple parading before his eyes was the prime minister-apparent of Canada and his wife, whose resolute smile and wary eyes give her countenance the mask of perfect ambivalence.

They could be a bride and groom departing a wedding reception, or he might be some sudden local celebrity — perhaps the Junior Chamber of Commerce man-of-the-year — or she might have been the first London woman to swim the English Channel, but there is so much wholesome, modest, ingenuous concentrate in them that the varlet, much less a tourist, must blink before the blinding reality that he is looking at a prime minister of the realm, a few days from now, and his consort. Furthermore, appearances are not only deceiving, but dangerously so, for beneath that transparent sweetness there is iron enough, in the woman alone, for all the anvils in Canada, and, as for Clark, a supple quickness and well-disguised fierceness of purpose that belie the awkward, ambling gait. Boadicea and Caesar would not have made a better pair for the strategies of conquest and the rule of pragmatism; it will be some time yet before the Tory party appreciates the bargain it struck in the leadership convention hall in Ottawa.

Fanfare, appropriate cheers and adolescent boos escort the beaming couple to the platform, an adequate reception from this largely stolid gathering that is, even when it is all in place, not impressive in its numbers. Were it not for the hecklers, it would be a lifeless crowd; but the waving of Trudeau's face on their placards and the Liberal chants goad the staid Tory partisans to the indignity of counter-demonstration.

Introducing the candidates, the master-of-ceremonies — could there be a chairman at such proceedings? — presents one of them as "a world-renowned authority on monetary policy," and the varlet cranes his neck to see such novelty and to gauge the effect upon the crowd of a man bearing this qualification for membership in the House of Commons. All is lost, however, in a renewed outbreak of dissent from the children of Liberalism, whose placards obscure his vision, while their shrill cries are all he can hear. (He makes a mental note for a revised edition of a campaign handbook: there are no better hecklers for plaza politics than children in their early teens, against whom no one has yet found an antidote.)

The thrust of Clark's speech, when his turn comes, is a rearrangement of a familiar medley, a brisk pop-orchestration suitable for a standing audience — reminding them that they are overtaxed and "underencouraged" and stressing the merits of voluntarism over federalism in providing community services. There appear to be no end of good works that can be safely left to the zeal of Rotarians and the ladies' auxiliaries. Like Jimmy Carter, Clark is running against government: "Will the cows continue to give milk without Pierre Elliott Trudeau? Will the grass grow without him?"

And then the clincher: "But the most important question: without Trudeau, will the mail get delivered in Canada?"

Thus, by "restoring a sense of responsibility back to individual citizens and individual communities across this country," only then would we be "strong as a nation."

The errant thought in the varlet's head is that Clark believes it! Himself the exemplar of his own home truths — a man could go a long way with such a faith, rising above his ordinariness and humble origins, without the subsidy of inherited wealth or power's patronage. "A man with not very much behind him," he could stretch himself enough to realize his fondest dream, given the goose of his own finger.

The only men who truly believe in luck are those who have never had any. In the entrails of Clark's belief in individual potential glows the formidable pride of a self-made man, alongside which the mere conceits of vanity are pale indeed. There is merit for politicians in such notions, but it would be safer lodged in one who bore some of life's lumps and scars on him, who had tasted his own blood and known pain. Was there ever a man who had come to power with so little tutelage in compassion? (The varlet could think of only one — Trudeau.)

After Clark's media message has been sent for the six o'clock newscasts, the crowd dissolves: the followers back to business, the children back to school, and the varlet, with

Sears, to a nearby restaurant. One might be wise to be well fortified for the rigours ahead — the Tories' "all-candidates" rally on the island of Montreal that very evening.

xvii

Once back on Charter 087, the varlet struggles to compose his thoughts on the true nature of this surreal experience, of life aboard this flying media complex, of the adroit manipulations and fierce attentions to minuscule detail, of the lack of exuberance and passion — had he ever known such joyless company? His apprehensions about future political campaigns, if this one were an augury, were profound and inconsolable.

The locus of the campaigns had shifted. They were no longer waged in earnest debate in the old Orange Halls in the countryside or from the secular pulpits of the cities. The age was too impatient for argument, too distracted to hear speech. Politics had become pictorial, a rush of fleeting images, from which the memory retained a montage of visual impressions relieved only by slogans. A curious development in democracy that the public comprehension of an election would come much more from what was seen than from anything heard or read.

As to what was said — since something must still be said — a political speech could now be safely couched in the common denominators plumbed in public opinion. Though a man must speak, he need not give offence by offering his own judgement; instead, he could demonstrate his wisdom by conforming to that of the majority. A touring politician without his polls would be as naked of inspiration as a circuit preacher without his Bible. No politician in Canada's history had stuck to his scripture as faithfully as Clark. As of this moment, it had promised a near certain salvation.

But this is not to say that Clark is the timid creature of expedience, a slave to his polls: a more honest and ungrudging conclusion is that he is not so egocentric as to fly in the face of them. A messenger might have lost his head had he brought a bad poll to Diefenbaker, but think of all the bleak, black figures Clark has put his fingers on; for a long time, the only thing worse than his press was his polls. That they are now in tandem with his ambition, as he is twinned to their findings, is no rebuke to Clark. Who can blame a man for trusting public opinion when it has the weight to make him a prime minister?

Even so, this is a politics without much soul in it, nor any gristle or tissue to it, and, if it could be managed, no surprises either. Perhaps that was the wretched part of it all, the dull predictability, the fact that those deeply involved in it knew too much; indeed, knew what everyone else knew even before they knew it, which was the dubious achievement of the malign science of voter projections.

As for the shift in venue of these trials of politics: they had been moved from the hustings to capsules such as this, Charter 087, in whose underside the blinkered eyes of the cameras rested between their assignments, while the reporters foraged at the Wagonmaster's table, awaiting their next summons.

The varlet counted himself (for once, in recent times) as blessed. He was fortunate not to have been raised a film-maker or camera mule, or to have the daily task of synthesizing the condensations of the compressed thoughts of Joe Clark, or of as many of them as he is prepared to divulge. It is the lot of the varlet's media companions to meet the needs of editors in filling the gaps of space and time, and in gulling audiences into comprehending the obvious as significant; none of this falls to him. He would sooner cover a sack race as be obliged to winnow such chaff each day for some kernel of hard news.

The reporters and camera crews do not have his envy, but they have his admiration. While every precaution is taken to ensure them against privation and other physical discomforts, there are no palliatives for the afflictions of tedium as relentless, in this campaign, as migraine. Furthermore, their role in politics is misunderstood.

A reporter with Trudeau recalled an event at which he had stood on a table to have a better view of the prime minister.

"Get down!" a woman spectator had shouted. "I can't see!"

"Madam," the reporter had said, turning to her, "you're speaking to a member of the fourth estate."

"I'm speaking to an ass-hole," the woman had responded. "Get off that table."

Too few understand that the game of politics is one played between the politicians and the media — the Wagonmaster is among those few with a perfect understanding — and, while spectators are useful, they are not vital, other than as ornament. Ultimately, the innovators will find a way to campaign without them; until then, those who attend political meetings should realize that no one is talking to them anyway, and the value in their presence is in their being seen rather than in their seeing. The public has its own illusion of reality: it imagines itself the arbiter in the running battle between the politicians and the media, with a slight bias against the media, which, it imagines, frequently distort the news when not actually lying about it. In the campaign of '79, the newsmen were more suspect than the politicians; more than once the varlet had detected hostility in the crowds when the reporters stepped from the buses and made their way to the areas reserved for them, always nearest the action. It was as though they were intruding on an event, when, in fact, they were creating it.

But the varlet's assignment was a far simpler one — to sift the day's dross for his own impressions. Even though the campaign had been a treadmill — with wings — and the polls had not budged beyond the margins of error since the beginning of it, there were still cosmic particles in the air, messages on the winds, and jetsam left by ebbing tides. Men, too, were changing, as they aged amid the waxing of their fortunes.

The leader's entourage — Gillies, the policy adviser, William Neville, the leader's principal aide, and Ian Green, the archetypical executive assistant — wound itself a turn tighter with each passing day, eyes beginning to bulge and sockets to jam; the varlet suspected there could not be a sphincter in the front of the bus that did not have a knot in it. They had been inching to Jerusalem (a figure of speech) since the October by-elections, a step at a time, one foot before the other, and were now so close, they could smell the blossoms in the promised land.

xviii

If Claude Ryan went on vacation to Acapulco, he would end up looking for the French fact; if a Tory went looking for the French fact, he would end up in Acapulco.

Old Saw

On the way in from Dorval airport, stopping at a traffic light on Peel Street, the varlet sees from his bus window, not twenty feet away, Duart Farquarson of the Montreal *Gazette*, standing in a doorway. He has not seen Farquarson for many years, having first met him during the Roblin era in Manitoba, and he waves frantically to catch his eye. He also attempts to raise the window but finds it to be permanently sealed. More maddening, Farquarson seems to be staring right at him! It is then that he realizes that, while he can see out of the bus, Farquarson cannot see in, a trick of the tinted, one-way window glass. Fortunately, he is sitting alone, so that no one notices his sudden fit of mirthless laughter over this mute, existential tableau.

It is at the Montreal all-candidates meeting in Lafontaine Park that he begins to compose his epilogue. When he arrives, with his media companions, his first view of the site of the rally — a semi-circle of benches rising in tiers against the slope of hillside overlooking a stage and bandshell — informs him that no one has yet arrived.

This is not quite true: looking down from the rim of the amphitheatre, he can see below him a dozen or so preadolescent children who are mindlessly marking time on the stage to the beat of a drum corps band. The rain, which had followed Clark yesterday, has preceded him to Montreal and left pools of water on the stage and along the rows of seats. Visible behind the bandshell is an artificial pond, half the size of a football field, and, to the right, behind a wrought-iron fence, stands the only crowd he can see, which, on closer inspection, turns out to be of Marxist-Leninist persuasion, under the casual scrutiny of a few police.

For an hour or more, during which time the majorettes continue to pump their legs with heroic endurance, the candidates arrive in a trickle, accompanied by their next-of-kin and clutches of supporters. A motley gathering, this one, representing the generations of bleak attrition that had been history's rebuke to Conservatism in Quebec. Under the sullen sky, in the fading light of the dampened day, there seems to be a rueful sheepishness in the gathering, as though the darkness could not fall upon them soon enough and shield them in anonymity. Even so, imagine the perversity stirring in the cells of this body of Tories! How did one remain a Conservative in Montreal?

As the crowd begins to jell — might there be two thousand in that sea of placards? — the candidates are summoned to the platform to be introduced to the cheers of their

Ted Grant

Behind a wrought iron fence stands the only crowd he can see, which turns out to be of Marxist-Leninist persuasion, under the casual scrutiny of a few police.

Ted Grant

A motley gathering, this one, representing the generations of bleak attrition that had been history's rebuke to Conservatism in Quebec.

supporters, and there is a special huzzah for the candidate for Laval-des-Rapides, Pierre Trudeau, whose resemblance to another by the same name ends as he appears. For all of them, however, there is a uniqueness in the moment: they have never stood before so large a gathering of Tories, which accounts for there being more enthusiasm on the platform than off it. Then Heward Grafftey enters from the wings, one hand brushing back his cowlick, the other acknowledging the crowd. A winner seven out of eight times running as a Conservative in Quebec, an eternal asterisk in the laws of probability, Grafftey's slight, stooped figure reminds the varlet of the unlikely shapes in which indestructibility may come disguised.

Out on the pond, a small craft moves silently upon the waters, half barge, half gondola, but wholly improbable, ferrying Joe Clark and Maureen McTeer to the Montreal rally. Standing together on the prow, holding firmly to a handrail, the Tory leader, his wife and their boatman inch their way to the near shore.

"They should've walked," an observer says, without emotion.

"Through submarine-infested waters today, Joe Clark . . . ," another remarks, working on his lead.

A re-enactment of history, it seems to the varlet — Wolfe slipping ashore behind the bandstand to take the Plains of Abraham by surprise! A tactical manouevre it is meant to be, since the Marxist-Leninist forces on the flank have failed to maintain watch on the pond and, when Clark steps from his contraption, he is already beyond the range of their verbal fire, and in the midst of his own crowd.

It is enough for the varlet to see; the campaign has peaked for him, in this contrivance of politics, sodden and pathetic as it is, here at the nadir of Tory fortunes. But it might be a boon to salvation yet. For there is Clark — as Doug Fisher had said of him a day ago, a tough and ruthless pragmatist — in the course of bidding farewell to the forlorn remnants of the party of all his predecessors, and to the endless season

Ted Grant

Out on the pond, a small craft moves silently upon
the waters, half barge, half gondola, but wholly
improbable, ferrying Joe Clark and Maureen
McTeer to the Montreal rally.

of an abject futility. Imagine, Clark speaking before two
thousand Tories, who would represent one of every fifty
votes his party would count on election day from all twenty-
four of the ridings in Montreal. Never again, for Clark,
would the varlet need to drag himself to Montreal for a
scavenger's feast like this.

The triumph of Joe Clark would shatter the mould of the
old politics and set the Liberal monolith of Quebec in new
perspective. The Tory leader would come to power without
the encumbrance of a French lieutenant — his absence
noted in the journey across the pond! — and without the
invisible strings of the Union Nationale, now defunct; and,
yes, without the dead weight of a hundred equivocations to
his policy. No Tory leader had ever been so unfettered by the
conventions of the old politics, which had for generations
guaranteed hegemony to Liberalism.

Indeed, a Phoenix-apparition in this impending débâcle:
there would be nothing left of the Conservative party in
French Canada once the votes were counted. But what a
blessed purgation for Clark, who would be a prime minister
without legacy or debt in Quebec. He could, then, begin
anew, so fresh a beginning as to invite the reasonable expectation of a Tory renaissance in the other of Canada's two
nations, a hope made even stronger by the fact that he had
been, even in his beginnings as a politician, uncommonly
sensitive and alert to the legitimacy of Quebec's distinctive
place in Confederation — the last Tory who would need to
be told it was not a province like the others.

The varlet could forgive the opportunism in the Tory
platform and overlook the intransigent bigotry and reaction
that would swell Clark's majorities in many a constituency.
Clark would not be the only man who had come to power
with a mandate riddled by contradiction. (Even de Gaulle
had told the cheering *colons* of Algeria, "I understand you!"
before he dispossessed them.) But Clark had been a shrewd-
er, wiser man than the legions of his detractors would admit.
In the only fateful issue confronting the nation, that of a

revised accommodation in Confederation, he had not sur-
rendered a single option to the exhausting rigours of his
campaign.

But that aside, the country needed much that Clark represented: a surcease from the habits of élitism; a revival of the
commonplace virtues of a God-fearing people; a recognition
of the "Western fact" in Canadian politics, worked out of
the new empire rising beyond the horizons of the old; and,
perhaps the best of it, the restoration of a less complicated
Canadian democracy.

Liberalism had achieved its predominance in Canadian
politics through its dominance of Quebec, and for so long a
time none could be certain whether the country was
governed with the interests of Quebec in mind, or merely
with the interests of the Liberal party in Quebec, or even
whether these were indeed indistinguishable. All one could
know was that, while the tensions and strains increased
within that province, Liberalism remained undisturbed in
its suzerainty. It was remarkable that so much could change
in Quebec that political parties would appear and disappear,
and politicians be consumed in the upheaval, while the
federal Liberal party would sail serenely onward, its
membership rarely changing, save for appointments to the
bench, the Senate, to boards and commissions, or by
intermittent acts of God.

There were, in fact, so many Liberal Sarums in Quebec as
to perpetuate distortions in the Canadian democracy,
rotten boroughs enough to frustrate the national will and
enshrine a dubious oligarchy. Clark — and random
fortunes, all of them good — may have now combined to put
an end to it, and nothing would serve the needs of
democracy more than a lengthy interruption to Liberal
dispensations in a province that had known no other.

We shall see, at least, how long Liberalism retains its
paramountcy without the avails of entrenched patronage
and preferment: these are, at last, now in the singular grasp
of a Tory prime minister with enough wit to respect their

uses. How will Liberalism then fare in the wilderness of its own redoubt? And should the reconfiguration of federal politics in Quebec once more come to resemble that of the rest of Canada, will not the parties themselves, Grits no less than Tories, become national in their ambit?

Yes, points of departure of epic promise — and no better moment for a resourceful pragmatist! The varlet, retreating from his brooding perch overlooking the stage at Lafontaine Park, the disembodied voice of Joe Clark fading in the night, seeks a taxi to carry the freight of his reconciliation to some place of celebration. There is wisdom in the numbers in this election after all, including the mournful tables in Quebec, and the emphatic majorities that will come pouring out of the West. And while Joe Clark may now see the country as a community of communities, and federalism as a blight to private enterprise, history may yet see him as the man who levelled the walls of regionalism and bridged the solitudes to allow Canadians the first clear view of their whole inheritance.

EPILOGUE

*Atmosphere structuring is terribly
important to the psychological interplay
which is encountered in a 50 day tour.*
The Wagonmaster

The varlet takes his leave of Charter 087 at Malton without
any ceremony of farewell to Clark. He has made peace —
perhaps a truce — with his own uncertainties about the next
prime minister of Canada and, as any man would be, bearing so much fragile hope, he is stiff with caution.

On the ramp, beneath the luggage bays of the aircraft, he
finds his portable typewriter. It has been dropped from
some height — perhaps from the height of the Wagonmaster's scorn for fractious passengers such as he has been
— and it rests in disassembled parts at his feet. Would not
any pilgrim, come to this last point of departure, kneel
before this symbolic heap — and pick up the pieces?